THE FIRST
LONDON
OLYMPICS
⁓ 1908 ⁓

THE FIRST
LONDON
OLYMPICS
~ 1908 ~

REBECCA JENKINS

piatkus

PIATKUS

First published in Great Britain in 2008 by Piatkus Books
This edition published in 2012 by Piatkus
Copyright © 2008 by Rebecca Jenkins

A CIP catalogue record for this book
is available from the British Library

ISBN 978-0-7499-2940-4

Designed and typeset in Legacy Serif by Paul Saunders
Printed and bound in Great Britain by
CPI Group (UK) Ltd, Croydon, CR0 4YY

Piatkus
An imprint of
Little, Brown Book Group
100 Victoria Embankment
London EC4Y 0DY

An Hachette UK Company
www.hachette.co.uk

www.piatkus.co.uk

CONTENTS

‹—⟩⊂—›

Acknowledgements *page vi*

Preface: Scene Setting *page ix*

1 ATHENS *page 1*

2 THE WHITE CITY *page 20*

3 THE STADIUM *page 46*

4 INTERNATIONAL SPORT *page 76*

5 FLAG FLYING *page 105*

6 THE TUG-OF-WAR *page 132*

7 400 METRES AND FAIR PLAY *page 160*

8 THE MARATHON *page 188*

9 THE QUEEN AND THE SUGAR BAKER *page 226*

Notes *page 262*

Index *page 266*

Acknowledgements

As always with writing, this book would not have existed without the assistance of others. In particular it would not have been written but for a timely and generous grant from the Royal Literary Fund. Thank you to Helen Stearman of Northern Film and Media whose phone call formed the first link that brought me to this story; to Peter Brown and Brendan Foster who introduced me to the human drama of the marathon, and to Christopher Sinclair Stevenson, my invaluable support for so many years, who listened patiently to my first ramblings on the subject. During my research I have benefited from the knowledge and skills of many librarians and archivists – in particular I would like to thank Beverley Cook, Curator of Social and Working History at the Museum of London and Amy Terriere at the British Olympic Foundation for dealing with my insatiable photocopying demands with such good humour. My gratitude to Virginia Owen, great-granddaughter of Imre Kiralfy and her husband Fred Owen, for so generously sharing family photos of Imre Kiralfy; to Hugh Farey for giving me the benefit of his research on the 1908 marathon course and to Lucia Luck for her translations of material relating to Dorando Pietri.

Thank you to Alan Brooke, my editor, whose patience I sorely tried and yet who has put up with me with good humour throughout; to Steve Gove for his careful attention to detail and to Denise Dwyer who put everything together with such skill and cheerfulness under the most extreme pressure. I could not write without the support of my friends and family – I am grateful for them all; but special thanks to Gail Jordan for reading every chapter, to Deborah Jenkins, Diane Roberts and Ivor Stolliday for their support and constructive criticisms, and to Tim Jenkins whose phone calls always come at the most useful moment. And finally, thank you to my agent Caroline Montgomery who keeps me sane.

www.rebeccajenkins.com

In memory of my grandfather,
H. L. Peet, sporting enthusiast and newspaper man.

Picture Credits

P. x British Pathe Limited; p. 3 Getty Images; p. 25 Courtesy of Virginia Owen; p. 51 © IOC; p. 65 © British Library Board, all rights reserved, zc.9.d.560; p. 73 Courtesy of the Desborough Collection, Hertfordshire Archives and Local Studies DE/Rv/F25; p. 125 © IOC; p. 131 Getty Images; p. 137 © British Library Board, all rights reserved, zc.9.d.560; p. 144 Courtesy of Nicholas Kingsbury; p. 238 The Arthur Conan Doyle Collection Lancelyn Green Bequest, Portsmouth City Council, all rights reserved; p. 259 © British Library Board, all rights reserved, zc.9.d.560.

Every effort has been made to identify and acknowledge the copyright holders. Any errors or omissions will be rectified in future editions provided that written notification is made to the publishers.

Preface
SCENE SETTING

In 1908 *The Sportsman* published in London the first of 13 volumes intended to become an authoritative survey of 'British Sports and Sportsmen past & present'. One volume is taken up with racing, the 'king of sports'; there are volumes on 'Yachting and Rowing', 'Polo and Coaching' and 'Country Life Pursuits'. 'Hunting' takes up a complete volume and 'Big Game Hunting and Angling' another. (The latter includes an evocative parade of 'rifle celebrities', studio portraits of well-to-do men with receding hairlines and expressions ranging from constipated, through vacant to stiff.) 'Athletic Sports' – including the track and field events – are bundled up in Volume 8 along with boxing, swimming, fencing, croquet, 'Highland sports' and 'tennis, rackets and other ball games', including fives and bowls. *The Sportsman*'s series would take a decade or more to complete and in that time the world of the Edwardian sportsman it commemorated would have vanished. It was overtaken by a new breed of international sport: a spectator sport carried far and wide into the homes and hearts of a new breed of sports fan through newspapers, photographs, radio, film and, eventually, television.

Almost by accident, the 1908 Olympics were the first to be

filmed. At the time the moving picture was still a novelty. The Pathé brothers' Cinematograph booths happened to be one of the sideshows in the Franco-British Exhibition grounds which housed the London Olympic stadium. The Pathé brothers' cameramen were reputed to have shot 80 miles of film every day capturing activities around the Exhibition and the events of the Olympic Games became part of the programme. In those days the film was coloured: 'The natural colours reproduced clearly and without a trace of blurring or jumping.' According to the advertising material at the time it was 'difficult to realise that one is looking from a darkened hall ... instead of really participating in the incident enacted'. The images that survive today are flickering and faded and

Pathé brothers' still showing a gymnast in the first week of the Games (note the empty stands).

the colour is gone. The stunning intimacy of film when it was new has been translated into distance. But what might seem at first merely a nostalgic glimpse into quainter times unfolds on examination into a surprising story.

By a series of accidents, in spring 2006 I was contracted to research the 1908 marathon for a film company. I took on the task as an opportunity to investigate what was to me virgin territory. I was intrigued by the underlying assumption – central to the Olympic vision – that sport is one of the few things that unites us all.

It would be hard to find a human being on this planet who has not heard of the Olympics. The faces of entire cities have been permanently altered by the quadrennial Games; half the world's population will watch the Olympics on television when that season comes round. Whatever the routine complaints about the massive complications of coordinating the efforts of hundreds of thousands of people, or about all the millions – even billions – spent on the project, the four-yearly Olympic circus amounts to a common good. All this has sprung from the dreams of a group of fin de siècle aristocrats who, inspired by the verse of Pindar, wanted to rekindle in the modern world the spirit of the ancient Olympic games.

Early on in my researches I was struck by a 1908 article written by one Dr Emil. In discussing the importance of the then forthcoming London Games Emil wrote of the emotional power for those who had – like him – found their 'most important experiences in sport … In a game of cricket there is a novel, a drama, a tragedy; there is a science and calculation; there is the uncontrollable element of chance; there is the mysterious power of personality; there is nearly the whole of human forces.'

When I first picked up a *Spalding's Almanac* – those yearly bibles of American sport from the early twentieth century – all I saw was page after page of statistics. Rankings in brittle, small print interspersed with grainy photographs of a man in mid-jump, or a man breasting the tape at the end of a race – pictures so blurred as to be almost generic, the name in the caption a mere courtesy. Human effort and aspiration reduced to statistics without personality, motivation or character – or so it seemed to me, at first.

But then there is that picture – 'the' picture from that year. It is the one thing people remember about the 1908 Olympics: Dorando Pietri, the little Italian with knobbly knees and a look of Charlie Chaplin, staggering towards the finishing line herded by a semicircle of officials and policemen. It is the iconic image of the 'ordinary Joe' almost killing himself to

The image that made the 1908 Olympics memorable: 22-year-old Italian Dorando Pietri staggering across the marathon finish line with the clerk of the course, J.A. Andrews (in the boater) supporting his elbow and race physician, Dr Michael Bulger, urging him on.

achieve his goal. That picture began to open me up to the drama Dr Emil wrote about. An investigation that began from curiosity to understand how the leisure interests of a certain portion of the population came to hold such sway over the rest of us led me into an entrancing story.

The first London Olympics were not a roaring success. The Fourth Olympiad has been relegated to short paragraphs and summaries a thousand times over on websites and in sporting compilations, in histories of the marathon, or of athletics or the Olympic movement. There is half a page here, a couple of pages there – and that photograph of Dorando. There is the authoritative blue book, one volume among seven chronicling each of the first Olympic Games of the modern revival, but otherwise the story has been overlooked as insufficiently substantial to warrant detailed reconstruction. But in light of the forthcoming Olympics of 2012 it seems appropriate to revisit the first London Games.

In the twenty-first century, mounting the Olympics in London takes an Act of Parliament, a London 2012 Organising Committee, and an Olympic Delivery Authority 'working with key stakeholders from national and city government and sport'. In 1908 a group of English sporting enthusiasts, headed by Lord Desborough, agreed to take on the mounting of the Fourth Olympiad in a bare two years, after the original host city, Rome, dropped out. As I write in summer 2007, the anticipated costs of mounting the third London Olympic Games are estimated at close on £9.3 billion. With five years to go, there are still concerns that facilities will not be completed in time. In 1908, the organisers of the Franco-British Exhibition built their stadium with seats for 68,000 and standing room for 23,000 in just ten months for around £85,000 – just over £6 million in 2006 values.[1]

[xiii]

The pattern of Edwardian sportsmanship: Willie Grenfell, later Lord Desborough, the man who brought the 1908 Olympics to London. Vanity Fair Spy cartoon, 1893.

In 1908 the Olympics were a showcase of amateur sport. Today they are a development agency to regenerate mankind. Sport is almost crushed with the load of expectations: land will be reclaimed, communities regenerated, we are promised a lasting legacy to 'benefit sport, the environment and the local and global community'.

For those of us who like milestones, the 1908 Games were the first Olympics in which national teams competed in an organised form. They were also the first to attract substantial media attention. They were not only the first to be filmed but the first to generate widely published photographic images. Across the Atlantic, Randolph Hearst was conducting his circulation war with William Pulitzer, expanding sports pages, employing photographs and cartoons and vivid reporting in the fight to grip the reader and take his two cents. Much of the drama of the 1908 Olympics was driven by the American papers; picking up complaints from the US team about biased British judges (the judges at the 1908 Games were all British), they assaulted British 'fair play' to the point where it was rumoured that King Edward VII was sufficiently offended to withdraw from attending the closing ceremonies in the Shepherd's Bush stadium.

This account is not intended to be a comprehensive record of the Fourth Olympiad. That book is Bill Mallon and Ian Buchanan's *The 1908 Olympic Games: Results for All Competitors in All Events, with Commentary*, a solid, authoritative 500 pages of statistics and facts and names, with extensive appendices. My narrative revolves around the White City stadium. I largely pass by the Olympic events held outside it and the winter Games. The 1908 Olympics would hardly have registered in the collective memory but for its alliance with the Franco-British Exhibition of that year and the massive stadium the Exhibition Company built to showcase the Games. This is a tale of the extraordinary endeavours of ordinary men – sugar bakers and policemen and market gardeners. And more – there is a White City of palaces built by a Hungarian showman who knew how to deploy his fairy lights; a heroically dutiful sporting aristocrat and the greatest stadium in the world (at the time); international controversy and a diplomatic queen, and a Red Indian struck down by strychnine.

I hope this book will amuse both the sportingly challenged, like me, and with luck the sporting faithful as well.

A note on statistics: Although the IOC ruled that Olympic performances should be recorded in metric units, in 1908 the Anglo-Saxon press generally used imperial measures. I have tried to list both measurements, but occasionally I have only found one. If the reader is confused by this switching between different styles, I apologise, but it reflects the lack of standardisation in 1908.

CHAPTER 1

ATHENS

Since the Olympic movement began no such
successful games had previously been held as
those of 1906 in Athens...

THEODORE COOK

ON THURSDAY 12 APRIL 1906, Theodore Andrea Cook, 39 years old, blind in one eye and half an inch shy of six foot, arrived at London's Victoria Station carrying his cricket bag. The bag contained his duelling swords, fencing mask, golf clubs and a lawn tennis racket. Cook was heading for Greece for the very first time. He was going as captain of the British fencing team to compete in the 1906 Olympic Games in Athens.

Theodore Cook was editor of the *St James' Gazette* – a paper published 'for gentlemen by gentlemen'. He was also a leading light of the Amateur Fencing Association, an enthusiastic promoter of the sport in England at a time when it was often overlooked as a European pastime practised by Frenchmen and the occasional Italian. During the social round of 1905 Cook met Mr Marinaky of the Greek Legation in London.

Theodore Cook in 1925: the passionate fencing amateur who recruited Lord Desborough to compete at Athens in 1906 and thereby made the connection that led to the mounting of the first London Olympics.

Marinaky just happened to be secretary of the Greek Olympic Committee.

'As soon as he explained that an athletic gathering of an important international character was to be held in Athens in 1906,' Cook recorded, 'I felt that it would be an unrivalled opportunity to take out a British Fencing Team and compete with the *épée de combat* upon that historic soil.'[1]

The journey to Athens was formidable* and not cheap. But for this cultured son of a headmaster and an artist mother – holder of a second-class Classics degree from Oxford – the lure of Olympic competition on Greek ground was irresistible. Athens in 1906 represented the harmony of Theodore Cook's two passions: his admiration for the classical world of ancient Greece and his commitment to pure-hearted sportsmanship.

---

* ' … it may without discourtesy be suggested that, until railway communication becomes better developed, some difficulty will be experienced by other countries in sending athletes to Greece', Theodore Cook wrote in *International Sport*.

It was 12 years since Baron Pierre de Coubertin had first gathered together a group of like-minded friends and aristocratic acquaintances at the Sorbonne in the spring of 1894 to discuss his dream of a modern revival of the Olympic Games of ancient Greece. There had been three 'Olympiads' since then – 1896 in Athens, 1900 in Paris and 1904 in St Louis – but after a moderately fruitful start in Athens, the two subsequent gatherings had not been a success. The Greek king and his government were keen to exert the prior claim of Greece to its own heritage. Prince Wilhelm, elected King George I of Greece in 1863, was born a Dane. For the relatively new Greek royal family, their endorsement of the Olympic revival served as a means to bond with their people. Inspired by the national enthusiasm aroused by the first revival of the Games in 1896, the Greek authorities declared that they would hold their

Baron Pierre de Coubertin, the fin de siècle *gentleman who inspired by the ruins of Olympia had the romantic notion of reviving the ancient Olympic Games of Greece.*

own Olympics in spring 1906 to mark the ten-year anniversary. De Coubertin stood aside from the 1906 Games. From his perspective they represented an unfortunate distraction from his 'official' four-year cycle in which the Games moved from capital to capital, but at this stage in the development of his vision he was in no position to do anything about it. (Today the Athens Games of 1906 are not officially recognised by the International Olympic Committee. They are referred to as the 'Intercalated Olympics'.)

Theodore Cook had been recruited to de Coubertin's Olympic movement the same year he met Mr Marinaky. In the summer of 1905 the well-known sportsman and MP Willie Grenfell, a British member of de Coubertin's International Olympic Committee (IOC), invited Theodore to join the newly formed British Olympic Association (BOA) which he chaired. A few weeks later Grenfell was created Lord Desborough, 1st Baron of Taplow.

'If one were asked to name the most typical Englishman of his generation,' once wrote the editor of *Vanity Fair*, 'one would be inclined to name Lord Desborough.'[2] A little over six feet tall, a reticent, well-proportioned man with a strong sense of duty, Willie Grenfell was the Edwardian ideal of the gentleman sportsman. As a schoolboy at Harrow he had demonstrated his talent for cricket at the yearly match between Eton and Harrow. While up at Balliol College he won his Oxford Blue, rowing to victory for his university against Cambridge. He was the first man to be president of both the Oxford University Boat Club and the Oxford University Athletic Club at the same time. In his youth he rowed as stroke to a crew of eight, crossing the Channel from Dover to Calais in a fragile clinker-built boat with sliding seats – a hair-raising trip during which capsizing and catastrophe were only narrowly averted by 'prompt and dextrous bailing'. Nothing daunted, he subsequently crossed the Channel a second time in a one-man scull. He shot tigers in India, lions in Africa and grizzly bears in the Rockies. He climbed the Matterhorn three times and twice swam across Niagara just below the Falls (once, it was said, in a snowstorm). And, according to Theodore Cook, his swordsmanship was 'as good as anything else he ever touched'. In short, Willie Grenfell, Lord Desborough, was a symbol of the sportsmanship that many of his English contemporaries liked to believe they gave the world. Theodore Cook admired him deeply. He was thrilled when Grenfell agreed to join the Athens expedition.

With Lord Desborough signed up, Cook had no trouble gathering four more 'thoroughly representative swordsmen' to defend Britain's honour in Athens. It was part of the code of honourable amateurism that gentlemen should pay for themselves, which put the trip beyond the pockets of the ordinary young athlete. Cook's five swordsmen ranged between 26 and 52 years of age and included two lords and a knight.

Charles Newton Robinson, the lightest, shortest and oldest of the bunch at 5ft 7in and 52 years old, had a reputation with the épée. Sir Cosmo Duff Gordon, 43, was a friend of Lord Desborough from the Bath Club (a London club of which Desborough was co-founder and president). A prominent Scottish landowner, Sir Cosmo was too much of a gentleman to participate in public tournaments as a rule, but was well thought of by the 'best judges' for his unorthodox and 'characteristic' style. Edgar Seligman, a lithe 38-year-old, was British amateur champion in both foil and épée. Another leading light in the revival of English fencing, he had been competing for five years and was good enough to come second in French competitions. The junior member of the

Five 'Thoroughly Representative Swordsmen' – the English fencing team at Athens 1906, snapped by their captain, Theodore Cook. From left to right: Charles Newton Robinson, Sir Cosmo Duff Gordon, Edgar Seligman, Lord Desborough, Lord Howard de Walden.

party was Lord Howard de Walden, aged 26, a competent swordsman with foil, sabre and épée who might, Cook suggested, become first rate if he would practise consistently. He was listed as the 'spare man'. Walden had other assets, most notably his seagoing yacht, the *Branwen*.

Lord Desborough's presence in the team transformed the expedition. Edwardian society was a world of personal connection. Desborough did not just bring with him those networks of sporting fellowship forged at public school and Oxbridge. He was a friend of the King. As Prince of Wales, Edward VII had been a witness at Willie Grenfell's wedding to Ettie Fane in 1887. When, at short notice, His Majesty's government received a formal invitation from the Greek government to send a pair of representatives to the Athens Games, it was natural – particularly since he was already going – that Lord Desborough should be appointed alongside Mr Bosanquet, Director of the British School in Athens. As it happened, King Edward VII, his wife Queen Alexandra, and the Prince and Princess of Wales were all attending the Games. (It was something of a family holiday – the King of Greece was Queen Alexandra's brother.) So from his first romantic notion of taking a group of English swordsmen to uphold the honour of their king on this 'historic soil', Cook found himself swept up in the skirts of exalted circles.

Theodore's baggage swelled with importance. The Foreign Office advised him that although court dress would not be required, 'top hats and frock-coats were almost certain to be wanted'. And his team received official sanction before they left. With eager pride he distributed among his band 'those

The Branwen *moored at Venice. The cruise was not entirely pleasant. The knights ran into some gusty spring weather near the Straits of Messina. Theodore Cook remembered the little ship taking the waves 'as a steeplechaser takes a hedge'.*

[7]

articles of clothing which are now among our most treasured possessions – the little Union Jack on our left arms and the white international cap with the Tudor rose that commemorates the first royal recognition of English swordsmanship by Henry VIII'. In contrast to the previous Olympic Games of de Coubertin's cycle at which British athletes had competed as individuals, Cook's men were going out as a team to defend the honour of their king and country.

Cook met Seligman and Robinson at Victoria Station. They travelled together to Paris where they joined Baron de Coubertin for a convivial dinner. The next morning they parted. Seligman and Robinson made their way across land to Athens. The more privileged Cook headed for Naples where he was to join Lord Desborough and Sir Duff Gordon on Lord Howard de Walden's yacht.

The Englishmen arrived in the aftermath of the eruption of Mount Vesuvius. Seligman and Robinson, travelling overland to Athens via Brindisi, found ash dust spread eastward from sea to sea. Even Paris had been visited by a brown fog one day when the wind changed. Ash had stopped falling in Naples but in places its streets were a foot deep in fine, grey silt.* In the bay, where the *Branwen*, Walden's 135ft, two-masted yacht bobbed in bright sunlight, the crew were working double shifts to keep engines, decks and brassware clean.

Inland hundreds of families were left homeless; scores of people had died. The Englishmen visited a devastated town, wearing driving goggles and respirators against the black pall that made it dark at noon. Cook was fascinated to walk on lava ten feet thick, the tip of his walking stick glowing

---

* Cook recorded that 'there was great discomfort, but no real danger' – once the authorities realised the need to shore up unstable roofs against the weight of the pumice ash.

red-hot as it poked through the crust. They watched mangled bodies being carried out of crumpled buildings by soldiers – but their real aim was the museum at Pompeii. There, hardly ten minutes from the edge of the recent lava flow, they strolled through forum and streets ghostly in the drifting volcanic smoke. The contemporary disaster added poignancy to Cook's contemplation of the petrified Roman corpses in the museum.

The *Branwen* left Naples harbour on the afternoon of 17 April, its gentlemen passengers swapping Homeric references in the original Greek. Cook spent happy hours poring over charts next to the captain, testing his pet theory that Homer's *Odyssey* was based on the Phoenician 'Pilot's Guide'. As he wrote in *International Sport*: 'The sea itself was mysterious, romantic, breathing old history upon its breezes: at any moment might have risen on the horizon the black ship of the old sea-rover, faring homeward from Troy's ruins to Penelope.'

Cook's published account of his Greek adventure is peppered with comical little drawings of small knights doing battle against unseen enemies in clouds of smoke. The doodles were Howard de Walden's contribution. They played on the nickname the team shared among themselves: 'the knights'. Allowing for an element of traditional English self-deprecation, that spring Cook was starring in his own romance. As they sailed across choppy spring waters through the Straits of Messina, towards the Gulf of Corinth, 'the thought of the Athens Tournament loomed like another siege of Troy'.

The *Branwen* dropped anchor in the Bay of Phalerum in the lee of an English cruiser squadron during the late afternoon of Saturday, 21 April. Desborough, Cook, Gordon and de Walden disembarked to catch the little local train from Piraeus up to the town. They shared a carriage with an enthusiastic footballer from Smyrna who was eager to know what they thought of the chances of his team. They were diplomatic – in view of the fact that no British amateur eleven had made its way out to Athens.

Their goal was the Imperial Hotel, close to Athens's central square. There they were reunited with Seligman and Robinson. The hotel was packed with visiting sportsmen. Just over 900 athletes had put their names down to take part in the Games. They came from all over Europe, from North America, from Australia; there were even a couple from Samoa and Egypt.

The next day, at the opening ceremony, Lord Desborough – dressed in his top hat and frock-coat – led the British contestants in procession around the white marble stadium. Built on the site of the original arena dating to the fourth century BC, the stadium represented Athens's commitment to the Olympic revival. The King of Greece had initiated the first excavations of the site in the 1870s. A rich merchant from Alexandria, Mr Avéroff, paid for the 'reconstruction' of the horseshoe-shaped stadium, including its stately columned entrance, in time for the first modern Olympiad in 1896. The local population had turned out in force to fill the 60,000 seats; they did so again in spring 1906. As was fitting for a knightly romance, royalty was much in evidence. The athletes paraded past a royal box dense with monarchs and princelings: King George I of Greece and his wife Olga (a Russian grand duchess), King Edward VII of England and his wife Queen Alexandra, the Prince and Princess of Wales and miscellaneous members of the Greek royal family. The contestants drew up for the formal salute to the King, between two columns topped by a pair of ancient marble heads recovered from the original

Greek boys giving a gymnastic display at the 1906 Athens Olympics. At the front, flanking the circle of mown grass, are the two heads recovered from the ancient site draped with wreaths of laurel – a reference to the wreaths which, according to tradition, were the sole prizes awarded winners at the original Greek games.

site and encircled with wreaths of fresh laurel leaves; while the Pantheon, that shrine of the Golden Age of Greece, looked down from the heights of the Acropolis.

At the opening ceremonies of the Games of 1896, ten years earlier, the audience filling the Athens stadium had been edified by a specially written ode, delivered in classical Greek by its English author – Mr George Stuart Robertson, a Wykehamist.* It began, in translation:

> *Up, my song!*
> *To this Athenian home –*
> *Yet not like Persian plunderers of old,*
> *But in frank love and generous friendship bold!*

* That is, he was educated at Winchester College public school.

There was much more in the same vein. No doubt it sounded better in the Greek, but these verses written and delivered so prominently in ancient Greek by an upper-class Englishman underlined the spiritual connection with the English public school. Baron de Coubertin's Olympic vision germinated from his admiration of that public school regime initiated by Dr Arnold, the famous early Victorian headmaster of Rugby School whose moral reforms and efforts to turn schoolboys into Christian gentlemen were developed into the Victorian ideal of sporting, honourable manliness. Although – as the knights discovered – their Greek was quite useless in modern Athens (the stresses and pronunciation being entirely different), as educated English gentlemen, brought up to venerate their Greek poets, they regarded classical history with proprietorial pride. As Cook remarked, 'We can imitate the songs of Pindar more closely than the inhabitants of Pindar's home.' The knights winced their way through a special performance of *Oedipus Tyrannus* in the stadium, the Acropolis brilliantly lit up in the night above them. The actors used modern stresses on the ancient stanzas and were 'quite incomprehensible'. (As the *Times* reporter at the same event commented sniffily: 'scientific study of the usages of the ancient stage seems to have made little progress at Athens'.[3])

When Theodore Cook first climbed the Acropolis, he was nearly overwhelmed with emotion by his first view of 'the chaste perfection of the Parthenon against a burning sky'. He saw before him the soul of the classical education that made an English gentleman, the inspiration of his physical ideals and the touchstone of his artistic taste.

Out of this mingled, hurrying modern life, with all its telegraphs and railway trains and daily newspapers, you

The Parthenon, the most important surviving building of Classical Greece, the temple to Athena built in the fifth century BC.

have walked suddenly into the Temenos of ancient Hellas, into the ordered shrine designed by men whose dream was harmony and balance and proportion, whose victory over the Barbarians had been won as much by the intelligence of their brains as by the courage of their heart, who here determined to put into tangible, eternal form those disembodied theories of philosophic reason which they knew and felt.

There were 77 athletic events contested at Athens. Apart from the fencing competitions, the largest amount of space in Cook's account of the Games was dedicated to those events 'which most faithfully recall the classical festivals of ancient Greece', the discus and javelin contests – sports reconstructed from a couple of ancient statues and a clutch of decorative pots. (Specifically, in the case of the discus, the standing

Discobolus in the Vatican and the Discobolus by Myron in the Palazzo Lancelotti in Rome. The difficulty of interpreting such inanimate sources was evident in complicated rules at Athens which, for instance, planted the discus competitor on a small downward-sloping platform and strictly prescribed the acceptable movement of his limbs.)

Inspired by the ancient Greece of literature, statues, friezes and classical ruins, in the white marble stadium of Athens that spring Theodore Cook glimpsed a manifestation of an intellectual ideal. It was a return to 'that purer dawn of physical culture when "personal expenses" were unknown, when the "shamateur" was yet unborn, and when the joy of generous contest and the strength and health of youth were considered the best blessings Providence could bestow upon a grateful nation'.

'Martin Sheridan throwing the discus "Athens style" from the slanting pedestal, as prescribed by the rules at the 1908 London Olympic Games.'

Struggling to express the feelings aroused by his partici-pation in such pure sporting contests carried out between good fellows in manly informality, Cook borrowed an English academic's description of the ancient Greeks' appreciation of Pindar's Odes: a combination between the emotion 'with which one listens to an anthem, and that with which one witnesses the victory of one's old school at cricket'.

Beyond the stadium, Desborough, as British represent-ative, led the fencing knights in a happy social round of receptions at the British legation, a delightful garden party given by Mrs Bosanquet, wife of the Director of the British School, and a lunch hosted by the Greek Crown Prince in the Aktaeon Hotel at Phalerum, where the healths of the royal family were drunk in 'every accent known to civilization'.

Amid all the conviviality and manly athletic contests there were IOC members at Athens with important matters to discuss. At a meeting in 1904 the Fourth Olympiad of the 'official' Olympic series, scheduled for 1908, had been awarded to Italy to be mounted in Rome. However, once back home, the good intentions of the Italian representatives had become mired in political rivalries. The authorities of Milan and Turin resented the idea of national resources and international attention being focused on Roman games. The eruption of Mount Vesuvius on 4 April 1906 set the seal on the matter. The Italian representatives arrived at Athens seeking an alternative host for 1908.

Relaxing on the *Branwen* out in the shining seas of Phalerum Bay, discussion among the knights turned to the possibility of mounting the Fourth Olympiad in London. At one of the many social events, Lord Desborough took the opportunity of having a word with the King. Edward VII expressed his approval.

So it was that at a meeting of the IOC in Athens, with the British King, Queen and Prince and Princess of Wales in attendance, the Italian representatives formally offered the English representatives the privilege of mounting the 1908 Games. Lord Desborough, on behalf of the English, accepted.

Massed royals processing at the opening of the Athens Games on Sunday 22 April 1906. King George I of Greece and his wife Olga lead, followed by Edward VII and Queen Alexandra. Imre Kiralfy ensured that the opening ceremonies of the 1908 Olympics were rather more elaborate.

⊷⇒ ⇐⊷

Having assumed the task of organising the Fourth Olympiad in under two years, with no funding in place and no appropriate stadium to serve as principal venue, Lord Desborough suited up to compete in the international épée team tournament. The Crown Prince of Greece had offered a special prize in addition to any Olympic medals, and the King of Greece's private secretary was president of the jury. At eleven o'clock on Tuesday morning of the concluding week of the Games, King Edward and Queen Alexandra, accompanied by the Prince and Princess of Wales and their hosts, the King and Queen of Greece and their sons, descended on the fencing ground. They examined swords and admired the colours and caps Cook had produced for his team until their opponents – the Germans – arrived rather late.

Lord Desborough and Edgar Seligman proceeded to beat every one of the German swordsmen, winning the round by nine points to two. Edward VII was so cheered by the victory that on his return to London His Majesty would send a message to Theodore Cook, informing him that henceforth the monarch would be the patron of the Amateur Fencing Association of Great Britain and Ireland. That afternoon Great Britain took first and second place in the mile swim across Phalerum Bay and as darkness fell there was a torch-lit procession around the central square of Athens. During the evening the British royal family left Greece for Naples full of the success of the Olympic Games.

Cook's team made it to the final. They were beaten by the French on points, according to Cook himself; according to *The Times* they drew to become joint winners. Whatever the truth of the matter, Duff Gordon became the first English fencer to hit four Frenchmen one after the other in the final heat of an international competition – an achievement of which the knights would always be proud.

The good weather held right through to the splendid climax of the Games, the conclusion of the marathon race. It was watched by 60,000 in the stadium and more outside. Greeks from every district south of Turkey packed the heights above the arena, marshalled by a solid line of soldiers picked out against the blue sky around the circling hills.

The next day the prize-giving took place in the white marble stadium. Theodore Cook and Lord Desborough each walked in their turn between the two columns with their ancient marble heads, up on to the royal stand to receive their medals from the hands of the King of Greece.*

'I still preserve the branch of olive from the ancient Altis of Olympia in Elis which accompanied our medals,' reminisced Cook fondly, years later. 'We must have looked rather like a bridal procession as we descended the dais from the royal stand and walked down the centre of the white marble amphitheatre, which was crowded with cheering Greeks.'

In terms of points and prizes, the British enjoyed limited success at Athens – unless (as Cook did) you classed the Canadian winner of the marathon, Bill Sherring, as British. Lieutenant Hawtrey won gold in the 5 mile race. Britons came first in the high jump, the hop, step and jump (now called, less amusingly, the triple jump), the 1 mile (1,600 metre) swimming race and the clay-pigeon shooting. Two British cyclists won the 2,000 metre tandem race and another the 20 kilometre cycle race. Contrary to Cook's philosophy, the freestyle discus was won by an American policeman, Martin Sheridan, a man of no classical education who had not attended an English public school but who nonetheless set a new world record of 41.46 metres.

In respect of the next step in the Olympic story and the British contribution to it, the importance of the Athens Games lay in personal connections and experiences. Both Theodore Cook and Charles Newton Robinson would serve on the British Olympic Council (BOC) that organised the

---

* In Cook's case, the trophies were those won by Seligman and Robinson, who had left early for another competition in Paris.

1908 Games. Lord Desborough would be the invaluable president and Cook would compile the official report of those Games. In Cook's opinion:

> Since the Olympic movement began no such successful games had previously been held as those of 1906 in Athens; and it is very largely due to that success and to the fact that it was witnessed and enjoyed by our own King and Queen, and by the Prince and Princess of Wales, that the organisation of the official Games of 1908 in London was undertaken and carried through.

Rather like that ancient citizenship defined by the reach of a herald's cry, Cook and Desborough's shining memory of that spring trip to Athens could not entirely be shared by those who did not have school songs or who had never been taught to pronounce Pindar in the ancient Greek. Nonetheless that sunny experience was the origin and glowing inspiration for the First London Olympics of 1908.

CHAPTER
2

THE WHITE CITY

The great attraction in London this year is, without
doubt, the Exhibition at Shepherd's Bush. It will take the
Londoner from his desk, and his business, from his
suburban home and garden, and land him, family and
all, probably more than once or twice, by one railway
system or another, in the midst of a new and gigantic
pleasure ground.

A PICTORIAL GUIDE TO THE FRANCO-BRITISH EXHIBITION, 1908

LORD DESBOROUGH RETURNED to the sobering light of
a damp London. The British government believed in
private enterprise; whatever expressions of princely support
might have been voiced in Athens, it was not offering any
Olympic subsidies. If Desborough failed to deliver there
was a chance that the Olympics might slip out of Baron de
Coubertin's grasp. In Athens, the Crown Prince of Greece had
been touting the notion that 1906 should become the first of
a Greek revival, initiating a new four-yearly cycle of Olympic
Games in the white marble stadium. In May 1906 that option
must have seemed the more logical course. Desborough had

no budget and no central venue in which to mount the London Games in two years' time. But he was not alone. He had the support of his British colleague on the IOC, the Reverend Robert de Courcy Laffan.

Robert Laffan had become a friend of Pierre de Coubertin in July 1897 when he stood to address an Olympic conference at Le Havre – in perfect French and with peculiar eloquence – on the moral uses of the sporting phenomenon. A striking man, with a 'face of rare *finesse*',[1] the English clergyman argued that through sport man came to know himself better and that sport served as a path to the establishment of the Brotherhood of Man. De Coubertin recognised instantly that he had found, as he later recorded, a 'collaborator of the most invaluable quality'.[2]

De Coubertin's chief apostle (according to Cook):
Robert Laffan, founder of the British Olympic
Association, a silver-tongued enthusiast with Irish roots.

Laffan's linguistic abilities were not his sole charm. He was attending the meeting as representative of the Headmasters' Conference. (The distinction of being a British 'public school' rested on the headmaster being a member of the Headmasters' Conference – admittance to which was by invitation only.) Like Rugby's headmaster, Thomas Arnold, Robert de Courcy Laffan was a Wykehamist. He graduated from Merton College, Oxford, with a first-class Classics degree and was ordained in the Church of England. In 1884, at the age of 31, he was appointed headmaster of King Edward VI School in Stratford-upon-Avon – an institution that counts Shakespeare among its alumni. Having joined the school at a low point in its history, he made a great success of it, but it was not a 'public school'. So in 1895 Laffan moved on to become headmaster of Cheltenham College, which was. Thus, when he addressed the IOC at The Hague he did so as the voice of the English public school – that manly, learned Christian gentleman, grown out of the teachings of Thomas Arnold, teachings which Pierre de Coubertin had studied and worked to transplant into the French educational system.

Before he left Le Havre, Laffan was co-opted on to the International Olympic Committee. As he would later describe it: 'I came to the Olympic Movement prepared to scoff and I remained to admire – and to work.'[3] He would remain a member of the IOC for the next thirty years. The encounter with de Coubertin came at a crossroads in Laffan's life. His move to Cheltenham College had not proved happy. He was looking for a new purpose. He found it in de Coubertin's Olympic vision.

The Olympic movement transformed Robert Laffan. As headmaster of Cheltenham College he was the Reverend Robert Laffan, who happened to have a middle Christian

name of 'de Courcy' in honour of a distant relative. As a
member of the IOC and the personal friend of Baron de
Coubertin he was ennobled; he became the Reverend de
Courcy Laffan. His horizons expanded. In thirty years he only
missed three meetings as the IOC gathered in the various
leading cities of Europe. He left his public school career to
become Rector of St Stephen's Walbrook, a post that allowed
him time for his new mission. In 1906 Laffan was 52, an
eloquent Irish dreamer disguised as a slightly pompous man
with an almost obsessive eye for detail.

In order to make the London Games a reality, Desborough
and Laffan had to create a national network. The British
Olympic Association was both new and unrepresentative.
Formed from a group of sporting gentlemen in 1905, it had
been set up to popularise the ideals of the Olympic movement
and represent British sport in IOC discussions. In 1906 the
BOA had no headquarters and no national representation. At
the IOC meeting in Athens, the British representatives had
agreed to host the Games on condition that their country's
principal sporting associations approved. So, once back in
London, Lord Desborough and Robert Laffan began to write
letters. They wrote to the leadership of every principal
national sporting organisation in Great Britain and Ireland
asking for their support and collaboration in mounting the
Fourth Olympiad in London.

In the pages of the *Tatler*, *Vanity Fair* or *Hearth and Home*,
Lord Desborough inhabited an insular and aristocratic
world. His wife's set of friends – the 'Souls', a social elite who
prided themselves on their conversational skills – regarded
him as a taciturn man, but he had been a popular mayor of
Maidenhead and he served on a range of sober, useful committees throughout his working life. His presidency of the

London Olympics proved his considerable administrative abilities. With Robert Laffan's assistance, he drew together a British Olympic Council of 40 men, comprising a handful of the most committed members of the British Olympic Association and the presidents or 'honorary secretaries' of Great Britain's sporting associations. All the principal sporting activities in the United Kingdom at the time were represented – save cricket and horse racing – from amateur athletics through clay-pigeon shooting, cycling, football, golf, life saving, motoring and swimming to yacht racing (motor and sail). The 1908 Olympic Games would be mounted through the volunteer work of these men and the honourable members of their associations.

On 19 November 1906, the *Sporting Life* scooped the news that that day the British Olympic Council would 'decide … that the fourth celebration of the original series of Olympic games should be held in London in the month of July, 1908'.

The sportsmen of Great Britain had rallied to the cause but the problem of a venue remained. Of all London's sporting venues there was none whose facilities approached those of the Athens stadium. However, to their good fortune, it happened that that autumn Lord Desborough and Robert Laffan were not the only ones to consider mounting a grand international event. Across in Kensington, in a small office, an exuberant, tireless Hungarian émigré of colourful life experience was planning the greatest exhibition London had seen since that held at Crystal Palace in 1851.

Imre Kiralfy was a master of spectacle. He was born Imre Konigsbaum, the eldest son of a prosperous Jewish clothing manufacturer, in the Hungarian city of Pest in 1845. During

The man the Duke of Argyll called 'le Roi des Fétes' –
Imre Kiralfy with his wife, Marie (née Graham),
an English dancer.

the uprising of 1848, his father lost his business supporting the Hungarian patriots against the Austrian Empire and the family name was changed to Kiralfy. Imre began performing Hungarian folk dances at the age of four. Throughout his childhood he toured the Austro-Hungarian Empire with his brother, Bolossy, jumping and performing trick turns in the

athletic folk dances of their birthplace, dressed in tiny hussar
jackets and knee-high boots. By their early teens the brothers
were established celebrities in the Empire, supporting their
large family with their dance act, constructed around fast,
acrobatic Magyar folk dances. When Imre was 23, their career
as child prodigies fading, the brothers organised their first
municipal fête in Brussels. They went on to build a name for
themselves in America as impresarios of vast dance-based
spectaculars featuring flamboyant sets, extensive female
chorus lines, and innovative special effects. (The Kiralfy
brothers' productions have been credited with influencing
both Busby Berkeley's prismatic dance routines and the stag-
ing of D.W. Griffith's epic film sequences.)

In 1887 – the same year Willie Grenfell married the Cowper
heiress, Ettie Fane – the Kiralfy brothers quarrelled violently
and never spoke again. Imre went into partnership with
Phineas Barnum of the Barnum and Bailey Circus, honing
the art of the grand historical spectacular with vast productions such as *Nero and the Burning of Rome*. Moving to London
in the late 1880s, he graduated to fixed exhibitions and was
appointed director of the Earls Court exhibition grounds. He
became a naturalised British citizen in 1901.

Imre Kiralfy infused American-scale showmanship into
the traditional nineteenth-century British exhibition. The
Edwardian public was mildly curious about the far-flung
world. The *Illustrated London News* regularly printed intriguing
plates depicting 'The examination halls at Nanchang Fu
Kiangsi China' or 'The strange dead city of Koh-I-Kouadja
in Eastern Persia'. A Cairo bazaar, a Burmese village complete
with tumblers, a Swiss mountain railway on miniature
plaster hills – Kiralfy's exhibitions offered safe glimpses of the
cosmopolitan and the exotic to a largely insular public.

With the assistance of his son Charles, Kiralfy produced a series of elaborate exhibitions at Olympia and the Earls Court grounds – many on the imperial theme. Early in 1893, Kiralfy was approached by representatives of the British Empire League. The League was considering the possibility of mounting a grand British Empire Exhibition combined with a series of Pan-Britannic games. The timing was appropriate. Imre Kiralfy was approaching 60; balding, with wings of bushy hair and a moustache that perhaps was helped a little with dye, he was restless. The Earls Court exhibition grounds had become too cramped for his vision. For Imre Kiralfy had had a dream.

> One night I lay awake in bed, and, as if by magic, I saw stretched out in my mind's eye, an imposing city of palaces, domes, and towers, set in cool, green spaces and intersected by many bridged canals. But it had one characteristic which made it strangely beautiful. Hitherto I had dealt in colour in the shimmering hues of gold and silver. This city was spotlessly white. I saw it all in an instant ...[4]

Kiralfy was a shrewd publicist. In fact principal elements of his vision – in particular, the white palaces – were borrowed from that year's grand Columbian Exposition in Chicago, where he and his son Charles had produced the spectacular half-pageant, half-play, *America*, as part of the celebrations. However, Kiralfy was determined to outstrip his inspiration. Decades before Disneyland, he would combine fairytale palaces with his passion for the romance of Venetian bridges and canals, to create a fanciful white city. It would be the pinnacle of his achievements, the climax of his long career.

A site was earmarked in Shepherd's Bush but the Japanese

war intervened. The British League's commitment faded. Kiralfy's vision had to be shelved for nearly a decade.

At the beginning of the twentieth century, the map of British foreign relations was shaped by the question of how to deal with the ambitions of the recently unified Germany under Kaiser Wilhelm II – and in particular, with the German Emperor's ambitions to acquire colonial territories to match those of the French and British. Queen Victoria and her ministers had favoured the Germans over the French in foreign relations. It was widely reported, however, that Edward VII did not like his nephew Wilhelm, the German Emperor (hence his pleasure at the knights' success at Athens). 'Willie' had been Queen Victoria's favourite great-nephew – in contrast to the famously difficult relationship between Her Majesty and her eldest son and heir. As Prince of Wales, Edward had passed enjoyable times in Paris and in the more fashionable French coastal resorts. As King he used his conviviality to initiate an alliance with France. In 1903 he visited Paris on a charm offensive. The following year he signed an entente with the French President settling a long-standing colonial dispute, by agreeing British jurisdiction over Egypt and French control over Morocco.

Imre Kiralfy perceived an opportunity. He went to see his friend Monsieur Mercadier and brought out the plans for his white city. It would be, he suggested, the perfect showcase for an Anglo-French exhibition, a peacock display of the products and resources of the two allies and their colonies.

As it happened, the French Chambers of Commerce were already pondering such a grand dual exhibition. (As a nation, the French were such keen exhibitors that they had a permanent government body, the Comité Français des Expositions à l'Étranger, to organise national participation in international exhibitions.) Mercadier was enthusiastic. He took the proposal to the French ambassador while Kiralfy approached the Duke of Argyll, who was married to Edward VII's younger sister, Louise. The Duke floated the idea with the King. The King expressed his approval. A committee was formed under the Duke of Argyll and the Earl of Derby. They set to work with the French *Comité*. A group of wealthy aristocrats, including Lord Rothschild, Lord Strathcona and Sir Ernest Cassel, provided substantial donations to set the project on its feet. The site earmarked years previously, a large area of industrial scrubland running alongside Wood Lane in Shepherd's Bush, was acquired on lease from the Church Commissioners. At a ground-breaking ceremony on 3 January 1907, the Count H. de Manneville turned the first sod on behalf of the French ambassador. Imre Kiralfy set about the business of constructing his white city in plaster, concrete and electric lights.

The Franco-British Exhibition was intended to outstrip the glories of the Crystal Palace Exhibition of 1851 – that famed high-water mark of Victorian confidence. At 140 acres, an area half the size of Kensington Gardens, the grounds would cover seven times the area of the 1851 Exhibition. Even the International Exhibition of 1862, previously the largest exhibition held in Britain, had covered a mere 23½ acres. In a machinery hall and palaces of arts and sciences, the Anglo-French alliance would display the evidence that together they represented the fount and arbiter of the Western civilisation that ordered the entire world.

Plans for the Franco-British Exhibition were well advanced when Lord Desborough returned from Athens. Every true Edwardian believed that athletic sports and games were part of the English character. It was a standard British boast that the principal rules of sport had been forged on the playing

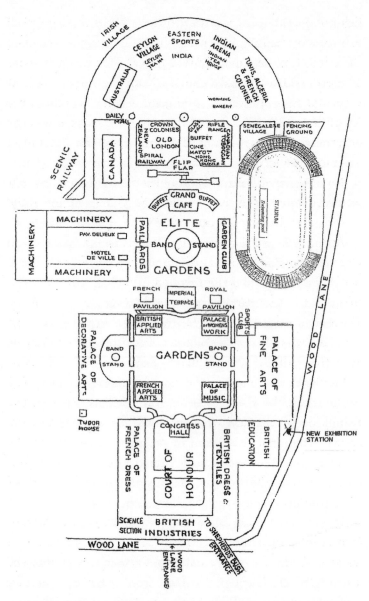

Map of the Franco-British Exhibition. Admission was one shilling (some £4 today) and season tickets could be purchased for a guinea (translating to around £80).

fields of the English aristocracy. If there was to be an imperial display sport had to play a part. The Exhibition was pencilled in for 1907 but the opportunity for Great Britain, motherland of sport, to host the quadrennial Olympic Games, 'revived at the instance of France', was too good to miss. Whether Imre Kiralfy sought out Lord Desborough, or whether it was the other way around, they found one another. The Exhibition was moved to 1908.

Kiralfy offered Lord Desborough a purpose-built arena. It would be state-of-the-art, a modern marvel to compare to the historic marble amphitheatre of Athens.

At a meeting held at the Bath Club, 34 Dover Street, on 20 December 1906, Lord Desborough put the proposition to his newly assembled British Olympic Council. The Franco-British Exhibition Company would build a stadium on the Shepherd's Bush site to the specifications of the BOC. The company would bear all the costs of constructing and operating the stadium (at an estimated cost of £44,000 – or about £3.1 million in 2006 values) and give the Council exclusive use of the facilities for two weeks in July 1908. In exchange the Exhibition would take three-quarters of the gross receipts earned from those two weeks – from the gate money, the stand receipts and the monies raised from sales of programmes and advertising (that is, fees paid for the use of the Olympic name).

In the past de Coubertin's Olympics had suffered from association with exhibitions. The Second Olympiad had been allied with the Paris International Exposition of 1900; the Third Olympiad had been tacked on to the Louisiana Purchase Exposition at St Louis in 1904. In both cases the exhibition organisers had borrowed the Olympic cachet and then run several of the sporting events as exhibition tournaments – so that many competitors were never clear whether they took part in Olympic events or not. Mr Fisher of the Amateur Athletic Association (AAA), a prominent member of the Council, objected that a virgin track would hamper Olympic competitors and result in slower times. Lord Desborough countered mildly that all previous Olympic races had been run on purpose-built tracks. Tube line extensions were being laid and new stations being built to draw the public to Shepherd's Bush. When they were finished, it was estimated that 75,000 people per working hour could be transported to the White City by tram, omnibus, tube and railway. The Exhibition would attract people to the Games, and the Games would attract people to the Exhibition.

No other venue was about to offer such advantageous terms. As Lord Desborough pointed out to the members of the British Olympic Council, all three previous Olympic Games had been run at a heavy deficit. The Franco-British Exhibition Company was proposing to indemnify the British Olympic Association against any losses and in addition advance them £2,000 against their share of the receipts to cover expenses in the run-up to the Games. At one stroke the London Olympic organisers would gain both a venue and freedom from financial worry. They put the matter to the vote. The council instructed Desborough to sign the agreement.

Over the next 18 months passengers passing the Shepherd's Bush site by tram or train watched industrial sheds torn down, canals and lagoons dug and gardens laid out. Twenty palaces and some forty other buildings arose, fashioned out of steel frames filled with fireproof concrete and 300,000 plaster slabs. At a cost of just over £2 million (which translates to somewhere in the region of £143 million in 2006), Kiralfy's dream took shape.

Thousands of cards, guides and booklets of views were printed to celebrate the Exhibition. They leave an impression of windswept size and the mad efforts of a plasterer with a penchant for cake decoration. Pinnacles, domes, arcades (Far Eastern, Arab and Gothic), rotundas and terraces, semi-circular balconies, Greek Doric columns and Arab minarets; filigree bits and twirls and fretted inlay and shallow ponds edged with municipal flower plantings. Architectural glimpses of Oxford and Cambridge and Siam mixed with impressions of India and Cairo; touches of Haussmann's Paris, fifteenth-century Florence, a sixteenth-century Dutch roof; a glimpse of the Taj Mahal or the Gare du Nord – anything that might seem exotic and foreign to the average Edwardian suburbanite was pressed and pushed together in one Shepherd's Bush plot.

The Exhibition opened its doors every day except Sunday, from ten in the morning until a quarter past eleven at night, from May to October 1908. In that time 8.4 million visitors passed through its turnstiles.

Under the external peacock gorgeousness many of the exhibits were endearingly homely: the British sports hall with its 'fishing rods, footballs, gymnastic apparatus and sporting powders';[5] an instructive panorama of the Whitstable oyster from spat to maturity in the British Alimentation hall or the 'battalions of toothpicks' and an arch made of packets of French chocolate in the French equivalent. In the French Social Economy hall, photographs of dirigible balloons hung next to 'excellent suggestions for simple and sanitary hotel furniture' offered by the Touring Club of France, alongside a large stall crowned by a bust of Louis Pasteur which unsettled observers with 'awe-inspiring cultures of various deadly diseases'.

One of the Exhibition's entrances in Wood Lane: once through the turnstiles 'indifferent walkers' could hire three-wheeled chairs or two-wheeled rickshaws to be pushed or pulled about the twenty miles of tiled paths, or catch the Rénard Road Train that shuttled visitors to the north end of the Exhibition with its colonial palaces and village displays.

The gleaming white palaces were arranged in a series of courts. The Court of Honour, where the British and French Palaces of Industry faced each other across an ornamental lake, the Court of Arts set around gardens, the Elite Gardens court with the Court of Progress branching off it. The Court of Honour was much admired. At its northern end stood the Congress Hall, a three-tiered, Siamese-inspired rotunda with a terrace and the Cascade Café. Here bands played above a glass staircase over which water flowed back down into the lake. Crossing the lagoon was a wide bridge of mixed parentage – Indian panels, Arab fretwork and Siamese balconies with domed canopies providing viewpoints from which court and lake could be admired. Swan boats, pedalled by men in white uniforms, took visitors around the lake and up and

The popular swan boats. After dark, flotillas of these swans would take visitors, at sixpence a ride, across the lagoon in the Court of Honour to admire the grand cascade lit up at the head of the lake.

down the canals that branched left and right into the Court of Arts and beyond. When darkness fell, thousands of electric glow-lamps lit the facades, and coloured lights behind the glass stairs of the cascade cast the water into rainbows of sparkling light.

On the edges of the monstrous quadrangle that was the Court of Arts were grouped the French and British Palaces of Applied Arts, of Fine Art and Decorative Art. The swan boats glided down the canal past the Palace of Music, the home of concerts and floral displays and of band performances in wet weather. In the French Palace of Applied Art there was always a crowd about the case displaying a blue diamond valued at £25,000 (equivalent to about £1.8 million in 2006). In the Palace of French Industries ladies inspected Paris fashions and, behind a heavy curtain, marvelled at Messrs Revillon Frères' illuminated tableaux of 'their agents engaged, alike in the desert and in the Far North, in securing costly skins'. In the Palace of Woman's Work the vista of cases displaying examples of needlework and crafts was broken by the carriage used by Florence Nightingale in the Crimea and a hospital set where real nurses tended bandaged dummies tucked up in bed. And should some lady have a practical domestic question on her mind ... 'At the enquiry office one can obtain information on every profession and calling that is open to women. A lady applied the other day for a lady gardener, and she was quickly accommodated with one.'

At the heart of the Exhibition, the Imperial Terrace stood between the Court of Arts and the Elite Gardens. On it the Royal Pavilion, built and furnished for the reception of King Edward VII, faced the Louis XV Pavilion, built by the government of the Third Republic to commemorate that last absolute French monarch, famed for ignoring oncoming catastrophe with a shrug: '*Après moi le déluge.*' As a central symbol of the imperial display it was somewhat unhappy. The English pavilion had originally been conceived as a 250-foot tower, only 23 feet less in height than the campanile of the Roman Catholic Cathedral at Westminster, but ambitions had to be truncated. In its final form the building resembled a fussy but economical single-tier wedding cake. It served as a useful rendezvous for lost parties.

The Imperial Terrace led into the Elite Gardens, set around a sunken bandstand where, for threepence, you could enter the enclosure to occupy one of the 1,500 chairs sheltered from chilly evening breezes and listen to military bands. To the west was the Restaurant Paillard, cut with a central arch leading through into the Court of Progress where modernity was paraded in vast halls of machinery. To the east, behind the Garden Club, the massive steel-strutted sides of the stadium loomed over the white daintiness and green, an uncouth reminder of the modern world.

Imre Kiralfy was determined that the Franco-British Exhibition would become the favourite resort of the fashionable in the summer of 1908. To that end he built the Garden Club (subscriptions £3 3s for gentlemen and £2 2s for ladies – in modern values, something in the region of £230 and £150) to attract the social elite. Two storeys with verandas in white-washed baroque, trimmed with a band of spindly trees, stood back to back with the stadium's royal stand. As a head-quarters for the organisers of the Olympic Games and to attract sporting aristocrats, he also built the Imperial Sports Club at the south-west end of the stadium.

The ladies and gentlemen had their clubs; the rest of the world had Mr Lyons's Grand Restaurant where the average man could entertain his family with light refreshments moderately priced. Grander patrons dined at M. Paillard's select French restaurant, a long, low building remarkable for its 'fantastic caryatides, representing nymphs and satyrs'. Lyons's mass catering did better business. According to the Exhibition accounts Lyons & Co. made £441,936 over the season compared to the fancy French restaurant's £65,065 (perhaps £31,730,000 in modern values for Lyons' share, contrasting with £4,670,500 for Paillard's restaurant).

The Court of Progress was reached via an arch bisecting the Restaurant Paillard, the resort of the aristocratic and rich. The importance of Progress was indicated in the main Machinery Hall, a massive Gothic structure with a twist of Gormenghast, and with a floor-print of 300,000 square feet. On this scale, Progress was rather overwhelming.

Exhibition-goers, clutching their Valentine's postcard views, were inclined to pool around the pretty array of model ships and the giant model railway set provided by the London and North Western Railway – 'which at stated hours is worked by electricity, to the unbounded delight of children, especially boys'.

The most remarked-upon piece of modern ingenuity on display in the exhibition was the Flip-Flap, a new take on the American Ferris wheel, an Edwardian predecessor of the London Eye. Two latticed steel, counterweighted arms, driven by electrical engine, lifted up passengers for a bird's-eye view of the grounds and the city beyond. The public were inclined to doubt its stability. Those not brave enough to 'flip or flap' preferred to spend their sixpence on the scenic railway, an electric train that speeded at up to 50 miles per hour over a mile of switchback track crammed with plaster mountains, valleys, wooden bridges and viaducts, lakes, waterfalls and 'charmingly lit caves'.

The Flip-Flap – the Edwardian version of the London Eye. Two cars hanging from cantilevered arms, 150 feet long, paused at the mid-point to give a bird's-eye view of the Exhibition and the surrounding metropolis. Carpers, determined to face the wrong way, objected that the view of the metropolis was confined to Wormwood Scrubs.

The Flip-Flap marked the fairground attractions grouped around the colonial palaces at the northern end of the grounds. The French had an Algerian palace, which shared its space with the products of Tunis and the other French territories. The British Indian government authorities contributed an airy palace of significant size. The India Palace had its own gardens where elephants, camels and zebus* drawing 'quaint

* Zebu (*Bos primigenius indicus*), humped cattle native to South Asia and Africa with large dewlaps and droopy ears.

[39]

little Indian carts' waited to give children rides. Beneath its minarets and domes there were sandalwood carvings from Mysore, Jaipur pots, silks and carpets from Kashmir. A Bengal village served as background to the Jute section sponsored by Messrs Thomas Duff & Co., and a vast wooden showcase displayed the delicate craftsmanship of native carvers in every kind of indigenous wood alongside motor-car bodies by Mr Press of Bombay. (The Franco-British Exhibition had practical purpose as a trade fair. The Commercial Bureau, sited in the British Liberal Arts section, offered visiting businessmen assistance in the form of a battalion of clerks and the latest quick-filing system to facilitate networking.)

The Canadian Palace was almost as large as the Indian Palace, if plainer in design. Exhibition-goers flocked to see its giant grain hopper towering to the roof, built entirely of grain and stalks, and its original tableaux of historical and topical scenes carved in butter.* The Australian Pavilion was smaller and resembled a biscuit box (not the most luxurious kind, but the sort you might give an aunt you see once a year at Christmas). The New Zealand exhibits were housed in a shed with perfunctory columns shared with the Spiral fairground ride.

For all its dignified intentions to forge the commercial links that would strengthen the Franco-British alliance, the success of the White City belonged to Kiralfy as a premier provider of mass entertainment. Who would linger among motor-car bodies or toothpicks when they could take their children to ride on elephants, camels or carts drawn by zebus? Or consider the virtues of Canadian apples when the Indian

---

* One group commemorated the King and M. Fallières, another the landing of Jacques Cartier at Montreal in 1535.

Arena beckoned with its thrice-daily production 'Our Indian Empire', with its 'realistic' tiger hunt during which a dozen fully grown elephants and their riders slid down a 40-foot precipice into a lake? The purveyor of American showmanship knew what the people wanted.

Behind the tea house (where you could buy a cup of tea from Messrs Lipton & Co.) was the Ceylon Village, a picturebook scene of Colombo, Gate of the Far East – coloured houses, bazaars and a pagoda built up on fake rocks, complete with imported native jugglers, dancers, cheerful children and chattering monkeys. Next door, the French colonial

A bird's-eye view of the Franco-British Exhibition: the great attraction of London 1908, offering the visitor, 'the opportunity of seeing all that is beautiful and ingenious in French, and what is equally beautiful and practical in English'.

government provided the Senegalese Village. For a shilling you could enter the stockade and watch 'scenes of domestic life' performed by a hundred men, women and children imported from the borders of the Sahara to live in straw huts 'exactly as they do in their native Africa'. The Ceylon Village was the more popular of the two offerings; admission cost only sixpence and they had better entertainers. And then there was the Irish Village.

Beyond the golden dome of the Daily Mail Pavilion, where special editions of the *Daily Mail* and the *Evening News* were printed before visitors' eyes, an anorexic round tower pointed skywards behind an entrance gate of pseudo-medieval towers complete with flags, marking Ballymaclinton Village. In this Irish theme park there was not a whisper of Home Rule. Smiling colleens stood about a reproduction of the thousand-year-old cross at Donaghmore and posed for snapshots in cottage doorways working lace. There was a Galway fisherman's cottage, the obligatory Blarney Stone, a Pig of Paddy and a mini herd of Kerry cows. For the American visitor there was a reconstruction – more of a reproduction or interpretation, perhaps – of the thatched cottage in which a grandparent of the late President McKinley was born, made out of the 'actual doors and windows, stairs, flooring, and rafters, the large iron griddle and crane, the lucky horse-shoe etc., from the old home at Ballymoney, County Antrim'. The sponsors of this 'typical Irish village' were McClinton's soap factory (specialities 'toilet, tooth and shaving soaps'), hence the name. The declared purpose was to 'represent Irish life and to direct attention to the rural industries of Ireland'. All proceeds, it was said, were to be devoted to the suppression of consumption in Ireland.

*A not-so-smiling
Ballymaclinton
colleen. A souvenir
postcard advertising
McClinton's soap:
'The Irish Colleens
use this soap, note
their beautiful
complexions.'*

A Ballymaclinton Colleen.
Franco British Exhibition. London. 1908.

POST CARD.

BALLYMACLINTON (McClinton's Town)
erected by the makers of McClinton's Soap.
The Irish Colleens use this soap, note their
beautiful complexions

Address.

Visitors crowded to watch English handmade glass produced by Thos. Webb & Sons of Stourbridge. They sat in the
dark to enjoy the novelty of moving pictures in the Pathé Frères
Cinematograph Hall, where 'classical tales and pantomimes'
alternated with 'representations of actual incidents' captured
around the exhibition and stadium the previous day. They
flocked to the Spider's Web, the rifle range and the Spiral –
'An absolutely new form of gravity railway with the delights
of the toboggan and the switchback cleverly combined'. They
were gloriously confused by the Hong-Kong Puzzle House, the
latest thing in mazes (the unsuspecting victim stepped into 'a
cylinder, and this revolving for a few minutes, he is, on leaving,
completely in the dark as to his whereabouts'). The most popular sideshow of all was the Johnstown Flood, imported from
America. From 11 am to 11 pm the public packed the hall to see
re-enacted the destruction of a manufacturing town in the
Allegheny Mountains one May afternoon in 1889 when a dam
burst after heavy rain.* There was the peaceful town on a May
evening and a glorious sunset; then a deluge of water swept the
inhabitants to destruction: 'Men, women and children struggle
for life amidst the debris in the seething maelstrom of waters.
Nothing can exceed the realism of the effect.'

Musical comedy gorgeousness, village hall displays and
colonial village sets: this stocktaking of the civilisation that
purported to lead the world was not what it hoped to be. In
answer to the Crystal Palace, that 1851 marvel of modern
engineering, the Franco-British Exhibition of 1908 offered
the truncated pretensions of a plasterboard pavilion.

---

* The show took some licence in the interests of dramatic effect. The actual
dam burst at 3 pm on 31 May 1889 after solid hours of heavy rain. Some
2,200 townspeople died when 200 million tons of water swept away the
heart of the city.

'In every exhibition of modern times one question has asked itself,' wrote the reviewer in *Blackwood's Magazine*: 'Is invention dead?'

> Neither in France nor in England has a beautiful style been evolved since the days of the Empire. Then continuity seems to have been snapped, and the artificers of today can do no more than copy the ancient patterns. We can assign no style to the Third Republic or to Edward VII. We admit all styles, and invent none … Our generation will pass away, leaving behind it little that is authentically its own. Its fame will be the fame of the collector.[6]

The White City was a pretty confection of the set designer's art, plaster crumbling at the edges and wooden props visible behind the hoardings.

'I felt it was necessary to surpass all my previous labours,' said Imre Kiralfy of the genesis of his White City. 'I must have something at once novel and commanding – something in keeping with the greatness of the project.' But he always knew that his plaster city was destined to be 'as evanescent as a summer's dream'. It was the noble purpose of the Olympic Games and the stadium he built because of the return of Lord Desborough from Athens in May 1906 that contained Kiralfy's hope of securing his White City lasting fame.[7]

THE STADIUM

England has led the way in manly sports. The games
which her sons first played, or reduced to order by rules
and regulations, have been adopted by many nations ...
she will suffer lasting disgrace if the Games of 1908 are not
only equal in extent and interest to those which have
preceded them, but so far superior as to develop a vast
increase of zeal for these international gatherings.

EVENING STANDARD, 24 NOVEMBER 1906

ON A PERFECTLY ENGLISH afternoon in early May the
employees of the White City prepared to open the
Shepherd's Bush grounds. French and English workmen took
down scaffolding poles; they bedded in the last few cartloads
of flowering plants and brushed green paint on the Flip-Flap.
The strains of the 'Marseillaise' drifted out from the Palace of
Music where the London Symphony Orchestra and a choir of
700 men and women rehearsed for the opening ceremonies.
In the Court of Honour a flock of electricians tested the triple
rows of electric lights and a band of engineers prepared to
flood the lagoon. The people of the Ceylon Village had arrived

with their elephants. The stockade stood ready for the West Africans who were expected any day. In the stadium 200 soldiers of the Coldstream Guards marched round the cinder track and negotiated their way across the freshly cemented cycle path. They climbed the new-painted steps up into the terraces and formed rows where the circular ends met the straight sides. At their officer's shouted command they began to mark time, their heavy boots ringing out on the concrete. Beneath them a district surveyor peered up at the steel skeleton while the London County Council surveyor and an architect watched from a safe distance. This scientific stress test was repeated at various points and pronounced a success. 'Everything secure, not a sign of vibration.'[1]

When he signed the contract with Lord Desborough back in January 1907 Imre Kiralfy had promised that the sporting

The Stadium, Franco-British Exhibition, London, 1908

An artist's impression of the stadium as Kiralfy originally envisaged it. The outer cladding with the tower was never realised as the Exhibition Company ran short of money.

[47]

facilities would be ready by June 1908; he kept his word. Lady Desborough placed the first stanchion of the arena on 2 August 1907 (she had help; Ettie, Lady Desborough, was not known for her construction skills). The cinder running track was finished by Christmas that year. Although construction took only ten months, costs nonetheless doubled from the original estimates. The Exhibition Company ran short of money. The steel-strutted oval was not quite the imposing edifice of the artist's impression but by May 1908 it was serviceable and ready for sport.

Determined to recreate the 'animated picture' of athletics enjoyed at Athens, the British Olympic Council ensured that the stadium could accommodate the broad spectrum of popular sports. The steel and concrete structure incorporated a cement cycle track, a grass track for hurdle races, a cinder running track and a swimming pool. The BOC's Running Track Committee (principally Lord Desborough and Mr Fisher of the Amateur Athletic Association, with Theo Cook acting as secretary), its Cycle Track Committee (again with the indefatigable Cook as secretary) and Swimming Pond Committee (led by Lord Desborough and Mr Henry of the Royal Life Saving Society) dedicated detailed attention to precise measurements and construction.

For all the charm of the Athens stadium, its running track had been, Theodore Cook noted, 'far from what an international racecourse ought to be'. Its corners were too sharp and its central turf was cramped to the extent that in spring 1906 the javelin competition 'nearly proved fatal to the runners in the five-mile race'.[2]

The London stadium was constructed around an ample oval measuring 700 feet by 300 feet in which javelins could be thrown with safety. Charles Perry, groundsman at the London

The newly finished stadium in summer 1908 showing the swimming bath which, at 100 metres long, was two times the length of the modern standard Olympic pool.

Athletic Club, who had been responsible for the track at Athens in 1896, supervised the construction of a cinder running track to satisfy Mr Fisher's exacting standards.* Running at three laps to the mile it had 'no awkward corners' and was 'admitted to be the finest track in the world'.[3] Around the outer edge of the arena, immediately below the seats, there was a concrete cycle track of two and three-quarter laps per mile. The Cycle Committee took a trip to Paris to inspect the renowned facilities in that city and came up with carefully considered contours banked up at the curves to a height of 10 feet and a home straight 35 feet wide. They called it the 'mile a minute track' for on it, the designers boasted, '60 miles an hour is

---

* Perry would go on to design tracks for the 1912 Stockholm Olympics and the 1920 Games in Antwerp.

attained with perfect safety'. And then, the *pièce de résistance*, in front of the Royal Stand on the west side of the stadium lay the swimming pool, 327 feet long by 48 feet wide. Fourteen feet deep at its centre to accommodate diving displays, it had the novel feature of a 55-foot diving tower that could be lowered into the water when not in use. (The water, however, was unheated, limiting its use to the summer season.)

One thousand feet long and 593 feet wide, the White City stadium was (as Kiralfy's publicity material liked to point out) as broad as the Circus Maximus of ancient Rome and longer than the Colosseum. Within its 346,283 square foot floorplan, it could hold the Albert Hall seven times over and the external breadth of the Athens arena would fit on its central oval of green turf imported from the Chiltern Hills. Whereas the Athens stadium had seats for 60,000, the ten miles of seating in the White City stadium could accommodate 68,000, with standing room for another 23,000.* Its construction involved some 3,000 tons of steel, 572,345 rivets, 13,656 tons of concrete and cost a reported £85,000 – somewhere in the region of £6.1 million in present values.

It was not just a stadium. It was a statement. The nature of that statement was underlined by the Imperial Sports Club – a white edifice with a central dome and a sheltered loggia situated just beyond the Court of Arts at the south-western end of the stadium. The Imperial Sports Club was flush with the trappings of patrician Edwardian conviviality. It had spacious dining rooms, drawing rooms, smoking rooms and a gracious circular hall 44 feet in diameter; there was even a

---

* According to Imre Kiralfy: 'By using a strip of twelve feet all round for standing room we could add another 50,000 spectators, but this will be done only if the crowd at the opening and closing ceremonies cannot be otherwise accommodated.' Interview in the *Daily Chronicle*, 22 June 1908.

The official poster of the 1908 Games designed at a cost of £49 1s 8d –
translating in modern terms to around £4,000 (in contrast to the £400,000
spent on the logo for the 2012 London Olympics).

private garage for those forward-thinking members who owned motor cars. Membership (available for gentlemen only, although ladies were admitted as guests) included free admission to the Exhibition, use of a private entrance to the stadium and for the two weeks of the Olympic Games, preferential access to a block of seats adjacent to the competitors' stand. As the *Sporting Life* reported:

> We understand that it is the intention of the Committee of the Imperial Sports Club to invite the foreign representatives of foreign nations who will be in charge of the teams, and also the Committee of Honour to be honorary members of the Club, and thus assure them a thoroughly sporting British welcome. This will have the effect of raising British sport in the eyes of our foreign athletic rivals to a higher plane than that which it even now occupies.[4]

Together the London stadium and the Imperial Sports Club announced to the world that in sport, as in all things, the British Empire led the world.

The Imperial Sports Club was a shrewd investment for the Exhibition Company. The British imperial elite were traditional in their lounges; Shepherd's Bush was not their natural haunt. Lord Desborough's presidency of the Club was an effective draw alongside his vice-presidents, the ambassadors of Russia and Austria-Hungary and the Swedish and Chilean ministers. Before the Exhibition had even opened 1,900 members had signed up – a hundred more than originally planned – including a swathe of the foreign diplomatic corps and an A to Z of lords from Lord Alington to the Duke of Westminster.

～ ～

Kiralfy and the Exhibition ensured that the London Olympics had the trappings of imperial status but it was up to the British Olympic Association to ensure that the Games were worthy of the Empire. The *Evening Standard* put the matter in its proper perspective:

> England has led the way in manly sports. The games which her sons first played, or reduced to order by rules and regulations, have been adopted by many nations. On racing and cricket, for example, she lays down the law in the full assurance that it will be obeyed without assistance from Dreadnoughts and Maxims. Holding the position she does and has done for so many years in the world of sport, she will suffer lasting disgrace if the Games of 1908 are not only equal in extent and interest to those which have preceded them, but so far superior as to develop a vast increase of zeal for these international gatherings.[5]

In the closing decades of the nineteenth century, fencers, runners, golfers, rowers, tennis players and other sportsmen from the UK, Europe, North America and Australasia travelled to compete in each other's championships with growing regularity. With the emergence of the revived Olympics, the need to establish international rules to govern sporting contests had become an increasing concern. The question was whose rules should rule. Towards the end of 1905, James E. Sullivan, the influential secretary of the Amateur Athletic Union (AAU) of America, crossed the Atlantic in pursuit of an 'athletic alliance' with England. 'Athletics have reached a stage,' he told the New York press, 'where in the interest of sport a binding agreement should be effected which will cover in detail every point in amateur athletics.'[6]

Secretary Sullivan naturally believed in the evident superiority of the AAU's rules. He was a persuasive man, but he was forced to return home without obtaining the agreement he sought when the secretary of the English Amateur Athletic Association fell from the top of a bus and was hospitalised. Still, the issue remained.

Baron Pierre de Coubertin was fond of saying that Germany had dug up the ruins of Olympia but the French had given them life. The British Olympic Council perceived in the London Games of 1908 an opportunity to regularise international sport on their pattern. If the Germans had excavated the inspiration and the French had supplied the vision, the sons of the British Empire would bind those ideals into an orderly and sustainable institution. The organisers of the London Olympics set about publishing rules for their Games with the intention of supplying the standard for future Olympics, and by that means for international competitions in general.

If the programme of the London Games was to remain manageable the number of contestants needed to be restricted. To this end the British organisers formalised a process that had already begun. One of the first threads of correspondence that flowed from Robert Laffan's pen (he was fluent in four languages) reached out to the other 24 countries represented on the IOC, encouraging those who had not already done so to set up national Olympic committees. The BOC announced that prospective contestants in the Fourth Olympiad would have to be properly accredited, their names forwarded by their national Olympic committee. Self-selected athletes – such as Theodore Cook and his team of 'thoroughly representative swordsmen' – need no longer apply. The athletes who competed in the Fourth Olympiad would to this degree – for the first time in the history of the modern Olympics – attend as members of national teams.

Each Olympic event in the London Games was organised and overseen by the relevant British sporting association. The association presidents and honourable secretaries on the BOC consulted among their members and drew up their rules – the precise approach that would be accepted in the high jump, the sort of pole allowed for the pole jump, the rules governing lane discipline and so on. Originally there was to have been a round of consultation with the various Olympic committees in the IOC membership. Lack of time truncated these good intentions. Robert Laffan gathered all the material together, translated it into French and German (emphasising that the English version of the rules was the official version) and printed it in pamphlets complete with diagrams to ship to the various national Olympic committees for distribution to contestants.

An effort was made to pass the rules before the IOC members for comment prior to their despatch around the world. No one raised any significant objections. It did not seem to occur to the authors that there might be any; after all Great Britain was the motherland of sport and the home of fair play.

The BOC's Arts Committee (Theo Cook, again, along with G.S. Robertson and two co-opted members of the Royal Academy, Sir Arthur Cope and Sir Thomas Brock) commissioned Australian-born sculptor Bertram Mackennal to produce a suitably classical-looking design for the prize medals. The intention was to provide the Olympic Games with a 'distinctive badge which no other form of athletic contest could imitate'. The London Games would leave to the Olympic movement a work of art worthy of representing the 'continuity of safeguarded record' and the status of the

Olympic record as the pinnacle of sporting achievement. In Cook's opinion, Bertram Mackennal's prize medal was 'as fine a thing of its kind as had been struck since the best work of the eighteenth century'.[7] The medals were struck in Paris in solid gold, silver and bronze and the dies preserved for future use. (They were employed again to manufacture the prize medals for the Stockholm Olympics of 1912 and the Antwerp Olympics in 1920.) The London prize medals were smaller than previous Olympic medals because of the value of the precious metals. The commemorative medals were larger, being cast in a light golden bronze. The charioteer depicted on the obverse of the commemorative medal and the athlete being crowned by Fame and Victory on the obverse of the prize medal were intended to become permanent patterns for future Olympic medals. The reverse sides bore an Olympic St George representing the London Games.

Prize-winners' medal: obverse.

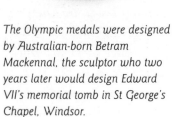

The Olympic medals were designed by Australian-born Betram Mackennal, the sculptor who two years later would design Edward VII's memorial tomb in St George's Chapel, Windsor.

Prize-winners' medal: reverse.

Commemoration medal: obverse.

Commemoration medal: reverse.

Diploma of merit for competitors. The Olympic diplomas were designed by Bernard Partridge, chief cartoonist for Punch.

The programme of the Fourth Olympiad was based on that of the Athens Games. There was some debate over which events were suitable for Olympic competition. Certain sports were deemed too specific to one nation; cricket was excluded for that reason. In theory, as one reporter summarised it in an article in the *Country Gentleman*, 'If any given sport is found to be popular in half a dozen countries, it is admitted, but not otherwise.'[8] The tug-of-war, which would hardly qualify under that definition, was retained from the Athens programme. Reflecting the military and hunting origins of many traditional European sports at the time, among the list of firearms events were 'Shooting: Running deer (single and double)', 'Individual Shooting against 1) moving and 2) disappearing targets' and 'International Military Rifle'. Some 'sports' were included as demonstrations rather than medal contests: bicycle polo, for instance. Fencing with the foil, too, was given exhibition status, the BOC, under Cook's influence, ruling it an art rather than a sport. (The knights felt privately that they had suffered from poor and partisan judging in the fencing contests at Athens, which may have influenced this particular categorisation.)

Robert Laffan submitted the BOC's proposed programme to the meeting of the IOC held at The Hague towards the end of May 1907. Dividing the Olympic events of 1908 into summer and winter Games, competitions ran from 27 April to 31 October. The principal two weeks of events in the stadium were to take place after the Amateur Athletic Association Championships and the Henley Regatta from 13 to 25 July. Before that, racquets, covered court tennis and jeu de paume competitions were to be held at the Queen's Club in London; lawn tennis at Wimbledon; polo at the Hurlingham Club; rifle contests at Bisley; and trap shooting at Uxendon Shooting Club.

Track and field, swimming, diving, cycling, gymnastics, wrestling, archery and fencing events, the tug-of-war and water polo would be contested in the stadium. The two weeks of Games would climax – as at Athens – with the marathon race, to begin in Windsor and end on the cinder track at Shepherd's Bush. A scattering of events would follow over the next two months – yacht races in the Isle of Wight, rowing at Henley-on-Thames, three days of 12-metre-class yacht races in August from Hunter's Quay in Glasgow, and two days of motor-boat races on Southampton Water. During the winter Games, running from 19 to 31 October, football, lacrosse, rugby, hockey and boxing contests would be held in the stadium, and concurrently, figure skating at the Prince's Skating Club.

The programme submitted to the IOC included proposals for aeroplane and automobile racing and a 'military riding' event favoured by a Swedish member of the committee, which never took place. A golf tournament too was abandoned. The Olympic golf champion from 1904, the Canadian George Lyon, had set sail for Britain to defend his title when the event was summarily cancelled because the Royal and Ancient Golf Club of St Andrews, the governing body of the sport, refused to come to terms with the British Olympic Association. (This did not prevent Theodore Cook – his eye on future international competition – including 15 pages of rules governing the sport in the *Official Report* of the 1908 Games.)

In the end, there were 23 sports incorporating 110 events, outstripping Athens' 'over-long' programme by a third.

The Hague meeting of the IOC in spring 1907 was a convivial one. It was attended by representatives from 11 European countries but none, significantly, from the USA. The delegates unanimously re-elected Baron de Coubertin president of the

IOC for a second term of ten years. The meeting gave its general approval to the British arrangements. The Baron expressed warm admiration for the British, citing their Olympic Council as a model of national Olympic organisation. The meeting agreed that certain parts of the British Empire – Canada, South Africa and Australasia (Australia and New Zealand were treated as one) – should have separate representation on the IOC and a separate identity at the forthcoming Games. In conformity with previous Olympic competitions, so that records could be compared, metric units of measurement would be used rather than the imperial measure of yards. (The reluctance of the British press to acknowledge this led to some confusion, with reports of the 109.3 yards race instead of the 100 metres and the like.) And it was agreed that all the judges at the London Games would be British.

The proposal arose from practical considerations. Given the restrictions of budget, how else could 110 events be administered except by drawing on the expertise at hand? A Greek representative on the IOC suggested delicately that there might be an international jury of appeal for cases in which the judges disagreed, but his motion was not carried. Instead the British committee was given the power to appoint foreign assistants to their judges. In general the Baron's aristocratic colleagues seemed happy that the London Games were safe in the hands of British sporting gentlemen. They even agreed a clause investing the BOC with 'full power to make in case of absolute necessity such changes as may be desirable in these Regulations'.

In spring 1908 the BOC moved its business out of the Bath Club into new offices rented at 108 Victoria Street and hired Captain F. Wentworth Jones, late 51st King's Own Yorkshire Light Infantry, and Deputy Assistant Adjutant General Lines of Communication, South Africa, to serve as assistant secretary to Robert Laffan. The triumvirate that built the British Empire was complete: the aristocrat, the clergyman and the soldier.

The Games were fast approaching. On Saturday 25 April 1908 the Polytechnic Harriers, who were in charge of organising the race, held a trial for the climatic event of the Games, the Olympic marathon.

For all its ancient-sounding origins, the marathon race was invented as a suitably classical-sounding component of the first modern revival of the Olympic Games in 1896. The race commemorated the exploits of a legendary herald, Pheidippides, who was supposed to have carried the news of victory over Persian invaders from the battlefield of Marathon to Athens in 490 BC. According to the story, Pheidippides ran non-stop, arriving with just enough breath to cry 'Victory!' before falling dead, his duty done. The marathon, with its connotations of human will drawn out to its very limits, became instantly iconic. It was the 'Everyman' race; a race in which the ordinary man – a shepherd, a baker, a postman – could become extraordinary through sheer tenacity and will and solitary training over long distances and longer hours. The race had particular significance for the Edwardians in that the British were supposed to have the best long-distance runners in the world, based on the public school penchant for cross-country running. That and the British climate, it was claimed, bred hardy men whose national temperament exemplified the stoic endurance necessary to triumph in this ultimate challenge.

The man in charge of setting the course and overseeing the Olympic marathon of 1908 was J.N. Andrews, secretary of the Polytechnic Harriers. A decade after its invention there was no agreement on the precise length of a marathon. The distance from the plain of Marathon to Athens was judged to be somewhere between 24 and 25 miles – the prestigious Boston marathon was 24½ miles long. At the end of April the final course and distance of the 1908 marathon was yet to be fixed. Andrews' trial race was run between Windsor and Wembley Park – a distance of 22 miles and 1,420 yards – in pouring rain that turned to sleet. Sixty-six runners started and 49 finished. One of the Polytechnic Harriers' own, J.G. Beale, came in second to Alan Duncan of the Salford Harriers, who had recently won the 10 mile flat championship at Stamford Bridge. F. Lord of the Wisbey Park Athletic Club came third and the fourth man was T. Jack of Edinburgh. All the front runners, save Duncan, finished the race pretty much done up, but conditions had been harsh. At the celebratory dinner held at the Frascati restaurant that evening, Lord Desborough toasted the contestants. 'In no other country,' he declared, 'could 66 gentlemen have been found to face the pistol and start on such a day for a 22 mile and 6 furlong race.' It was to clubs like the Polytechnic, he said, that the country must look for help to keep up the reputation 'for fair play and high honour which had always been associated with the name of Great Britain'.

'With regard to these athletic games,' he pronounced, 'we are beginning with a pretty good show.'[9]

The following Monday the first Olympic contests of 1908 took place: racquets* competitions at the Queen's Club in

---

* A forerunner of the modern game of squash.

West Kensington. There were only seven competitors; they were all British. (In fact, racquets was largely only popular in Britain.) The contests passed almost without comment. The season was just beginning and the British press was distracted by Empire Day.

On Thursday 4 May 1908, the Prince of Wales (the future King George V) opened the Franco-British Exhibition and dedicated the White City stadium in the pouring rain. The Flip-Flap was refusing to move and several of the palaces were yet to open. Looking out over a sea of umbrellas, the Prince spoke a few well-chosen words about Empire, brotherhood, peace and prosperity; Mme Albani sang the national anthem and there was a display of diving in the stadium swimming tank.

'A Mass Meeting of Umbrellas' at the opening of the Franco-British Exhibition. 'I was proud to know that actually one quarter of it was ready for me to see. I should have seen it, too, but for the rain,' wrote the cynical Bystander reporter.

The stadium hosted its first proper athletic meeting a week later. The cinder track was tested to the designers' satisfaction when H.A. Wilson lowered the standing 1,500 metres record to 3 minutes 59⅘ seconds, improving by five seconds the time established by J.D. Lightbody of Chicago at Athens.

The Olympic jeu de paume* contest opened at the Queen's Club. This time there were 11 contestants. It was a purely Anglo-American event dominated by the best player of the era – American Jay Gould. The glamorous Gould, son of the well-known robber baron of the Gilded Age, who was barely out of his teens, was in town to defend his title to the English championship at the same venue. There was never much doubt he would take the Olympic gold medal. The newspapers carried a photo or two of the pin-up boy of the jeu de paume, with his matinee-idol looks, but not much else. The Covered Court contests (indoor tennis) fared even worse. Again only two nations (Great Britain and Sweden) had players entered. It was one of the few Olympic events that admitted women contestants. Women had originally been barred from Olympic competition by the first International Olympic Committee on the grounds that public sport compromised a woman's femininity and therefore offended decency. (In 1902 Baron de Coubertin declared that women's participation in the Olympics would be against the laws of nature.) But the Paris Olympics of 1900 slipped from de Coubertin's control and women slipped in – Charlotte Cooper of Great Britain becoming the first of 12 women to win a gold medal in the Second Olympiad. Forty-four women registered to compete in the Fourth Olympiad, 39 from Great Britain and the bulk of

* The original racquet sport once played by Henry VIII – otherwise called 'royal' or 'real' tennis.

them (25) entered in the archery contests. Miss Eastlake-Smith won the first Olympic gold medal for Britain in the London Games, triumphing in the ladies' lawn tennis singles. She celebrated by getting married to another tennis player, Wharram Lamplough, two days later. The newspapers barely noted her victory, preferring to concentrate on the burning topic of whether or not the figure-hugging curves of the new Directoire gown were scandalous or merely fashionable. 'Now a woman without petticoats is pretty much like a lobster without a shell,' pronounced *Vanity Fair*. 'The Directoire sheath may do very well for the Mesdames Jumpabouti, who

Taken from the Bystander *showing tennis player Miss Eastlake-Smith, winner of Britain's first gold medal in the 1908 Olympic, and Jay Gould who won gold for America in the men's competition.*

delight the hearts of stockbrokers in musical comedy, but for an English gentlewoman at an evening party or on the lawn at Ascot, the thing is wicked and unthinkable.'[10]

'The Olympic Games are rather overdone,' sighed the commentator of the *Bystander*. 'From the point of view of public interest the Racquets competition was a comparative failure. Much the same may be said of the Covered Court Lawn Tennis.'[11]

The *Bystander* commentator was no fan of the Fourth Olympiad. 'I prophesied that it would prove to be too ambitious,' he pronounced smugly when the abandonment of the golf tournament was announced, 'and that, speaking generally, the whole business would turn out to be a nuisance.'[12]

The London Games were in trouble. The grand two weeks in the stadium were fast approaching and the vast arena that had risen out of such wonderful private enterprise and volunteer dedication was in danger of becoming a white elephant. The Games were struggling to attract column inches among the breach-of-promise cases, murders and battles on the Khyber Pass in the popular papers. The more upmarket prints, such as the *Tatler*, *Vanity Fair*, the *Bystander*, even the middle-class *Illustrated London News*, were firmly wedded to the beats of the traditional London season: Eights Week, Ascot, Wimbledon, the Eton v. Harrow match, Henley, Goodwood, Cowes. For all their affection for Lord Desborough they carried only a paragraph or two on the Olympics. Now, the first fragments of 'Olympic' contests, far from building interest, were trailing an air of failure before the Games proper had even started.

The situation was becoming critical. It would take the sale of two million tickets to fill the stadium for the two weeks of the London Games in July. The problems of volunteer organisation, too little time and no proper funding were about to produce a crisis.

It was Ascot week, 'the maddest, merriest week of our entire summer'. The south of England was enjoying a heat-wave. 'We have now reached the summit of the season,' announced the *Tatler* – paying no attention to the Olympics – 'and shall soon be rushing down the gay and giddy slope that leads to Cowes, Marienbad, Scotland and the general end of all things.'[13] Lord Desborough, president of the Coaching Club that year, was preoccupied as he drove his party of family and friends from his home at Taplow Court to Ascot in his coach. Registration of athletes for the Games had just closed. In Victoria Street, Captain Whitworth Jones was busy processing paperwork for 2,666 competitors of 21 nationalities (2,022 of whom – 1,978 men and 44 women – would eventually compete). Athletes had begun arriving from Australia and New Zealand. The King had still not decided whether he would open the Games and the £2,000 advanced to the BOC by the Exhibition Company to cover expenses had run out. The Games in the stadium were barely a month away and there was no money left. No means to entertain the foreign guests, no money to pay the bills – the BOC even found itself in the embarrassing situation of having to postpone paying Mackennal's account for the design of the prize medals.

On 20 June Lord Desborough circulated a letter to every editor he could think of, bringing the crisis to their attention. Papers up and down the land, from the *Liverpool Courier* to the *Morning Post*, carried his words on their letters pages.

England has a reputation to maintain in the conduct of sport, and it is hoped that on this occasion we may be able in showing some hospitality to our visitors to maintain our reputation for national hospitality as well. To fail in this would be to fail in one of the most essential objects of the Olympic Games. For this purpose funds are urgently needed to meet the necessities of so great an undertaking, and the time is short.

Short indeed. Surprisingly, to modern notions, tickets for the Olympic Games in the stadium were only put on sale on 22 June, 21 days before the Games were due to start. 'I don't think the public realise yet the unique character of the Olympic Games,' Imre Kiralfy told the *Daily Mail* plaintively.[14]

The British public remained unmoved. There were so many other subjects to occupy the press that season, what with the Directoire gown and the hot weather, the Pan Anglican Congress* and the Olympia Horse Show. And 1908 was a year of exhibitions, quite apart from the Franco-British – no less than seven opened in May, three more in June and another six in July and August.[15] The Olympics might promise the biggest gathering of international athletes ever seen but the capital was already full of foreigners. It was estimated that there were 450,000 visitors crowding London's hotels. In one nine-day run the Exhibition counted two million people through its turnstiles. (The engineers had finally got the Flip-Flap going. On its second day of activity it held two cars of what the newspapers christened 'flappers' in mid-air for over an hour while the machinery rested.)

In desperation, Lord Desborough sought out a fellow member of the Pilgrims, a cross-Atlantic dining club founded

---

* The international conference of bishops from around the Anglican Communion which met every ten years (it is now known as the Lambeth Conference). In late June 1908 it gathered in London – according to London's chattering classes there was much fun to be had with 'Panglers'.

a couple of years earlier to foster the Anglo-American alliance: Lord Northcliffe, owner of the *Daily Mail*.

The *Daily Mail* had a special relationship with the Exhibition. Its gold domed pavilion, where visitors could see daily editions of the *Mail* and the *Evening News* run off the presses, was one of the attractions of the north end. It was not, however, a newspaper that either Lord Desborough or Theo Cook would buy. Their class tended to find the commercialism of the *Mail*'s proprietor offensive. Lord Northcliffe was an energetic newspaper magnate; a modern, forward-looking kind of peer. He was multiplying his readership at a rapid rate with his own version of the techniques pioneered across the Atlantic by Joseph Pulitzer. *Vanity Fair*, which had a particular antipathy to Northcliffe, condemned his 'ha'penny papers' and his introduction of marketing gimmicks such as coupons. But at this crisis Lord Desborough needed a paper with the ear of the great British public. The *Daily Mail* was a dab hand at running campaigns with a patriotic spin. In May it had been the *Daily Mail* Cup, an international rifle competition to celebrate Empire Day; then The Flag, an appeal to raise money to add a wing to the capital's United Servicemen's Club. Lord Northcliffe agreed to help.

The *Daily Mail* appeal made the first Olympic story fly. Here was imminent crisis, a slur on national pride and a sideswipe at incompetent government combined. Papers across the board picked up the story. One such, in the *Tatler*, was headlined 'Games Which Cost Money':

Lord Desborough, the president of the British Olympic Council, has been making an appeal for the necessary funds to carry on this year's Olympic Games, but so far the monetary support has not yet been forthcoming. He complains, quite rightly, that the council receive no subsidy from the Government, and as the only source of revenue comes from one fourth of the gate money, there will probably not be enough funds to give a lunch or a dinner to the foreign competitors when they arrive. If this should happen a great slur will be cast on British hospitality, and it is to be hoped that the public will not remain deaf to Lord Desborough's appeal.[16]

The *World* said much the same with a ditty and a cartoon:

> *A pretty state of things*
> *If Britain can't stand dinner!*
> *Each day new athletes brings;*
> *A pretty state of things*
> *If ne'er a summons rings*
> *To cheer the man that's inner!*
> *A pretty state of things*
> *If Britain can't stand a dinner!*[17]

At the eleventh hour, fund-raising for the Olympics became a matter of patriotism. Cheques, banknotes, postal orders poured into the *Daily Mail* offices. Lord Desborough's town residence, the newspaper reported gleefully, was 'bombarded with money'.[18]

Celebrities – from the Prince of Wales and 'the Maharajah of Cooch Behar' to the professional strongman, Eugen Sandow – gave their bit for publicity and patriotism; and sporting associations too, of course, large and small. The Football Association gave £250, Lord Desborough's friends at the Bath Club sent in four subscriptions totalling over £400, £5 5s came from the Worthing Cycling Club and the ladies of the Automobile Club sent £25. The Corinthian Football Club presented £100, in 'memory of the princely hospitality received during their foreign tours' (and this despite the fact that they were unable to take part in the winter Olympic Games due to some dispute between the Football Association and the Amateur Football Association). Thirty pounds was collected from 30 MPs and hundreds of ordinary readers sent in donations of a few pence at a time.

Five days before the Games in the stadium were due to start, Lord Desborough stood before a meeting of the BOC to announce that 'the subscriptions raised by the *Daily Mail* on behalf of the expenses of the British Olympic Council had now reached a sum considerably over £10,000'. The BOC could now settle its bills. It celebrated by voting to raise the allowance for dinners to ten shillings per head.

'Britain's fair name is saved,' announced the *Daily Mirror*, 'and there will be no occasion for her guests from a score of countries throughout the world to return home with stories of her churlish lack of hospitality.'[19]

In less than four days, Desborough and his colleagues arranged a reception at the Grafton Galleries, five official banquets, a ball at the Holborn Restaurant, drives and excursions and other courtesies to the visiting sportsmen – including Exhibition passes for competitors and 'seats in the Stadium for distinguished visitors and donors'.[20]

On Friday 10 July Lord Desborough mounted his carriage box, gathered the reins of his matched team of bays and drove his second boy, Gerald, from their home at Taplow Court to attend the cricket match between Eton and Harrow at Lords, 'the smartest of picnics'.

'Nowadays "Lords" means the beginning of the end as regards the gaieties of a London season,' noted the *Tatler*, ever watchful of the social calendar. 'For after that date balls and parties are few and far between, and we go in strong for outdoor frolics such as days on the river, motor trips to the country, balloon parties at Hurlingham or dinners at the Franco-British Exhibition.'[21]

London Society had been following the same rhythm for decades. The Eton v. Harrow match was the sunny sward on which the ruling elite, bound together by public school, college and marriage, gathered to recapture that familiar comfort of happy connection that is the best of school days. The old school match was an occasion when the famed English reserve would fall away and gentlemen walking in Bond Street could be seen calling out to strangers on the mere recognition of a light blue ribbon (for Eton) or a dark blue ribbon or a buttonhole of cornflowers (for Harrow). When Lord Desborough was a boy of 20, twelve hundred carriages could be counted at the game. A vast concourse of members of the upper classes perched on their carriage boxes, picnicking out of enormous hampers while they watched their golden youth, exchanged gossip and flirted. Now only Desborough and a few last members of the Four-in-Hand and Coaching clubs made their appearance in the old way. On the ground where the carriages used to meet a huge stand had sprung up. The entrance fee, fixed to keep out those who merely liked cricket and had no social reason to be there, was no longer holding the line. The British Establishment was not as secure as it seemed.

Britain had been enjoying the perfect Edwardian summer of story books – blue skies, full-canopied trees and record hours of sunshine. The previous Friday, 3 July, was the hottest day of all. That night, at two in the morning, a tremendous thunderstorm woke Londoners up with a theatrical lightning show and deafening thunderclaps; the rain fell in torrents, marking the end of the heatwave.

A man bearing a remarkable resemblance to Lord Desborough accosts John Bull and Britannia seeking cash for Olympic expenses.Cartoon published in the World, *6 July 1908, in the middle of the 'hospitality crisis' a fortnight before the stadium Games were due to start.*

A few hours earlier, across Europe, a small but historically significant event had taken place. Count Zeppelin, after a long history of accidents and reverses, successfully completed a 12-hour flight in his military dirigible. He steered his airship across the Swiss border, sailed over Lake Constance and the Swiss city of Lucerne before floating back to land again on German soil. The *Daily Mail*'s editorial on Saturday morning was clear about the significance of the event:

The Command of the Air

Not without reason has the Emperor William – no mean judge of the importance of contemporary events – declared that Count Zeppelin's balloon voyage into Switzerland marks 'the beginning of a new national era'. For this is the first occasion upon which a military dirigible has crossed an international frontier, sailed above the territory of a foreign state, hovered over its towns, exchanging messages with the inmates of hotels in these towns, rising and descending at will, and finally returning at high speed whence it came.

This was the counterpoint to the ladies in their picture hats with their straw-boatered swains, enjoying the perfect summer weather in Kiralfy's White City. For all the musical comedy aspects of an elderly German aeronaut exchanging notes with foreign visitors planted on hotel balconies, the image of the vast canvas Zeppelin hovering uninvited over non-German cities crystallised the unease that impelled the Franco-British entente. The race to master the air was one of the stories of 1908. The 70-year-old hero of the Franco-Prussian war and his Zeppelin airship were of a piece with the doubling of the German fleet, the mammoth new German warship launched in spring 1908 and the Kaiser's unsettling pronouncements about the destiny of the unified German peoples.* Europeans wanted to believe that the German Emperor was – as he frequently said – a man of peace, but it was difficult to be confident.

De Coubertin's dream of reviving the ancient Olympic Games of Greece had begun with his experiences as a young man witnessing Paris's humiliation at Prussian hands in the occupation of the French capital in 1870. As Lord Desborough explained to a *Daily News* journalist in the run-up to the London Games:

* It was in 1908 that H.G. Wells published his disquieting short story 'The War In the Air'.

The underlying hope is that the youth, and especially the athletic youth, of the different nations represented, by meeting each other in friendly rivalry, will get to know each other better and appreciate each other more. Perhaps, indeed, through these Olympic Games good feeling between nation and nation – the good feeling which helps to prevent the outbreak of war – may be at least as well promoted as by diplomatists sitting round a board.[22]

In the haven of their aristocratic imagination where sporting knights met in good fellowship on the greensward of Athens, de Coubertin, Desborough and Cook dreamt that sport could transcend the political habits of humankind. In the Shepherd's Bush stadium they were about to get a reality check from another rival nation poised to transform the world – the nation that would shape the Olympic Games into their modern form, the United States of America.

INTERNATIONAL SPORT

The athletic victories of our modern gladiators carry a
corresponding value to those secured by diplomacy,
commercialism and war. The desire to excel is inherent
in the American citizen, and the natural inclination to
indulge in physical exercise has built up a nation of
brawn and muscle.

NEW YORK TIMES, 23 JULY 1905

ON 9 JANUARY 1907 TWO hundred prominent American
sportsmen gathered for a dinner at the New York Athletic Club. They had come together under the tastefully hung
bunting to celebrate a new president of the Amateur Athletic
Union of America, 46-year-old James E. Sullivan.* The first of
the telegrams read out against the backdrop of a vast American flag carried the cordial greetings of a former Governor of
New York, President Theodore Roosevelt. Introducing the
man of the hour, Barlow S. Weeks, chairman of the dinner

---

* The 'E' was to distinguish him from other Sullivans with profiles in New
York sport – for example, John Sullivan, the prince of the old-style boxers,
and a young runner on the 1908 US Olympic team, James P. Sullivan.

and a former president of the club, described the characteristics that made Sullivan 'the greatest present force in athletics today'. His influence was, Weeks declared, 'derived from the fact that he invariably tries to do right, no matter whom it aids or hurts'.

To cheers, James E. Sullivan arose, a solid, silver-haired man with a grey moustache and wearing a bureaucrat's suit. Having allowed the tumult to die down, 'the leading figure of the government and administration of amateur athletics' in America spoke.

The success of the AAU, he told his audience, was evidenced in the victories won by American athletes. Their victories were not just athletic but ethical, for 'our American

James E. Sullivan, president of the American Athletic Union – the czar of American athletics at the turn of the twentieth century. Given his role in shaping modern athletics it is surprising how few pictures of Sullivan survive.

athletes as a whole are a clean, wholesome lot of boys'. There was a need for uniform athletic rules throughout the world, declared the new president of the AAU, and it was time for America to step up and show the way.

> The projectors of the international games in England next year have invited us to send a team abroad, and the cables tell us they propose to carefully scrutinize our list of competitors to see that they are amateurs. I want to say that we will carefully scrutinize them, as we always have, before we send them, and if they reject a single athlete on the list we will withdraw the whole team. Outside Oxford and Cambridge, the English amateur athlete is a joke. We make laws honestly and enforce them honestly to keep athletics pure, and we do not propose to accept the judgement of England or any other country upon the amateur status of a man we guarantee. We believe in international athletics and want to foster every international meeting held, but we do not propose to be stigmatized by self-constituted critics whose government is far more lax than our own.

These sentiments were greeted with a volcanic explosion of shouts and cheers; men stood on their chairs, waving their arms and straining their voices in a hoarse rendition of 'Tammany',* broken by shouts of 'Sullivan! Sullivan! Never tiring, he's inspiring! Sullivan!' It was, wrote the *New York Times* reporter, 'an avowal of loving fealty probably not enjoyed by any other single man in sport'.[1]

---

* An anthem of Tammany Hall, Democrat headquarters in New York and at that time a stronghold of the Irish-American and white working-class constituency.

This was the man President Roosevelt was sending as his Commissioner to the London Games.

James E. Sullivan ascended the heights of athletics administration in the United States on a platform of purity in amateur sport. His supporters praised him as 'manly, straight-forward and vigorous'; his critics stigmatised him as bullying and rude. But he was a brilliant administrator and networker. The faces of the guests at that testimonial dinner represented the personal connections that made him the 'power in athletics': Barlow S. Weeks, a former president of the grandest of the city's sports clubs, the New York Athletic Club, and an active colleague in the AAU; P.J. Conway, the vigorous founding president of the Irish American Athletic Club (IAAC); A.G. Spalding, sports entrepreneur and publisher; Gustavus Town Kirby, the college athletic administrator of Columbia University and a leading light of the Intercollegiate Athletic Association; Martin Sheridan, all-round athlete and discus gold medal winner from Athens 1906. These men represented the relationships on which James E. Sullivan constructed his unparalleled influence in American amateur sport.

James Edward Sullivan was born in New York on 18 November 1860, the son of an Irish immigrant who made his living working on the construction sites of the growing city. Throughout his life Sullivan's home would never be more than a few blocks from his birthplace in the region of West 114th Street. As a teenager James joined the Pastime Athletic Club, at the time one of the most successful of the New York athletic clubs. He competed as a runner and twice won their all-round championship. He was an industrious young man, a good Irish Catholic boy, close to his mother and three sisters, imbued with a strong sense of duty and of right and wrong. In his late teens he went out in the world and found his way into the newspaper business.

He began reporting sport in New York at a golden moment. The popular newspaper was hitting its heyday – a time full of excitement, innovation and vigour before film and radio intervened to fragment the world of popular media. And New York was the energetic centre of the business. For in New York Joseph Pulitzer was building the *World* into the most widely read national daily by combining sensational headlines with vivid writing, illustrated by line drawings and pointed cartoons, for a mere two cents a copy. His competitors – Charles Dana's *Sun* and James Gordon Bennett's *Herald* and the rest – responded. Newsprint multiplied with morning dailies, evening editions and increasingly elaborate Sunday papers. By 1904, when the national population stood at 82 million, the US Bureau of the Census would record 2,453 daily newspapers and 1,493 weekly periodicals in print across the Union.[2]

As the newspapers evolved, sports coverage grew increasingly elaborate – particularly in the emerging Sunday papers. In 1892 Pulitzer's *World* would fill three lavishly illustrated pages with coverage of a football game between Yale and Princeton. Sport was being turned into a popular spectacle accessible to readers across the continent. Editors and journalists made celebrities of college football players, baseball players and boxers with 'colour' interviews, line illustrations and biographical detail to supplement accounts of matches and meets. The liveliness of the coverage accelerated in the 'yellow press' war of the mid-1890s, when Randolph Hearst bought the New York *Morning Journal* and set out to challenge the *World*'s position as the nation's most popular daily.

James E. Sullivan wrote for the *Morning Journal* and the

New York Sporting Times. His 'vigorous' style attracted some attention. 'Mr. J.E. Sullivan degrades modern journalism,' spat the *Spirit of the Times*, 'He is a renegade Irishman, the purveyor of shameful and malicious falsehoods.'[3] But Sullivan was building a power base. At weekends and in evening meets he had turned his attention to club administration.

In parallel to what was happening to the daily newspaper, the 1870s and 1880s were a veritable boom time for amateur sport in America, and particularly in New York. Since 1868, when 'father Bill' Curtis, Henry Buermeyer and John Babcock founded the New York Athletic Club as the first of its kind, 1,250 sports clubs had sprung up nationwide. By 1905 the *New York Times* claimed that almost one-eighth of the population took part in organised sport, an army of 10 million athletes (amateur and professional). James E. Sullivan was riding the wave. He was endlessly energetic and thorough. Before long he was president of the Pastime Athletic Club.

Sullivan's vision was large. By his late twenties he had carved out his mission in life: to advance organised sport in America for the betterment of society by discipline, regulation and coordination. His commitment to amateurism was rooted in a different soil to that of the European members of the IOC. Whereas to sportsmen like Lord Desborough or to Baron de Coubertin the concept was about perpetuating the spirit of a gentlemanly code, Sullivan's evangelical determination to root out sham amateurs – athletes who performed for money – was about a battle to distinguish socially valuable sport from the 'sinful' world of seedy gambling parlours and rigged boxing matches that flourished in the big city.

Sullivan was fired by an almost religious belief in sport as a mechanism for the betterment of society. Watching children play dodging traffic in New York's congested streets he was inspired to become a successful campaigner for playgrounds and sporting facilities. He helped found the Public Schools Athletic League which, within three years of its creation, would accumulate 150,000 competitive members recruited from among the schoolchildren of New York. Sullivan would argue that the Public Schools Athletic League was the 'greatest athletic organization in the world ... greatest in size, greatest in conception and greatest in beneficial influence'. By being taught to play fair the schoolboy would learn morality and through teamwork in sports he would be educated in citizenship and distracted from mischief. The League both encouraged sporting heroes as role models for disadvantaged youth and helped feed the athletic clubs of New York.[4]

In 1888, Sullivan helped found the Amateur Athletic Union. Serving as its influential secretary, he worked industriously to build the organisation, affiliating increasing numbers of athletic clubs across the country, with the aim that one day the AAU would become the governing body of all amateur sport in America.

Then in 1892 Sullivan was offered a golden opportunity by which he would spread his message across the land to every man and boy with a sporting interest. Sports entrepreneur A.G. Spalding invited him to become president of the American Sports Publishing Company, with the responsibility of editing and overseeing the Spalding Athletic Library.

A.G. Spalding made his name as a baseball pitcher in champion Boston and Chicago teams in the mid-1870s. He left the infield to set up 'Spalding's Complete Line of Athletic Goods'. He was so successful that, by the end of the nineteenth century, if you bought a baseball or glove, or a golf ball or club, anywhere on the East Coast it was quite likely to be Spalding's. In 1892 Spalding introduced Spalding's Athletic

The 1909 Spalding's Athletic Almanac *in which James E.Sullivan published his record of the Fourth Olympiad, available at 5 cents from all major US retailers. Theodore Cook's* Official Report of the Fourth Olympiad, *in contrast, runs to 830 pages bound in gilt embossed red cloth at a price only the rich could afford.*

Library. Beginning with *Spalding's Official Base Ball Guides*, by 1909 the library would contain over 300 publications. These cheap pocket editions offered easy-to-read instruction manuals complete with helpful diagrams. There were titles on how to play baseball or basketball or football or handball; how to figure skate or play golf; the Science of Swimming, a Manual for Boxing; 'Tennis for the Junior Player, the Club Player, the Expert', 'How to Bat Like the Big Leaguers' or how to coach

Little League; not forgetting 'Tumbling for Amateurs', how to exercise with clubs, dumbbells, pulley weights or punching bag; how to use a medicine ball ('Indigestion Treated by Gymnastics') or proper 'Pyramid Building Without Apparatus'. If there was a physical exercise, indoor or outdoor recreation, Spalding's Guides explained how to play the game, how to train and how to be a good sport.

Spalding's Library made James E. Sullivan *the* popular sporting authority in the average American home. Through the guides he not only popularised the AAU's rules but also formed the record. Year by year, Spalding's almanacs provided 'the really first authentic records of events and official rules that have ever been consecutively compiled'. At the turn of the twentieth century the history of American sport coalesced on their cheaply printed pages.

Sullivan was only one of an American generation inspired by the potential of sport as a means of social improvement. Towards the end of the nineteenth century, comfortable commentators from among the prosperous classes began to ponder the effects of the rapid industrialisation, fuelled by immigration, that was transforming the United States into the greatest economic power in the world. They observed a burgeoning new reality where prosperity multiplied on the backs of regimented working stiffs pressed together in vast cities. They saw the small-town, rural community that had previously been enshrined as the moral heart of America being shouldered aside. The sight of the overweight city capitalist and his armies of pallid clerks inspired a new philosophy. The health of the Republic required a vigorous citizenry. Athletics and good honest exercise offered salvation from the moral degeneracy threatened by urbanisation. The puritan work ethic would be multiplied through the disciplines of sport. A new sense of community would be forged on the urban playing field. The athletic club would bind immigrants and native workers together in common Republican values and shared pride in the success of their sporting heroes.

Prominent among such commentators was Caspar Whitney, the editor of *Outing* magazine – 'the Illustrated magazine of Sport, Travel, Adventure and Country Life'. Whitney attended Harvard with Theodore Roosevelt. As the 26th President of the United States would later reminisce, he did not stay long. Young Whitney left 'like a good many other Harvard men of that time and took to cow-punching in the West. He went on a ranch in Rio Arriba County, New Mexico,

A New York Times *cartoon published in the first week of the stadium Games. A robust President Roosevelt, puffing on his businesslike cigar, faces down the spindly and decadent Brit.*

and was a keen hunter, especially fond of the chase of cougar, bear, and elk.'[5] When he returned to the big city, Whitney built a following among the college-educated and prosperous at *Harper's Weekly*, writing lyrically on big-game hunting and on intercollegiate sporting contests (especially football and baseball). His theme was the intrinsic virtue of 'pure' amateur sport as compared to the 'other kind'. He wrote from the idea that men learnt to be men in the open air and that the true Republican spirit rested in the injunction: 'To play like gentlemen; to avoid strength without fairness ... to be a man, win or lose.'[6]

Whitney bought *Outing* magazine in 1899. He expanded his readership, publishing articles such as 'Wyoming Summer Fishing and Yellowstone Park' next to 'An Elephant – Tiger Fight' and 'How to Make Totem Poles for Shacks', interleaved with atmospheric adventure stories by the likes of Rudyard Kipling and Jack London. In the words of the editor of one contemporary journal, Whitney taught 'that travelling and camping and climbing are a joy in themselves, but that their real value is not their joy; it is not even that they reveal character; it is that they build character as unmistakably as books and companions'.[7]

The world of *Outing* was that of the 'strenuous life' philosophy embraced by President Theodore Roosevelt. If Lord Desborough was the symbol of Edwardian sportsmanship, then Roosevelt was the American equivalent. As a speaker at Sullivan's testimonial dinner in January 1907 put it, America's youngest President* was 'American in essence and substance from the crown of his head to the soles of his feet'.

---

* Vice-President Roosevelt moved into the White House after President McKinley's death by an assassin's bullet, a few days shy of his 43rd birthday.

He believes in fair play, but is a doughty antagonist. Because every muscle, every fibre, every nerve, every cell of his strong brain is alive and awake and mindful of the crisis to be met. He has contributed vastly to the maintenance of clean, decent, improving amateur athletics. He believes in a square deal all round. His example is an inspiration which, if properly studied, dissipates discouragement. Theodore Roosevelt is the spirit and embodiment of amateur athletics.

When the first revived Olympics came along in 1896, Caspar Whitney and his like perceived an opportunity to display to the world, in the words of historian Steven Pope, this 'virile national sporting identity'.[8]

The first American intimately involved in the Olympic movement was a professor of European history at Princeton, Dr William Milligan Sloane. In 1889 Baron Pierre de Coubertin, aged 26, made his first trip to the United States. On a visit to Boston he met Sloane, a fluent French speaker and Francophile 13 years his senior. The pair became firm friends. Sloane travelled to Europe to be part of the creation of the International Olympic Committee at the famous Sorbonne conference in June 1894. He was one of the IOC's first members and served continuously until 1925, the year de Coubertin stepped down as its president. It was Professor Sloane who gathered a handful of students from Harvard and Princeton prepared to pay for a European vacation that incorporated athletic competition, and thereby ensured American participation in the first Olympiad of the modern revival in Athens. The Ivy League boys made a remarkable showing in 1896, winning eight track and field events. Back home the commentators took note. Various journals published articles about the Olympic revival, and, in particular, the nature of the American youth that had won at the Athens Games.

A key story was that of a Princeton student called Garrett. A shot putter and a weight man, the day before the Olympic discus contest Garrett was in the stadium watching the Greek athletes practising their ancient and newly revived sport. The young college jock thought he would give it a try. He picked up a discus and practised a little. The next day he out-distanced the competition with a freestyle discus throw of 95 feet 7½ inches (29.15m) and won the gold medal.[9] The competition was not all that impressive – in 1906 Martin Sheridan would throw more than 136 feet – but the message of the story was clear: the land of the free bred better sons. The American democrat had demonstrated his natural superiority without even trying too hard.

In 1893, Baron de Coubertin returned to the United States. Professor Sloane arranged for him to meet a small group of athletics officials from prominent eastern universities. De Coubertin failed to persuade them to join his Olympic movement; they were preoccupied with domestic competition. However, one of their number, Gustavus Town Kirby of Columbia University, suggested that the Baron needed to speak to James E. Sullivan. Sullivan, he told him, 'is your man in the United States capable of organizing an Olympic Committee'.

De Coubertin met Sullivan a short time later and the pair took an immediate dislike to one another. Sullivan thought the Baron a fussy dreamer incapable of driving the kind of administration that he felt international sport required. The Baron listened to the AAU secretary's ambitions to create an international body to regulate track and field sports and correctly identified the project as a threat to his Olympic movement. Sullivan caused further offence by writing to the Baron, with characteristic bluntness, that William Sloane was 'a lovely gentleman … [but] he knows nothing about athletics … certainly he is unknown in the athletic legislative halls of this country'. Sloane, it must be said, was equally uncomplimentary about the AAU secretary. 'Sullivan is ghetto-poor Irish-American,' he wrote to his French friend, 'a man whose great faults are those of his birth and breeding.' But, the professor added regretfully, 'he is unfortunately a representative man and holds the organized athletes of the clubs in the hollow of his hand'. [10]

The success of the American college athletes in the track and field events at Athens drew Sullivan's attention. Assuming the title of 'Assistant Director at the Olympic Games', he took charge of American Olympic participation in the Paris Games of 1900. Sloane was reduced to reporting developments and gossip to de Coubertin. President McKinley acknowledged the new reality by appointing Sullivan his 'Special Commissioner from the United States to the Olympic Games'. Sullivan would be awarded the title by both McKinley and his successor Roosevelt for the next four Olympic Games,* but what he really coveted was a seat on the IOC – a boon Baron de Coubertin was not about to grant him. Instead, Caspar Whitney, who had published complimentary remarks about the new Olympics in *Outing*, was elected to join the IOC in 1900.

The American athletes took all the sprinting and field events at Paris 1900 except the discus, which was won by a Hungarian. (The long-distance runs – the 800 metres, the

---

* That is, he was appointed Special Commissioner to the Olympic Games of 1900, 1904, 1906, 1908 and 1912.

1,500 metres and the 4,000 metre steeplechase – went to British athletes.) In his journalism James E. Sullivan promoted a point-scoring system that favoured track and field events. This accounting proved to the satisfaction of the American papers that the United States had 'won' the championships and their interest in the Olympics grew. Sullivan published a succession of articles driving home his point that track and field events were the essence of Olympianism and that America's success in this international arena was a measure of her sporting superiority among nations. He was outspoken in his criticism of the chaotic French management of the Paris Games. Word filtered back to the Baron that the secretary of the AAU was calling him an 'inept leader' and 'a powerless and pathetic figure'. Sullivan had made himself the key figure in American participation in the Olympic movement. Baron de Coubertin knew by now that his Olympic vision could not survive without American involvement.

The two men had to do business together, but it was an uneasy relationship. They clashed over the 1904 Olympics. De Coubertin wanted the Third Olympiad to be staged in New York or Chicago. Sullivan was material in moving the 1904 Games to the great World's Fair held at St Louis that year. Under the title of 'chief of the department of physical culture' at the Exposition, the AAU secretary took over the organisation of the Third Olympiad from de Coubertin. Despite Sullivan's pride in his superior organisational skills the Games foundered, subsumed in the St Louis Exposition. Few foreign athletes ventured into the Midwest. Back in Europe, hearing of the tasteless addition of 'aboriginal games' in which native peoples were challenged to perform Western sports in pseudo-scientific competition to measure racial abilities, de Coubertin shrugged and sighed, 'only in America'.

Still, Americans won every track and field event bar two (a French-Canadian won the throwing of the 56-pound weight and the sole Greek contestant won the weight-lifting). The St Louis Games served to advance Sullivan's campaign to promote track and field events to journalists at home as the face of Olympic competition. The American daily press, with the help of his scoring method, began to embrace the idea that the Olympic Games were the international championships of sport.

Baron de Coubertin offered Sullivan an olive branch, awarding him one of the early Olympic medals in recognition of his organisation of the St Louis Games (Sullivan was the first American after President McKinley to receive the honour). But the medal was late in arriving and Sullivan was not pacified. It was no substitute for a seat on the IOC. He

Irish emigrant and stalwart of the Irish American Athletic Club, 35-year-old John Jesus Flanagan, who dominated international weight-throwing at the turn of the twentieth century.

turned his mind to organising an American team to compete at the 'unofficial' Olympic Games in Athens from his AAU offices at 233 Broadway, New York.

Caspar Whitney, meanwhile, had also fallen out with the Baron. Whitney always had a tendency to find fault. He used the pages of *Outing* to air criticisms of the IOC, blaming it (somewhat unfairly) for the poor organisation of the St Louis Games. To his annoyance – despite the fact that he had never actually attended a single organisational meeting – Whitney was dropped from the IOC. De Coubertin's loss was Sullivan's gain. In January 1906, Whitney was elected president of the American Committee of the Olympic Games, the latest incarnation of the ephemeral committees Sullivan set up to oversee American Olympic participation. The editor of *Outing* declared his new allegiance with an essay: 'Right Man in the Right Place'. 'Sullivan is a great AAU president, who not only sees right, but has the courage to fight for it.'[11]

Thanks to Sullivan's administrative skills and drive, by the time of the second Athens Games, the organisation of American involvement in the Olympics stood out as the most advanced of all the nations taking part. Athletes from across the nation were identified on the basis of past performance. Money was raised to transport the chosen competitors as a team to Greece with trainer and managers at a projected cost of $25,000 (around $570,000 in 2006 terms).[12] Press interest was growing. The daily newspapers, in New York at least, recorded the successes of the athletes sent over on the SS *Barbarossa* on their sports pages.

Just as for the British, the Athens Games proved an experience for the Americans to look back on with rosy nostalgia. James E. Sullivan described the meet as 'the most imposing athletic spectacle that the world has seen'. US trainer M.C. (Matt) Halpin, an official from the New York Athletic Club, led the American contingent in the opening parade. He liked to tell the story of how, when he dipped the flag he carried in salute before the royal box, 'the King staked me to a smile that made me feel that I belonged'.[13]

Athens 1906 set the stage for London 1908. In the words of G.S. Robertson, an active member of the 1908 BOC and a contestant at Athens, all other nations save Great Britain and America were 'in an absolutely prehistoric condition with regard to athletic sports'. The French were superior only in fencing and on the bicycle, he argued, and German abilities were confined to gymnastics. (Robertson did not think highly of gymnastics: 'An Olympic wreath is far too precious a thing to be squandered on good form in hopping over a horse or swarming up a rope.') The Latin countries he dismissed as being constitutionally 'opposed to active exercise'.

The US athletes went home with victory in 11 out of the 22 track and field events. Such successes made it difficult for the British to cling to their assumption of sporting superiority. G.S. Robertson admired the effort which the Americans made to participate in the Athens Games, pointing to 'the natural enterprise of the American people and to the peculiarly perfect method in which athletics are organized in the United States'.[14]

Theodore Cook, in contrast, argued that the Americans' success had been achieved at a cost to all-round sportsmanship. For Cook, as for Baron de Coubertin, the Olympic vision was intended to encompass a broad spectrum of sporting excellence, reflecting the variety among nations. The American successes at Athens, Cook agreed, 'were very great, and they thoroughly deserved them; but outside the "track athletics" in the stricter sense, they did very little. So that, if we take the whole of the 72 events mentioned in the card, we get the somewhat curious result that neither the British nor the American athletes did best all round. That distinction must go to our friends the French.'[15]

By Cook's reckoning – using James E. Sullivan's own scoring system of five points for first prize, three for second place and one for third – the French came first with 92 points, the British second with 78, the Greeks third with 76.* The Americans he put fourth with 75 points.

James E. Sullivan disagreed. In his view the only truly international sports were the track and field events. Neatly laid out in charts and lists, his measurement of the international standing in sports was much more appealing to his national press. Trumpeting 'American Athletes Champions of the World' in *Outing* magazine in August 1906, Sullivan calculated that 'America won eleven firsts; Great Britain, with all her possessions – England, Ireland, Scotland, Australia and Canada – won four firsts; Greece won three firsts; Sweden won two firsts; Russia, Austria, and Germany each won one first.' In short, 'The athletic supremacy of the world was settled; every country being represented by its strongest men.'

By 1906 the American daily press had begun to catch on to the Olympic story. It had drama and vital young men pitting their brawn and brain against true-life challenges. The newspapers of Pulitzer and Hearst thrived on tales of Everyman up against the privileged and powerful. It is traditional that in all the best stories the plucky young hero requires an opponent old in sin. As the London Games of 1908 approached, the

---

* The Greek points were garnered from, among other things, eight firsts in 'putting the stone (running), two-hand weight lifting, ladies' single lawn tennis, rope-climbing, sixteen-oar galleys, duelling pistols at command, champion shot (kneeling), and revolver at fifty paces'. Cook, *International Sport*.

American press was clear that the opponent the fresh-faced young American underdog aimed to beat in international sport was the stuck-up and decadent Brit.

Sir Arthur Conan Doyle, a great admirer of Americans, liked to talk of them as colonial cousins. It was an Edwardian habit to speak of Americans as members of the 'John Bull family'. This was not intended to be condescending. It was supposed to be friendly. Both President Roosevelt and King Edward VII considered the maintenance of friendship between 'the two great English-speaking powers of the universe' a keynote of foreign policy. But the Edwardian English were rather complacent in their reliance on 'the community of sympathies, of interests, of traditions, and of ancestry'[16] between the two peoples. The notion glossed over the fact that the Republic had been torn from the grasp of the British king and that a hundred years had not yet passed since a British fleet sailed up the Potomac to burn America's fledgling capital. Language about the British in the popular American press of the time betrays something of the simmering frustration of an overlooked younger sibling who has been nursing unacknowledged grievances for years. The common comic stereotype of the Englishman was of a stuck-up toff with a monocle and cane who prided himself on never showing an honest emotion. At a time when the USA challenged Great Britain for the political and economic domination of the world, the Olympic Games simplified the contest in terms easily understood by the American newspaper reader. When the Irish question and the Boer sympathies of German immigrants to the United States were added in, popular American attitudes to the British were not entirely cordial.

American preparations for 1908 marked an evolution in the history of US involvement in the Olympic Games. For the first time an American Olympic Committee made preparations on a national scale, with regional tryouts rather than selection by past performances. On 8 June 1908, a 'joint conclave of the executive and selection committee of the American Olympic Committee' gathered under the chairmanship of James E. Sullivan for an all-day session at the Astor House Hotel in New York. With careful deliberation they sifted through the long list of three different tryouts and two intercollegiate champ-ionships. They sat in judgement over the college men – the cream of university athletes from Princeton, Harvard, Yale and Cornell, Penn State and Ann Arbor – and the club men, working men from the big cities like Chicago, San Francisco and New York, looking to identify possible Olympic medal winners. The 122 men they selected (women were excluded from the 1908 US team) made up by far the largest team mustered to date for American competition abroad. And the majority of them – 70 per cent – would compete in track and field events.

A team uniform was ordered: white with a trim of red, white and blue stripes down the outer trouser seam, white jerseys with a United States emblem on the breast, and a blue cap with the same repeated in a badge. Arrangements were made for the team to sail together on the American liner *Philadelphia* at the end of June, in time to arrive some ten days before the opening of the Games. The projected cost of this national presence at the London Olympic Games, according to the *Chicago Daily Tribune*, was $30,000 (perhaps equivalent to $680,000 in 2006). In advising the successful candidates of their selection, the American Olympic Committee made it clear that every athlete would be 'subject to the jurisdiction of such members of the committee as happen to be in London during the games. The manager and trainer will have absolute control of the men.'

The 'members of the committee' referred principally to the members of the Comité d'Honneur. A feature of the early Olympic Games, the Committee of Honour was composed of three or four representatives from each nation taking part. All four US representatives were prominent in the New York sporting establishment: Sullivan, Barlow S. Weeks and Gustavus Town Kirby were joined by another New York resident, General J.A. Drain, captain of the US shooting team. In addition there was the team trainer, Mike Murphy, a university coach who had trained student athletes at Yale for many years and was now based at the University of Pennsylvania, and manager Matt Halpin, who had accompanied the 1906 team to Athens. Murphy, a 'wizened-up old man',[17] was selectively deaf and supposedly had only a quarter of a lung working, but he dominated his young men. The *Spalding's Athletic Almanac* of 1909 contains a picture of Murphy wearing a bowler hat and a big coat, muffled up like an Edwardian London cabby, his eyes shrewd above his brush moustache. Halpin, as befitting the upper-class New York Athletic Club, was in contrast clean-shaven and given to boaters and blazers.

The US team of 1908 was dominated by Sullivan and his fellow New Yorkers. More than thirty of the city's athletes, nearly all members of the venerable New York Athletic Club and the newer Irish American Athletic Club, competed at the London Games.

The Irish American Athletic Club had been founded a decade earlier by a group of Irish-American sporting enthusiasts led by P.J. Conway, a close associate of Sullivan. At the turn of the century the Irish-American immigrant still suffered considerable prejudice in the American community at large. The stereotype was illustrated in contemporary comic strips popularised by the Pulitzer and Hearst newspapers. Cartoon characters such as the 'Happy Hooligan', an Irish-American tramp, or the iconic 'Yellow Kid' called Mickey Duggan who lived in Hogan's Alley and played outside Demsey's Saloon, were endearing rogues who were never expected to amount to anything. Conway, in contrast, epitomised the increasing prosperity and respectability of the established Irish-American community in turn-of-the-century New York. Arriving from Limerick at the age of 20, he had worked his way up to become a man of property who owned his own business, a stable and blacksmith's servicing the city's dray horses.[18] Conway's Irish American Athletic Club organised track and field events, bicycle and handball tournaments, Irish football and hurling games from its Celtic Park ground in Queens. Its emblem was a winged fist, the motto reading (in Gaelic) 'Strong Hands Forever!'. The design of this badge was no doubt intended to contrast with the famous 'winged foot' emblem of the New York Athletic Club, but it also indicated the strong nationalist sympathies of its core members. The activities of the Club were regularly featured in the *Gaelic American*, a New York weekly journal 'devoted to the cause of Irish Independence, Irish Literature and the interests of the Irish Race'; a publication devoted to exposing British tyrannies and exploding the self-satisfied myth of the White City's Ballymaclinton village and its smiling colleens.

The Irish-American community of New York contributed more than its share of stars to the 1908 US team. Martin Sheridan, 1906 discus winner (who also competed in pole vault, standing broad and high jumps and javelin), and America's champion hammer throwers John Flanagan and

Matt McGrath, were all Irish born; others like 1,500 metres runner J.P. Sullivan – known as '4.22 Jim', he was the first native-born American to run the mile in 4 minutes 22 seconds – and marathon runner Johnny Hayes were the sons of Irish immigrants. Mel Sheppard, a record holder in the 800 metres, was a member of the Irish American Athletic Club, as were Harry Porter, regarded as the best running high jumper in the

HERE AND FOLLOWING PAGE *Contemporary cigarette cards depicting some of the New York sporting champions of the US team in 1908.*

TOP *27-year-old Martin Sheridan, pin-up boy of the Gaelic American and star of the 'Winged Fist' (IAAC) who won nine Olympic medals for the US after emigrating from Ireland aged 16.*

RIGHT *'Peerless Mel' Sheppard, the 25-year-old from New Jersey, who won both the 800 and 1500 metres for the Irish American Athletic Club.*

LEFT *Matt McGrath, another Irish emigrant to New York, star hammer thrower for the New York Athletic Club.*

RIGHT *Little Johnny Hayes, 22-year-old second-generation Irish-American marathon runner, pictured in the Olympic uniform of the US team.*

LEFT *Charles Daniels, champion sprint swimmer of the New York Athletic Club, who in 1908 held every American record from 50 yards to one mile.*

United States, and J.P. Sullivan. Sheridan, born in Ireland in County Mayo and an immigrant to the USA only eight years previously, claimed that 'if one were to go right through the team the difficulty would be to pick out those who haven't at least some strain of Irish blood in them'.[19]

At its 1907 meeting in The Hague the IOC had confirmed that individual competitors could represent either the country in which they were born or the country in which they lived. They had agreed that Canada, South Africa and Australasia, although officially parts of the British Empire, could have separate representation but, conscious of the delicacy of the subject for the British hosts, had avoided mentioning the Irish. Eire would not be granted political existence until 1922. Irish men and women were fighting and even dying for their independence. Many Irish Americans and others were eager to draw parallels with the American war of independence 132 years earlier. Whatever the hopes of Lord Desborough and the British Olympic Council, when a team so infused with Irish-American heritage arrived to compete in the capital of the British Empire the issue of Irish independence was bound to enter the stadium.

'Irish Athletes May Revolt' reported the *New York Times* at the end of June:

There are indications that the Irish athletes will refuse to do battle for England in the coming Olympic games. In which case the American representatives would have what is commonly called a cinch in the field section of the sports – jumping, weight-putting, and hammer-throwing.

Recently James E. Sullivan, President of the Amateur Athletic Union of America, expressed the opinion that it would be a shame if Ireland, which has supplied many of the world's finest athletes, should have to hide its identity behind the geographical description of the United Kingdom, and now the Gaelic Athletic Association has issued a warning to its members that they must not, under penalty of expulsion, take part in the Olympic games unless the land of their birth receives official recognition...

With Irishmen out of the way, the Americans would have no serious competition. Lord Desborough and others of the management of the Olympic games are quite upset by the incident.[20]

Behind the headlines, few athletes in the US team showed active interest in the Irish situation. Martin Sheridan, a convinced nationalist, spoke on the subject but mostly the contestants, young men in their late teens and early twenties, were fixed on their sport. However, the personal opinions of the actual contestants were insignificant when journals such as the *Gaelic American* saw the potential of the London Games to bind its advocacy of Irish nationalism to a wider story with cross-American appeal. For such advocates, the sporting stars of the Irish American Athletic Club were just the kind of all-American heroes to show the world the true nature of the British oppressors.

'Let us export,' Baron de Coubertin once said to a group of early supporters, 'our oarsmen, our runners, our fencers into other lands. That is the true Free Trade of the future; and the day it is introduced into Europe the cause of Peace will have received a new and strong ally.'[21] Egged on by the pages of the *Gaelic American*, the expatriate sons of Ireland were going to London to give the imperialist aggressor a bloody nose.

~⇒ ⇐~

The American Olympic team sailed on the morning of Saturday, 27 June 1908. An enthusiastic crowd packed the New York pier. Above them towered the steamer *Philadelphia*, a band playing 'Yankee Doodle' from the deck. Below on the dock thousands of little American flags were held aloft to the roar 'A-m-e-r-i-c-a!' as a group of young men walked up the gangway. 'Fit as so many Warriors,' gushed the *World* reporter, 'four score and three, bronze-faced, red-blooded soldiers of the track and field ... They went prepared for battle, but not with guns or cannon. Instead their implements of combat are speed, strength and a confidence that they will conquer the world in the London stadium.'[22]

At half past nine the final call rang out across the decks: 'All ashore who's going ashore.' A perspiring youth pushed his way through the crowd. G.A. Dull, a steeplechaser, had taken the wrong trolley car and ran the last mile carrying his suitcase. Manager Halpin, checking the arrivals off on his roster, discovered that there were still two men missing, one of whom was Martin Sheridan, the pride of the 'Winged Fist'. Sheridan, John Flanagan and Matt McGrath were a trio of New York policemen. When their places on the US team were announced, their police chief had refused to give his athletic patrolmen leave, considering Olympic competition in far-off London a poor excuse. But James E. Sullivan and his Irish-American lobby had influence. Pressure was exerted from the mayor's office and the police chief relented. Now the steamer was about to depart and it looked as if Sheridan might miss the boat after all.

Sailors were preparing to lift the gangway when a car drove on to the dock. Sheridan leapt out, another victim of New York's congested transport system. Then the final missing man, runner and hurdler Harry Coe, was shoved through the crowd and bundled aboard the *Philadelphia*. The band played louder and the flags fluttered as the steamer's engines rumbled into life. The athletes waved from the deck as the crowd on the pier three times yelled 'A-m-e-r-i-c-a!' before a final cry of 'Success!'

Lord Desborough hoped that the Olympic Games in the London stadium would be an opportunity for the best of young men from different nations to get to know one another better and appreciate one another more. Joe Hickey, correspondent for the *San Francisco Chronicle*, despatching his copy from London on the eve of the stadium Games, knew better. 'While all the countries in the world will figure, more or less,' he wrote, 'the actual fight will reduce itself to a titanic struggle between Uncle Sam's representatives and the athletes of Great Britain.'[23]

5

FLAG FLYING

RAIN MARS THE OPENING OF BIG GAMES IN LONDON
King Edward Starts Olympiad Before Crowd Which Fails
to Come Up To Expectations – Athletes Parade

CHICAGO DAILY TRIBUNE, 14 JULY 1908

FOR LORD DESBOROUGH and his colleagues, the climax of all their hard work was approaching. To their great relief, in the last days of June, King Edward VII had finally indicated his 'gracious consent' to become patron of the Olympic Games and, more importantly, to preside over the opening ceremonies in the Shepherd's Bush stadium. All sorts of voices and accents could be heard around the tracks and turf each morning as contestants came to practise – South African and Austrian, Canadian, Swedish, Australian and French, Danish, German and Italian. The English Amateur Athletic Association championships held in the Shepherd's Bush arena on Saturday 4 July were awash with foreign competitors, enjoying a record entry of 254 contestants. More than 20,000 watched Canadian Robert Kerr win the 100 yard dash in ten seconds flat, finishing a yard in

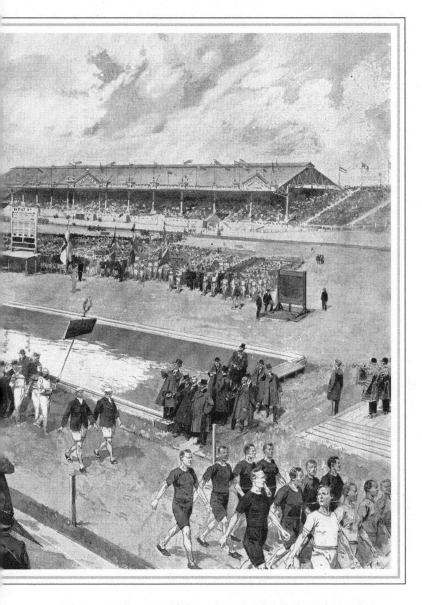

Print of the opening parade of the Games issued with the Daily Graphic, *18 July 1908, showing the Danish team with their contingent of lady gymnasts passing the royal box.*

[107]

front of R.E. Walker of South Africa. US commentators were keen to point out that Americans had been breaking the ten-second barrier since the 1890s – their record being 9²/₅ seconds by Dan Kelly of Oregon. The track was slow, said the British papers, due to the heavy rain that had fallen in the thunder-storm the night before. The English favourite, J.W. Morton, British championship holder for the past four years, only managed to come in third in the 100 yards. But Lieutenant Halswelle of the Highland Light Infantry upheld British honour, winning the quarter-mile run with a four-yard lead in 48²/₅ seconds.

At the Athens Games in 1906, 'moved by a generous desire to give all their visitors a chance of knowing one another well, and living together at a moderate cost', as Theodore Cook phrased it, the Greek authorities had offered their visiting athletes accommodation in the Zappeion, 'a fine white build-ing in a park near the stadium'.[1] At the time, their British guests complained privately of rowdy behaviour from con-testants returning home in the small hours and they did not like the food. The BOC abandoned the idea of communal living. Instead, contestants arriving for the London Games were provided with a booklet printed by the London Poly-technic containing a handy guide to hotels and boarding houses in the area.[2]

The American managers were not happy with their London lodgings. They had barely arrived in the British cap-ital before Pulitzer's *World* was reporting that 'the arrange-ments which have been provided for the American Olympic team here in London are unsatisfactory to Manager Halpin, Trainer Mike Murphy and the athletes'.[3] There were various reports as to the reasons behind the dissatisfaction. The Americans found the weather depressing. The stadium was too crowded and Murphy felt his athletes were not given the access they needed to practice facilities.[4] (Amos Alonzo Stagg, an athletics official from Chicago and a member of the US team's management committee,[*] who contributed regular articles to the *Chicago Daily Tribune*, added that Murphy, a martinet to his men, was annoyed by his athletes cutting practice to slip off and sightsee.)

'The American contestants have not had much courtesy shown them,' stated the *Tribune*. 'In training quarters, in privileges at the stadium, in the arrangement of "events," they appear to have had bad fortune.'

Suddenly James E. Sullivan and his colleagues removed the entire team to Brighton. The shift to the seaside seemed to mend tempers. 'The men put their minds on their work,' reported Stagg cheerfully, 'and trained twice daily with such excellent results that everybody is in fine shape and Murphy smiling and happy, indicating great expectations.'[5]

At the British Olympic Council offices in Victoria Street the atmosphere was fraught. Reverend de Courcy Laffan could not find the time to complete his usual meticulous minutes. In the last days before the stadium Games began Messrs Lyons were persuaded to reserve 200 seats in the Palace of Music Restaurant for members of the BOC and VIPs (cold lunches to be served to competitors in an adjacent hall from 12.30 till 2.30 at 2s 6d per head); Imre Kiralfy had 112 press desks fitted in the seats under the royal box; Lord Desborough announced that the wearing of Olympic badges would be accepted as granting free admittance to the Exhibition;[†] and Captain Wentworth

---

* He would later become well known as a football coach.

† It seems that Olympic badges were distributed to competitors, members of the BOC and track officials as well as managers of the teams.

was still awaiting delivery of the 500 caps sewn with a Union Jack badge on order for the British competitors.

The hospitality crisis continued to reverberate. The *Bystander*, as usual, was sourly critical. The 'happy go lucky' way in which the BOC had arranged their finances was 'deplorable', its commentator scolded.[6]

From a different quarter, 'Desmond', a commentator in the *Irish News*, was equally harsh. The donations sent in response to the *Daily Mail*'s 'wild series of shrieking appeals', he maintained, had come largely from foreign-born philanthropists, not Englishmen at all – citing the £1,500 from the German strongman, Eugen Sandow, and £500 from Vanderbilt, the American millionaire. He pointed to the American team's removal to Brighton as an expression of justified disgust at the shabby breach of international hospitality displayed by the British authorities:

> Greece is a small and poor country, but its people did not make such an exhibition of themselves when Olympian Games were held in the Athenian Stadium … Athletes from all countries were treated generously, and feted, and made to feel they were the guests of the State and Nation: and there were no frantic appeals for 'charitable contributions' … The poor Greeks made their guests feel honoured in a home; the rich English people have managed matters so that … John Flanagan, the mighty Irish hammerthrower, will feel indebted to the 'The Lord Monkbretton' for his chop [and the] French gymnast will rejoice that his trip to Richmond in a motor-bus has been paid for by a twirl of Miss Maud Allen's diaphanous skirts.[*][7]

---

[*] Maud Allen and her Salome dance were all the rage in London society in summer 1908. Performing barefoot, in what was for those times a

The BOC could draw consolation from the relative success of the rifle competitions. Out in Bisley, in a camp bright with bunting, international riflemen gathered in reasonable numbers and took shots at distant and moving targets despite squally weather that made accuracy difficult. It was the first real contest between the British and the Americans. The first round went to the British Empire when 61-year-old Irishman Colonel Joshua Millner – the oldest contestant in the Games – defeated 31-year-old Captain Kellogg Casey of Delaware in the 1,000 yards free rifle,[†] winning the first gold medal of the Olympic rifle shooting contest on 9 July. Two days later the American marksmen had turned the tables.

'General Drain and his Sharpshooters Beat the Riflemen of Every Country Whose Men Can Shoot', proclaimed the *World*, recording America's 'sweeping victory' in the international rifle and pistol matches with glee. It was all very good-natured and gentlemanly. General Drain, interviewed by the *World*, praised the sportsmanlike attitude of all the competitors, the hospitality of the English and the excellence of the welcome.

'The arrangements for the competitions gave us great satisfaction. We were afforded every facility for practice and everything was done to make us comfortable. Please tell the people at home,' he assured the reporter, 'that we have

revealing 'Greek' dress, she was quite as famous as Isadora Duncan to contemporaries. She had given a sell-out performance of her 'Vision of Salome', contributing the proceeds to the Olympic hospitality fund. Apart from her slightly risqué costume, Allen was considered notorious by the overtly respectable for having a brother who had been hanged for a gruesome double murder in San Francisco.

† For some reason the rifle and pistol shooting contests were measured in yards, contrary to the Olympic rule agreed by the 1907 Hague Meeting of the IOC.

experienced nothing but kindness and hospitality from the English people. We have been welcomed not as strangers, but as friends and comrades.'[8] It would be the last positive comment a member of the American Committee would offer on the record for some time.

On the evening of Saturday 11 July the British Olympic Council members turned out brushed up in their best at the Grafton Galleries in Bond Street to host the first of the receptions for visiting sportsmen paid for by the *Daily Mail* subscription. The next morning, readers across the Atlantic opened their Sunday newspapers to learn of 'some little friction' between the British hosts and the American camp.

'The Olympic authorities will not allow a hole dug for the pole vault,' reported the *World*, 'and it is said that they intend to have the high jumps without the sand pit, while the toe board for weight men is also questioned.' It was almost as if the British organisers were deliberately endangering the health and chances of the American athletes.

James E. Sullivan's AAU was determined to challenge the hegemony of the British AAA. The American Committee lodged an official protest over the pole vault regulations. American AAU rules allowed the vaulter to dig a hole to give his pole more grip, in contrast to British AAA rules that did not. The British officials pointed out politely that the Reverend de Courcy Laffan had circulated the rules governing the Shepherd's Bush contests in plain print in advance. The US managers insisted that their men were being unfairly disadvantaged by being forced to adopt an alien practice. The British would not budge. Their rules were the rules. The American managers were even more concerned when the lists went up for the first contests in the stadium. Four of their best contenders had been drawn against one another in the preliminary heats of the 1,500 metre race. J.D. Lightbody of Chicago, a medal winner at Athens, and the Irish American Athletic Club's fancied runner J.P. Sullivan, were placed together in the first heat, and the American managers' two star middle-distance runners, Mel Sheppard of the Irish American Athletic Club and J.P. Halstead of the New York

San Francisco Chronicle *cartoon published on Saturday 19 July at the end of the first week of the Games after the tug-of-war controversy had raised the temperature of the cross-Atlantic contest.*

Athletic Club, in the second. It was a particularly unfortunate chance that the two New Yorkers were drawn together. In the American Committee's plans, Sheppard was expected to win the 800 metres and Halstead the 1,500. The 1,500 metre distance was not known as Sheppard's speciality but he had done so well in the longer distances of late that the managers entered him in the 1,500 metres as a back-up, in case Halstead should meet with unforeseen difficulties.

British AAA officials were determined that the drawings were a private affair and would not admit observers. The American Committee suspected duplicity. 'It is either extraordinarily bad luck,' observed James E. Sullivan darkly, 'or it is the manner in which the drawings have been made that has resulted in such unfavourable conditions for the Americans.'[9]

On the surface the British AAA's method of drawing heats was simple and straightforward. Names were put in a hat, shaken up and picked out in turn for the first heat, the second and so on. The first problem from the American point of view was that the draws were made in private. The second was that under British AAA rules only the outright winner of each heat went on to compete in the next round. The Amateur Athletic Association was somewhat peculiar in this. In the preliminary swimming rounds, for instance, governed by the British Amateur Swimming Association, those coming first and second in each heat went through to the next round, just as under the AAU rules which had governed the 1904 Olympic Games at St Louis.

Theodore Cook explained that the British organisers worked on the principle of dividing the nationalities as equally as possible between heats. However, when a country fielded more contestants than there were heats, inevitably there would be some doubling up. 'In such cases,' Cook wrote, 'all competitors were considered as Olympic representatives of equal value, their positions in a heat being then entirely guided by the luck of the draw.'[10]

The American managers, however, were strategists. It seemed more than mere chance to them that their two best men should find themselves pitted against one another in the very first round. James E. Sullivan and trainer Mike Murphy's budding suspicions of a conspiracy were not helped by the manner in which their concerns were dealt with. The tone of Mr Fisher and his AAA officials was not particularly diplomatic. They had always run things this way and their sportsmen did not complain. When the American Committee protested that, in theory, every one of a nation's contestants could be drawn in the same heat to the evident negation of 'international' competition, the British AAA officials responded smoothly that the possibility was so remote it need not be taken into consideration. The US managers were already feeling besieged and the stadium Games had yet to begin.

On Monday 13 July Lord Desborough opened his curtains to steady rain. Grey clouds crouched over London all morning. Men wearing oilskins sturdily went about the damp business of readying the stadium for the ceremonial opening at three o'clock. Kiralfy's flag man, James Pain, directed his minions as they unpacked flags and ran them up the poles on either side of the royal box. Just after lunch the sky was seen to lighten and the rain turned to drizzle. By two o'clock it had almost stopped, but there were gaping spaces in the ten miles of seating. The American and colonial supporters bunched together in the covered stands, forming blocks of colour and animation complete with flags of all sizes. The members of the Imperial Sports Club ensured that London Society made a respectable show in the stands either side of the royal box, but, as an American correspondent noted, 'it would have been a small affair so far as attendance was concerned'.[11]

Beneath the seating the athletes were getting ready in their dressing rooms for the opening parade.* According to the parade regulations, drawn up by Robert Mitchell of the London Polytechnic:

> It is expected that every athlete taking part will be in the athletic costume of his country, or of the sport in which he intends to compete. In the event of it being a wet day, it is left entirely to the discretion of the manager of each team as to what precaution should be taken for the protection of his various members.[12]

At a quarter to three the contestants began to assemble at the rear of the stadium facing Wood Lane. According to the instructions relayed via megaphone by the chief marshal, Mr H. Elliot, they formed up in ranks, four abreast, team by team, 'behind their respective representatives, [bearing] the flag and entablature of their country'.

Sightseers had gathered, clotting together along the route the King and Queen were to travel to the stadium. They gave a cheer and a rustle of applause as King Edward and Queen Alexandra left Buckingham Palace with Princess Victoria in a landau drawn by four horses.

Soon after three in the afternoon the first of the noble guests began filing into the royal box fitted up on the west side of the stadium. The Duke and Duchess of Sparta arrived

---

* Only France and Great Britain each had their own dressing room; other nations had to share in groups of two or three. The United States shared with Austria.

first, their children in tow. The Duke and Duchess of Connaught came with the Crown Princes and Princesses of Greece and Sweden. The King's sister, Louise, Duchess of Argyll, and her husband arrived just ahead of the Prince and Princess of Wales, accompanied by their sons, Prince Henry and Prince Albert. (The kings of Greece and Norway had been expected but had sent their apologies at the last minute.) The Princess of Hesse was seen chatting to the prime minister of Nepal while Ambassador Reid, the American representative, made conversation with his fellow ambassadors from Russia, France and Austria.

At eleven minutes to four the band of the Grenadier Guards struck up the national anthem, signalling that the King and royal party were at the gates. Lord Desborough,

King George		Queen Mary		
The Duke of Argyll	The Earl of Derby		Imre Kiralfy	Lord Desborough
			The Hon. Sir John Cockburn	

A rare photo taken soon after King Edward VII's death in 1910, showing the two men without whom the London Olympics could not have taken place: Imre Kiralfy and Lord Desborough. The Duke of Argyll, King Edward's brother-in-law, was the influential chairman of the Franco-British Exhibition project.

Imre Kiralfy and a group of dignitaries representing the
Franco-British Exhibition welcomed their majesties. Lord
Desborough presented Baron de Coubertin, who bowed low.
The Baron, in turn, introduced a long line of members of the
International Olympic Committee in their top hats and tails,
representing 11 nations in all. Then their majesties were
ushered up the outer staircase to the royal box.

British officials mustering the parade at the rear gates
became aware of a ripple of consternation among the waiting
teams. It transpired that Kiralfy's flagman had made a faux
pas. During the last meeting held at Victoria Street before
the BOC moved its business to the Imperial Sports Club for
the duration of the Games, the members had agreed to pay
Messrs Edgington £5 for the hire of 'Flagstaffs and Flags'.
Messrs Edgington must have delivered a job lot, for among
the flags of the nations fluttering damply on the poles to
either side of the royal box hung those of China and Japan,
although neither country was involved in the Games. The
Swedish flag, however, was missing.

The Crown Prince of Sweden, president of the Swedish
Amateur Athletic Association, had been one of the most reli-
able supporters of the Olympic Games since their revival. He
and his government had – unlike the British government –
provided substantial subsidies to send the third largest
national team to the London Games.[13] And there was Prince
Gustavus standing in the royal box, an honoured guest of
their British majesties, with his country's flag singularly
absent. But that was not all. The Stars and Stripes was missing too.

Prince Gustavus was smooth about the omission. The
American Committee were less diplomatic in concealing their
feelings. However much Imre Kiralfy apologised and pleaded

the oversight of a minion, a deliberate insult was suspected. The Americans produced their own Stars and Stripes and that mistake was hurriedly rectified, but the Swedes, who had not thought to pack spare flags, for the time being had to make do with the single flag carried before their team in the parade.

A bugle sounded, the Royal Standard was unfurled and the gates to the arena flew open. The athletes marched out in formation, team by team, behind their national flag.

The organisers of the London Games had set out to add extra pomp and ritual to the simple procession of dignitaries and athletes around the stadium that had opened the Athens Games in 1906. As a young boy, Imre Kiralfy loved to watch military parades. The spectacular productions of his middle years were famous for their blocks of marching dancers performing synchronised movements while waving colourful flags. The opening ceremonies at the White City stadium betrayed the Kiralfy touch. Nearly 2,000 athletes marched in national teams, each behind two standard bearers, one carrying the name of the nation and the other its flag. The unforeseen difficulty was that when athletes, rather than actors, march with flags, politics follow.

Theodore Cook explained in the official report of the 1908 Games that the definition of the word 'country' presented questions of 'no small difficulty' to the BOC. Several of the 'nations' marching in the stadium were not officially nations at all. The rule established by previous Olympiads defined a country as 'any territory having separate representation on the International Olympic Committee; or where no such representation exists, any territory under one and the same sovereign jurisdiction'. Bohemia, for example, was a part of the Austro-Hungarian Empire. However, a Bohemian member of the IOC was a good friend of Baron de Coubertin. He arranged for Bohemia to compete in the Olympics of both 1906 and 1908 as an independent nation. In the 1908 Olympics Bohemia fielded 18 contestants and Austria a mere seven (although Hungary's contingent of 65 athletes outnumbered them both).

The continental teams came first, marching in alphabetical order with Austria's band of seven at their head, followed by a larger group of Belgians. Queen Alexandra's countrymen from Denmark* were accompanied by 22 fresh-faced lady gymnasts with upswept chignons in the then fashionable style, shorter-than-fashionable skirts and amber stockings. Denmark's lady gymnasts were to prove a popular attraction in the first week of the Games but they were present only as part of an 'exhibition' feature. The privilege of competition was reserved for the 78 male athletes marching in front of them.

The countries that employed conscription made the best show, their athletes marching with military precision. The teams of Sweden, Norway, Denmark and Finland were particularly admired for their neat and uniform appearance. The French contributed the second largest team to the 1908 Games but only 27 joined the parade. Wearing kepis and full of Gallic confidence, they marched in knee-length boots, showing off their muscles in figure-hugging jersey and white twill breeches. The Germans, who followed them, had less than half the number of contestants entered by the French but paraded a formidable band of 61. Fifty men walked behind the flag of the Netherlands, followed by the Hungarians, the Italians and the Norwegians. The Swedes put on a display to make their prince proud: 150 strong, marching in

* Edward VII's wife, Queen Alexandra, was born a Dane.

tight formation in gleaming white nautical-style uniforms, as trim as sailors in a musical comedy stepping out behind a line of officers in full military rig complete with plumed helmets and swords. They included the youngest competitor at the Games – diver Erik Adlerz, who was barely 16 years old.

Sixty-four Finns arrived at the stadium almost at the last minute. Their ship had been stricken by boiler trouble outside Hull and they were lucky to make it to Shepherd's Bush in time. They had brought their own flag and were keen to march behind it in the parade. Finland was at the time a part of Russia. The Russian athletes did not take part in the opening parade* (there were just six entered, including one figure skater who would arrive later for the winter Olympics). But the Russian representative was adamant that the Finnish flag could not be paraded in a London stadium. The BOC, caught between the two sides, reached a compromise at the last minute and the Finnish athletes joined the parade out of order and without a flag. They marched behind their standard bearer, Bruno Zilliacus, a shot putter, who displayed a name plate reading 'Finland'.

The US team led the English-speaking nations into the stadium. With their 122 contestants, the Americans might have fielded the fifth-largest team in the parade; but trainer Murphy did not think parades important. He kept his boys in training at Brighton until called on for 'more serious work'. Only those athletes who were to compete that afternoon marched among the 15-strong band representing the USA. They walked along in their street clothes behind the shot

---

* Three participating nations other than Russia did not take part in the parade, all three represented by a single individual: Argentina (a figure skater), Iceland (a Greco-Roman wrestler – although Iceland was officially under Danish sovereignty in 1908) and Switzerland (a hammer thrower).

putter Ralph Waldo Rose, the strapping 6ft 6in law student from California who carried the Stars and Stripes. The height of the Americans was much remarked upon, Rose and Lee J. Talbot of the Irish American Athletic Club and 'the other giants of the team towering over the majority of their competitors on the field'.[14]

Then came the British Empire: 13 South Africans* (all white men, this being the Empire) walking behind the flag that the BOC had decided should be employed for the occasion just a week earlier, the Red Ensign with a springbok in the corner.[15] There were thirty or so Canadians neat and orderly in white flannels, white cricket caps and cable jerseys with a maple leaf badge. Three New Zealanders and 11 Australians marched as 'Australasia', led by their flag bearer Henry St Aubyn Murray, a New Zealand hurdler. The antipodeans strode along in macho casual, the swimmers in their bathers and the rest in white shorts and dark jerseys.

Finally, the hosts, Great Britain, brought up the rear behind a Union Jack carried by John Edward Kynaston Studd, the eldest of three famous cricketer brothers, a former captain of Cambridge – over 200 men in baggy shorts and bare legs, the college boys sporting ill-fitting summer blazers buttoned up tight over jumpers to keep out the cold.[†] In the event, despite the efforts of the Gaelic Athletic Association, the Irish athletes marched among them, but they did so under protest.

---

* South Africa would not become an independent nation until 1910. In 1908 the designation referred to a group of four British colonies each with its own government: Cape Colony, Natal, Transvaal and the Orange River Colony – later the Orange Free State.

† In total Great Britain had 736 contestants entered in the 1908 Games: 697 men and 39 women. I have not been able to ascertain whether any of the British women marched in the parade.

The parade drew up in formation before the royal box, the Americans in the centre flanked by the Canadians and the British. Austria, Belgium, Bohemia, Denmark, Italy, France, Germany and Australasia were to one side, South Africa, Greece, Holland, Hungary, Norway, Sweden and Finland to the other. The flag bearers stopped three paces in front of their columns. Then, in unison, the flags were lowered in salute to the British king; each flag, that is, except the Stars and Stripes held by Ralph Rose. 'This flag dips to no earthly king,' the law student is supposed to have said. The mood in American quarters was distinctly different from the happy days of Athens when Matt Halpin had raised three cheers for the Greek king.

A fanfare rang out from the trumpeters of the Life Guards stationed on the wrestling stage. Lord Desborough bowed to the King: 'Will your Majesty graciously declare the Fourth Olympiad open?' he asked.

Led by an Oxford Blue, a Cambridge Blue and a former member of the Eton Eight, the British team parade, their loose formation betraying the absence of conscription in the United Kingdom.

'I declare the Olympic Games of London open,' replied King Edward.

The watery sun shone through the clouds and 30,000 spectators applauded. The band of the Grenadier Guards struck up the national anthem as the massed ranks of athletes gave three cheers. The teams then wheeled off in a column of companies giving the military salute as they passed the royal box, the flags dipping once more – all except the Stars and Stripes. The parade lapped the stadium and disappeared into the tunnel leading to the dressing rooms under the stands. The Games of Shepherd's Bush had begun.

The British papers largely ignored Ralph Rose's small discourtesy. But it was a sign of the sense of siege that was building rapidly in the US camp, fuelled by a heady mix of Irish-American pride, competitive instinct and James E. Sullivan's sensitivity to his exclusion by de Coubertin and the aristocratic inner circle of the IOC. The *Gaelic American* picked up Rose's little flag rebellion and made much of it, and the anecdote was repeated sufficiently in the American press to be long remembered as the first 'scandal' of the 1908 Games.

The parade had barely disassembled when the first heat of the 1,500 metres began the stadium contests. Kings and queens, princes, peers and plebs watched F. Meadows of Canada dash out in front for the first lap; then de Fleurac of France took the lead, only to be passed in turn by J.M. Smith of Great Britain with the home crowd cheering him on. Three hundred yards from home, J.D. Lightbody, the American winner at Athens, made his move. He flashed in front with team-mate J.P. Sullivan and F.A. Knott of Great Britain on his heels. Sullivan overtook them both and won by a good six yards. The Stars and Stripes was run up the flag pole and

The French performing during the team gymnastics competition that was the highlight of the first week for the European nations. The Americans did not compete and the British came last.

thousands of American throats roared in appreciation – the *World* reporter among them.

Almost before the enthusiasm of the American spectators had cooled enough to allow them to look at the track with normal eyes, 'Mel' Sheppard, the idol of the American team of middle-distance runners and an Irish-American A.C. man and J.P. Halstead of the New York Athletic Club, were leading a trailing field around the track. Halstead ran like the wind, but Sheppard was like a leaf before that wind, and with both straining every nerve and muscle they flashed across the tape with Sheppard a yard in front.

In order to maintain his lead, Sheppard was forced to break the Olympic record made by Lightbody at Athens...

Staggering behind Halstead in this heat came Butterfield, England's former mile champion. Again the Stars and Stripes were floated over the Stadium and again the spectators broke into a delirium of cheering.[16]

As it happened, the fastest time that day was achieved by N.F. Hallows, a 21-year-old Doncaster student who was studying at Keble College, Oxford. He, as the *World* acknowledged, set a new English record cutting two seconds off the previous one with a time of 4 minutes 3²/₅ seconds.

> N.F. Hallows, a rangy Oxford Blue three-mile runner surprised himself and everybody else by sprinting over the course like a frightened deer. When it was found that he had even bettered Sheppard's record of the previous heat, the Englishmen shook off their indifferent air and roared. Even King Edward forgot his dignity long enough to clap his hands at the performance.
>
> ... The five other preliminary heats were run off, but none of the Americans got a place in them. H.A. Wilson, of England, the 'dark horse' in the race, won the seventh heat easily.

In fact Wilson, a 22-year-old from Lincolnshire, was not so much of a dark horse. He was the English favourite, the winner of the UK Olympic 1,500 metre trials. The surprise over Nat Hallows' victory, however, was shared by everyone including Nat himself.

That afternoon, Lord Desborough and Theodore Cook could look out with satisfaction on something approaching the animated scene of Athens. The blue skies were lacking, of course, the stadium was made of concrete and steel rather than snowy marble and the spectators might cluster in patches under their umbrellas. But men raced on the turf track while the preliminary heats of the 400 metre competition churned the waters of the swimming pool and contestants in the 2,000 metre tandem cycling event circled the concrete path.

James E. Sullivan, meanwhile, was busy preparing to lodge a fresh protest – this time against the eligibility of the Canadian, Tom Longboat, to run in the marathon.

In the pre-race speculation Tom Longboat was often picked out as favourite to win the upcoming marathon race. An Onanagan Indian, born on a poor smallholding on the Six Nations reserve near Branford in Ontario, he was a sturdy, good-natured 21-year-old who had been competing in amateur races for a year and a half. In 1907 Longboat ran in the prestigious Boston marathon and broke the standing record by five and a half minutes. Since that time the president of the AAU had been trying to out him as a professional.

'Longboat will never run as an amateur in the United States,' Sullivan told the New York papers at the time. 'He has been a professional from the time he began his athletic career. He is taken from town to town ... with bands and carriages and silk hats. He runs all kinds of races at country fairs for money.'[17]

The man who paraded Longboat with those bands and silk hats was his manager, Tom Flanagan, a leading figure in Toronto gambling circles. Flanagan was a slick Irish Canadian who 'recruited' young Canadian track-and-field talent, ostensibly for the Irish Canadian Athletic Club in Toronto. When his win in the Boston marathon made Tom Longboat a sporting celebrity, Flanagan took over control of the young athlete's career, overseeing his training and paying his costs.

Flanagan was a wily operator. On his home turf in Canada he promoted meets, using Longboat's celebrity to pull in paying spectators by the thousands. In accordance with his amateur status, Longboat received little more than his costs (though Flanagan put him in charge of a cigar kiosk in a Toronto hotel he part-owned). His manager raked it in, taking a proportion of gate receipts, bets and the fruits of creative expense accounting. He treated his athlete with little respect. He would bet a crony over a drink that 'his' Indian could beat a horse-drawn buggy over 18 miles. When Longboat obliged, his manager thought it no more than his due. The Indian Wonder was his creature.

Tom Longboat as 'The Indian Wonder'. By 1908 Canadian sponsors were lining up to offer lucrative endorsement deals. His manager, Flanagan, had his eye on the greater riches that an Olympic champion could command.

James E. Sullivan had built his success on a platform of 'amateur purity'. He needed to pick the occasional fight to endorse his image in the press as the unflinching moralist. Tom Longboat's gambling manager made him a useful target. The fact that the Indian Wonder represented the greatest threat to American chances of winning the 1908 Olympic marathon was no doubt irrelevant.

The president of the AAU barred Flanagan's pet from defending his title and competing in the 1908 Boston marathon. He expected the London Olympic organisers to take his word that Longboat was a professional.

Under the British AAA rules which governed the 1908 marathon:

> An Amateur is one who has never competed for a money prize, or monetary consideration, or for any declared wager or staked bet; who has never engaged in, assisted in, or taught any athletic exercise as a means of pecuniary gain; and who has never taken part in any competition with anyone who is not an Amateur.

This definition could indeed be interpreted to exclude Tom Longboat. However, if strictly applied, it would also exclude many of the New York athletes on the US Olympic team. Just three years earlier in 1905, Sullivan, then secretary of the AAU, suspended as unproven amateurs a handful of the Irish American Athletic Club's star athletes, including their darling, Martin Sheridan and the Olympic steeplechaser, George V. Bonhag, accusing them of making financial profit from their sport. Apparently at the same time a blanket protest was lodged impugning the whole of the New York Athletic Club track team. The Irish American Athletic Club had threatened to secede from the AAU and set up their own rival amateur governing body, taking their dispute to the Supreme Court before a compromise was reached.

'President James E. Sullivan of the Metropolitan Association,' reported the *New York Times* at the time, 'said … that he was satisfied in his own mind that if a call were made for athletes in this division to show their winnings of prizes and trophies not more than 25 per cent would be able to do so.'[18]

When Sullivan became president of the AAU in late 1906 he proclaimed his intention to promote the training of a new breed of long-distance American champions, with the aim of defeating the British in the one athletic line where they were still considered invulnerable. (The English reputation in long-distance running was greatly enhanced by A.A. Shrubb, an all-triumphant long-distance man who had, however, turned professional by 1908 and was therefore barred from the Olympics.) 'I am going to do all I can to encourage a revival in this branch of athletics,' he wrote in the *New York Times* in January 1907. 'The Olympic games which will be held in London in 1908 will afford an excellent opportunity to match our best distance runners against the English cracks.'[19]

Under the BOC regulations (in an attempt to stop frivolous objections), any protest had to be accompanied by a £1 deposit which would be forfeited if the protest was not upheld. As the second day of the stadium Games drew to a close, Tom Longboat was pounding the muddy roads around Limerick in Ireland where Tom Flanagan had brought him to train away from prying eyes. Meanwhile, back in London, James E. Sullivan signed a letter to Lord Desborough disputing Longboat's amateur status and enclosed the obligatory fee with a slightly derisive flourish.

⇥ ⇤

The opening day of the stadium Games closed with an exhibition of bicycle polo at six o'clock; a match in which the Irish Bicycle Polo Association beat the Deutscher Radfahrerbund from Germany. The journalists headed off to lodge their copy for the next day's papers. *Vanity Fair*'s reporter concluded that the Americans were likely to sweep the board in hammer throwing, weight throwing, the sprint and the hurdle races and the high jump: 'Indeed, it looks to us at present as if the sports would be a triumph for the United States and their severe methods of training. Yet the English made a good beginning ...'[20]

The *World*'s reporter was more robust. His headline was:

YANKEES WIN FIRST BLOOD IN OLYMPIC GAMES

The Irish playing the Germans in an exhibition match of bicycle polo on the opening day of the Games – a recently invented sport, the brain child of R.J. Mecredy, the editor of the Irish Cyclist. *The Irish won 3–1.*

THE TUG-OF-WAR

The rivalry between the great nations in the field of sport is
one which by common consent does much to bring their
citizens together. It fosters good fellowships, it encourages
mutual respect, and it builds up enduring friendships.

DAILY MAIL, 13 JULY 1908

O N THE OPENING DAY of the stadium Games the *Daily
Mail* printed a special Olympic supplement. In it one
R.C. Reed offered a general forecast for the contests to come.
Great Britain, he felt, could be expected to win the 400, 800
and 1,500 metre foot races and the 5 mile race,* the 110 metre
hurdles, the walking races and the running high jump. The
Americans, he conceded, were almost certain to take the
400 metre hurdles, the standing broad jump, the standing
high jump, pole vault, discus throwing (both styles) and
the hammer and weight events. He was not sure about the
steeplechase, but thought either the British or the Americans
could win it. He only mentioned two other nations: he

---

* The 5 mile race was only contested at Olympic Games twice, in 1906
and 1908.

ROOTING

'Rooting' – cartoon from Pulitzer's World, *15 July 2008. A prim French Lady Liberty sits slightly apart as Uncle Sam and a chubby John Bull root for their teams with a Prussian officer and a fierce Italian looking over their shoulders.*

thought Tom Longboat the chief opposition to a British win in the marathon and that Robert Kerr, also of Canada, would be likely to win the 100 and 200 metre sprints. His single reference to a continental nation was his prophecy that Norway would take gold in the javelin (though why was not entirely clear, since the world champion was a Swede. Perhaps Mr Reed got his northern geography mixed up). Other British and American forecasters had different expectations but they were all united in one thing. The real contest was between the United States and Great Britain. Removed from the white marble stadium of Athens and its historic associations, the Fourth Olympiad was reduced to business: the business of winning the international championship of sport and, by implication, deciding which of the two Anglo-Saxon world powers was top dog.

'There is more or less suspicion of the hippodrome in connection with each "meet" now,' stated the *Chicago Daily Tribune*, setting the scene for its readers at the commencement of the Games. 'The well-known amusement promoter, Kiralfy, is to get 75 per cent of the "gate" at London. As 30,000 to 50,000 people are expected and seats have been sold from a dollar up to a guinea, it looks like a good business proposition.'[1]

In respect of good business, as it happened, the paper was wrong, for in the first week of the London Games the traditional British summer reasserted itself with a vengeance. On Tuesday, the first full day of contests, barely 18,000 spectators trekked out to the Shepherd's Bush stadium to peer through the drizzle and murk. That day honours were even, the United States and Great Britain winning two golds each. The hammer throw, as Reed predicted, was an American event – or more particularly a contest of Irish émigrés: two Irish Americans and an Irish Canadian. John Jesus Flanagan, born in County Limerick, a New Yorker for the past 11 years, battled it out with rival Irish New Yorker Matt McGrath. Flanagan, a stocky 35-year-old, was the standing Olympic champion.* McGrath was the young pretender snapping at the old champion's heels. At first it looked as if youth would conquer experience – until Flanagan stepped up to the mark for the last throw. He made a tremendous effort. The hammer flew from his hands and when it landed Flanagan had won gold again, breaking the record set by his fellow American, Gilles, at the AAA championship ten days earlier. Matt McGrath took silver and

---

* He had won gold in the hammer throw at both the 1900 and 1904 Olympics.

Cornelius 'Con' Walsh, born in County Cork, took the bronze for Canada. Flanagan's winning throw was 170 feet 4¼ inches (51.92 metres), almost 2 ft 6in beyond McGrath's best throw. (For a modern comparison, at the time of writing, the current Olympic record is 84.80 metres, thrown by Sergey Litvinov of the Soviet Union at the Seoul Olympics in 1988.)

Years later, Flanagan recalled:

> It was, without doubt, one of the most satisfying com-
> petition wins of my life. Matt McGrath tended to be a
> little arrogant and I had the feeling he believed he was
> certain to win. When it all came down to my last throw I
> knew I had to put everything into it, and as it turned out
> I did. If I have any regret at all now, it is that I was not
> competing for Ireland on that day.[2]

The 1,500 metres, the race the British had 'counted on' for H.A. Wilson or Nat Hallows, became the second American gold medal victory that day courtesy of a 'dashing finish' by the Irish American Athletic Club's Mel Sheppard. Wilson came second, beaten by two yards, and Hallows won the bronze. At least the British pedestrians had it all their own way. Few of the Olympic contestants could afford to stay in London for the full two weeks. In response, the cycling and gymnastic events, the walking races and most of the middle and long-distance races were packed into the first week. As a result, some contestants taking part in more than one discipline had to pick themselves up from competing in a heat for one event in the morning then make another supreme effort in the final of another in the afternoon. (British commentators argued that the reason that Joe Deakin, a much-tipped English favourite, did badly in the 1,500 metre race was because he was saving himself for the first round of the 3 mile team race later the same day.) The 3,500 metre walk provided an example of what Theodore Cook admitted was the occasional 'unavoidable hardship'.[3] George Larner demonstrated true British pluck, winning the final against wind and rain around an increasingly soggy cinder track, having completed the same distance in the morning heats.

Attendance dropped as the weather worsened through the week. The *Bystander* was quite smug:

> The notion of reviving the Olympic Games was a sufficiently far-fetched one to start with, and as the resemblance of the modern imitation to its ancient prototype becomes smaller and smaller, so much the tendency to regard it as a superfluity and a farce increase. Too much has been attempted ... The chief thing that will be remembered in connection with the Olympic Games of 1908 after they are over will be that they *are* over.[4]

The *Daily Mail*, in contrast, did its level best to drum up support. Every day the paper carried calls to the public and 'British Youth' encouraging them to take a day or two's holiday to visit Shepherd's Bush, 'as you are not averse to doing when the Derby brings half a million of you to Epsom Downs'.

'Were this contest taking place in the United States or Germany or France, it would have aroused universal enthusiasm,' lectured one editorial:

> We have carried with us our dress clothes and our games throughout the world, but when an event of vast international importance is taking place in London for the first

time in its history, and with the certainty that it will not be repeated in this country for sixty years, the British public are for some strange reason coldly apathetic.

If the British public did not come and fill the stands at Shepherd's Bush soon, the paper warned, the 'foreign Press' would 'go to their homes with the news that the British race is showing signs of deterioration and … that we are decadent alike in sporting instinct and in physical endowments'.[5]

The Europeans, meanwhile, were enjoying the gymnastic displays. The gymnastic events were perhaps the most popular contests of the Games, with 326 athletes competing from 13 nations. Every day (with the occasional postponement for truly dreadful weather) teams of Italians, Germans, Danes and others marched out on to the muddy turf in 'full

Spartan endurance: rain-soaked competitors awaiting their turn. During the first week of the Games athletes had to contend with the weather as much as each other.

gymnastic costume'.* The judges graded their routines on
such qualities as 'physique and carriage' and the ability to
perform movements in unison – 'especially in marching and
running'. Unsurprisingly, the nations with military conscription outstripped the competition. Sweden won with 438
points out of a possible total of 480. Norway came second
with 425 points and Finland third with 405. Great Britain
came last with 196 points. (There was no American team.) The
clear favourites of both the stands and the British press, however, were not competitors. The 22 Danish lady gymnasts who
executed Swedish drill in perfect synchronisation were much
admired, as were the 'graceful proportions of their nether
limbs' encased in amber stockings.

*'The drill that makes woman physically perfect': the big
attraction of the first week, the Danish lady gymnasts.*

---

* 'All competitors must be attired in full gymnastic costume, viz.: gymnastic vest (which must cover the armpits); long trousers to the ankles, or
short trousers with stockings to the knee (tights or woven knickers not
permitted); and light shoes.' Official Report, p. 186.

Another European admired for his well-proportioned physique was the Swedish javelin champion, Eric Lemming. The javelin was first introduced to the programme at Athens in 1906, but 1908 was the first time the event was contested at an 'official' Olympic Games. The British had yet to build up an interest in the sport but spear throwing seemed to appeal to northern nations – the top throwers included two Swedes, a Norwegian and three Finns (alongside two Greeks and a Hungarian). Lemming, gold medallist at Athens and world record holder, was the favourite from the outset. The 6ft 3in Swede was photographed in statuesque poses by several newspapers. His winning throw that Wednesday morning was 178 feet 7½ inches (54.44 metres). It was some ten feet short of his personal best, a world record he set earlier in 1908 at the

Sweden's gold medal javelin champion: Eric Lemming,
a 28-year-old policeman from Stockholm.

Swedish championships.* (Lemming threw a wooden javelin. With the assistance of new materials such as fibreglass and carbon fibre, javelin throwers in recent decades have extended their reach to the point where they might be considered to threaten safety within the confines of a stadium. In 1984 the East German contestant Uwe Hohn threw 104.80 metres. That year the competition javelin was redesigned, shifting the centre of gravity down the shaft to give it a downward pitch, making it harder to throw. Nonetheless, the modern Olympic javelin record stands at 90.17 metres, set by Czech Jan Zelezny at the 2000 Olympics in Sydney.)

On the morning of Wednesday 15 July 1908 the British won the 3 mile team race, Joe Deakin crossing the line first. The US team won silver and the French bronze. Four of the athletes running in that first race – two Brits and two Americans – went on to compete in the heats of the 5 mile race that afternoon. Three of them were unable to finish the second race, but Englishman Archie Robertson won his heat. This amazing feat, sadly, did not earn him a medal. He finished fifth in the 5 miles final held three days later.

The BOC, at their daily lunchtime meeting in the Imperial Sports Club, recorded the receipt of Mr James E. Sullivan's protest on behalf of the American Committee against 'the entry of T. Longboat (Canada) for the Marathon Race'. Sullivan hinted to journalists that the BOC would find a reason to shelve the protest 'on the grounds that it was not properly presented'. In fact, Lord Desborough wrote back to the American Commissioner requesting that he supply

---

* Two javelin events were contested at London in 1908 – free style and 'held in the middle'. But since most competitors used the traditional middle grip anyway, there was little difference between the two contests and in future they would be amalgamated into one event.

evidence to support his allegations. Sullivan, oddly enough, did not reply. Instead the American papers reported that the American Committee was taking the line of magnanimous sportsmanship: 'If the committee should decide to allow [Longboat] to run', Commissioner Sullivan was quoted as saying, the American Committee 'will abide by that decision so as not to interfere in any way with the success of the sports'.[6]

On Thursday 16 July barely 4,000 hardy souls clustered shivering in the stands. The rain fell without relief all day. The designers of the 'mile a minute' cycle track and the cinder track with its 'magnificently planned corners' had had such hopes of fast times. But with the rain driving across the vast expanse of the empty arena new records were few and far between. By mid-afternoon the running track resembled a canal.[7] (Fortunately there were no foot races scheduled.) In these conditions, 'dripping with rain and plastered with mud', Leon Meredith (Great Britain) broke the standing world record in the second heat of the 100 kilometre cycle race with a time of 2 hours 43 minutes 15²⁄₅ seconds, nearly six minutes faster than the record set by a Frenchman ten years previously.* That, as enthusiastic British reporter Louis Tracy emphasised, was like cycling 'all the way from London to Brighton and then a good stretch of the road to Worthing, with a nasty fall thrown in – a fall from which he alone among three was able to rise and ride on to ultimate victory'.[8] (And falling at speed on a wet concrete track with no padding or guards, let alone a helmet, was no small thing.) It was a fine piece of endurance.

The poor attendance was causing the authorities real concern. 'The Crown Prince of Sweden has thought so much of the past week's events that he has not, I believe, missed one

---

* The race is no longer contested in the modern Olympics.

attendance,' protested Lord Desborough to the *Daily Mail* reporter. 'Yet the cheaper seats have been empty.'[9]

People blamed the high ticket prices. 'The prices of the seats have been fixed by experts selected from athletic associations in consultation with two committees,' explained the *Chicago Daily Tribune* chattily. 'They range from 23 cents to $3 for the afternoon performances, and practically about half that amount for the morning.'[10] The best seats cost £1 1s in the afternoon (when most of the best events were scheduled) and the same seats 10s 6d in the morning. The cheapest afternoon seats cost two shillings and even standing room was priced at a shilling. New York's lone socialist daily, the *Evening Call*, claimed that this was a deliberate policy to exclude the working classes – and as a consequence the patrician British organisers had made a 'dead failure' of the London Games.

The *Tatler* almost agreed. That upper-crust journal wrote tartly:

> The general public, who I suppose are the principal patronisers of these affairs, objected, and most rightly too, to be placed for their modest one shilling or two shillings, somewhere in the altitude of the flip-flap and refused to be comforted with the information that the greatest athletic meeting in the world was taking place somewhere far away in the distance.[11]

An enterprising *Daily Mail* reporter interviewed a representative of 'Messrs. Keith, Prowse and Co., the well-known ticket agents'. That expert agreed that the prices were much too high. He also identified a surprising lack of advertising:

> Day by day, thousands upon thousands of people are visiting the White City, but little or nothing is done to

draw their attention to the fact that within a hundred yards of them athletic contests of surpassing interest are taking place. They see the wall of a structure which they may or may not identify as the Stadium, and here and there they may see notices that firework displays may be seen there on certain evenings. Why should not huge posters be displayed in such a way that visitors could not but know that at certain hours certain events were being decided? Then if prices for seats were more reasonable, numbers would look in to to witness the contests.[12]

Still, with or without spectators the Games went on. In the swimming pool, with the rain pitting the water, Henry Taylor of Great Britain beat Henry Beaurepaire of Australia to win the 400 metre swimming event. It rained so hard that the gymnastic displays had to be postponed and even the band failed to turn up to play. In the daily meeting at the Imperial Sports Club the BOC accepted – at rather short notice – an offer from the Venerable Archdeacon of London to hold a special service for the Olympic contestants at St Paul's Cathedral on the coming Sunday.

The final of the 1,000 metre cycle race was a 'fiasco'. With the rain pouring down, the four leaders were so determined to force one another to make the pace that they wobbled slowly around the track until the judges called an end in disgust, declaring the time limit had been exceeded. That contest was cancelled. No rain, however, was about to stop the Americans. World record holder and defending Olympic champion Martin Sheridan* won his third gold medal for throwing a discus free style from a seven-foot circle 'without follow'. His

---

* Sheridan would win nine Olympic medals in his career, including five golds (counting those won at the 1906 Athens Olympic Games).

LEON MEREDITH   E. PAYNE   C. B. KINGSBURY   B. JONES
(London)   (Worcester)   (Portsmouth)   (Wigan)

Due to the bad weather in the first week when the cycle races took place the track was usually flooded. 'This may have troubled our foreign visitors,' commented Theodore Cook, 'for the United Kingdom won five out of the seven events, but the English, it must be added, were peculiarly unfortunate in the number of their punctures.'

winning throw was 134 feet 2 inches (40.69 metres). The contest was an all-American event, Merritt Griffin winning silver and Marquis Horr, known as Bill, taking bronze. (The modern Olympic discus record at the time of writing is 69.89 metres, thrown by Virgilijus Alekna of Lithuania at Athens in 2004.)

'The hurdles, jumps, pole-vaults and weight-throwing events, all require, in addition to the necessary physical equipment, decided perfection of technique,' explained American commentator Arthur Ruhl in a confident overview of American prospects in *Outing* magazine. 'This is something which Englishmen, with all their sporting enthusiasm, are curiously inclined to neglect, just as it is something which Americans instinctively incline to acquire.'[13]

His words were put to the test in the shot put when big
Ralph Rose faced Irishman Denis Horgan on behalf of Great
Britain. Twenty-three-year-old Rose had been the AAU shot
put champion for the last two years and held the gold medal
from the St Louis Olympics of 1904. Horgan, aged 37, another
Irishman from County Cork, was the current British AAA
champion and had held the title in nine previous years.
Horgan had not competed in previous Olympics and the AAU
and AAA champions had never met before. Rose won. His
throw of 14.21 metres (46 feet 7½ inches) was well short of his
own world record,* but it exceeded Horgan's throw by nearly
two inches, leaving the Irishman with the silver medal. The
bronze was won by another American, John Garrells.

'It is the international interest that forms the real excitement of the games,' declared the *Daily Mail*:

> To our foreign visitors every beat and every contest has
> been of international importance; as the cyclists and the
> runners neared the finish it was not the name of the
> individual athlete that leapt to their countrymen's lips,
> but that of their nation, just as the names of Sparta and
> Athens must have resounded over the plains of Olympia.[14]

The American press were eager to know precisely how the
respective wins were to be tallied. 'No official announcement
is obtainable as to how the British Olympic Association is
going to decide the Olympic Championship,' reported the
San Francisco Chronicle. The writer speculated that the 'system
adopted by the London sporting papers' would be used to fix

---

* Rose had set a world record of 49 feet 7¼ inches (15.12 metres). The
  modern Olympic record (as of 2007) is 22.47 metres, set by Ulf Timmer-
  mann competing for East Germany at Seoul in 1988.

the respective positions: that is, one point for each first place winner, ignoring seconds and thirds, and including all sports contests under the Olympic name, whether inside the stadium or without.[15] Under that ranking, by Thursday of the first week, Great Britain had 20 points, the United States 8 and the nearest competitors, Sweden and Norway, 2 points each. What with all the rowing and yachting and winter Games to come, complained the *San Francisco Chronicle*, 'it will be the end of the year before the trophy of the championship can be awarded and Great Britain will win'.

'We came here as we went to Paris and Athens, with a field team, and we are making a fight in the field events, caring nothing for other sports,' James E. Sullivan declared to the Associated Press. 'We asked that the championship trophy be put up for the field sports separately but this request was not acted on. So we will simply take the score in the field events, counting first five points, second three points, and third one point and figure out the American score on this basis.'[16]

On Sullivan's basis the Americans led with 31 points, Great Britain trailing them with 20 points (the nearest other nation, Sweden, had 5 points).

Commissioner Sullivan had received a reply to some of the American protests. Lord Desborough had apologised in writing for the mix-up over the missing Stars and Stripes at the opening ceremonies. The complaints over the pole vault, the BOC chairman explained, had been referred to the AAA. The AAA had decided not to allow American competitors to dig a hole in the vaulting contests the following week, but it had acceded to the request to have pits filled with sand to soften the athletes' landing.

-→━○ ○━←-

The depression holding unsettled weather over London seemed anchored for the duration. Friday was cool and windy with intermittent rain. Attendance was still miserably low as the archery contests took centre stage on the boggy grass. Archery had been contested at both the 1900 Paris and 1904 St Louis Games. In Paris the contest was almost exclusively French. At St Louis the field was entirely American. (It seems that archers were too genteel to travel far.) In London in 1908 the archery contests had the highest concentration of female competitors of any sport – the 25 British women archers entered even outnumbered their 16 male countrymen. There were three events, two for men and one for women. The bulk of the contestants were British, with 18 Frenchmen shooting in the men's events and one American.

The 'half a gale of wind' blowing 'produced very tricky eddies owing to the curved seats of the surrounding Stadium'.[17] William Dod of Great Britain surmounted these conditions best and won the Gentlemen's Double York Round.* Appropriately, Dod was a descendant of the commander of the British archers at Agincourt, Sir Antony Dod of Edge. He had not been expected to win (though he went on to win the British championship in 1909). William Dod was a classic example of the gentleman amateur of means who, having sufficient funds, spent his time pursuing his sporting interests (which in addition to archery included golf and big-game hunting). His sister was one of the leading women competitors. 'Little Lottie Dod', as the papers liked to dub her, was quite a celebrity of the day. She was 36 in 1908. At the age of 15 she had been the youngest ever Wimbledon champion, winning her first ladies' singles title in 1887; she won the title four

---

* In this round arrows were shot in threes: 72 arrows at 100 yards, 48 arrows at 80 yards and 24 arrows at 60 yards; 288 arrows in all.

more times before she grew bored with it and retired from tennis competition aged 22. Lottie Dod then focused on other sports – archery was but one. She also played hockey for England and won the British Ladies' Amateur Golf Championship in 1904. Despite the press attention focused on Miss Dod, the ladies' event was finally won by Miss Sybil Fenton 'Queenie' Newall, who was four months short of her fifty-fourth birthday and thus became the oldest woman ever to win an Olympic gold medal. (She went on to win British championships in 1911 and 1912.)

'Miss "Queenie" Newall'.

That afternoon the weather began to clear and gradually a few more spectators trickled in to take seats in the stands. The stadium almost looked busy. Small but enthusiastic crowds of spectators clustered around each group of athletes, cheering on their favourites. Germany scored her first gold in the swimming pool when Arno Bieberstein came first in the 100 metre backstroke. George Larner was busy winning the 10 mile walk around the cinder track in an all-British final with Eric Webb following in second place behind him (just as he had done in the 3,500 metre race), and the tug-of-war teams gathered on the turf.

The tug-of-war was not a popular event. Originally seven teams were entered but those of Germany and Greece failed to materialise. Of the five teams remaining three were British, one American and one Swedish. The three home teams were all made up of British policemen. There was one team from the Liverpool Police, another of London City Police and the third from 'K Division'. On the afternoon of Friday 17 July the United States team was to meet Liverpool Police in the first heat.

The Americans arrived first in their trim white uniforms with the red and blue stripe down the trouser seam. They fielded a team made up of their best 'heavy' field athletes, hammer throwers and shot putters including John J. Flanagan and Matt McGrath, big Ralph Rose, Lee J. Talbot and M.F. 'Bill' Horr, under the captaincy of Martin Sheridan. Of the eight, two were from the New York Athletic Club and three from the Irish American. (Sheridan was also a member of the IAAC but as captain, he did not pull.*)

Then the police team walked on the field, eight solid, square, bull-headed men under their captain, C. Foden.

---

* In addition to Sheridan, Flanagan, Talbott and Horr were all from the IAAC; McGrath and A.K. Dearborn were members of the New York Athletic Club.

*Upholders of the British law: the Liverpool Police tug-of-war
team who defeated the Americans and won the silver medal.*

The Americans had taken note of the printed rules, in
particular that 'No competitor shall wear prepared boots
or shoes or boots with any projecting nails, tips, sprigs, points,
hollows or projections of any kind.'[18] Their team were wearing
normal athletic shoes. Matt Halpin, the American manager,
took one look at the Englishmen's feet and hurried over to the
official in charge of the event. The Liverpudlians, Halpin expos-
tulated, were wearing illegal footwear. The official, puzzled,
told him that the boots were those ordinarily worn by the Liverpool Police and were quite in order. Halpin protested that
there were steel rims to the heels. The official repeated that the
boots were not prepared in any way and did not break the rules.

Halpin almost took his team off the field there and then.
On reflection, however, as he told the eager American press,
he decided to go ahead with the first pull 'in order to show
how unfairly the Americans were being treated'.

The Americans – big strong lads, most of them over six foot tall – lined up on the rope opposite the burly officers of English law. The referee cried 'Heave!' and the policemen hauled the pride of America across the line. 'The United States remained as competitors for easily the shortest time on record,' observed the *Daily Graphic*.[19] To the Americans it was clearly a fix.

'As soon as the United Kingdom team put their weight down the heels of their shoes cut through the turf and gave them a hold that was almost impossible to break,' reported Joe Hickey of the *San Francisco Chronicle*.[20] The Americans' 'ordinary shoes' slipped on the damp grass, pointed out a New York colleague. And anyway, the American athletes deliberately 'made almost no effort' in order to protest the foul. They allowed themselves to be pulled across the line, the American journalists said. 'Rose, the anchorman, did not even wind the rope around his body.'[21]

Theodore Cook's version was a little different. 'The Tug of War is a game in which the English teams had carefully specialised, and they knew their business well,' he wrote in the official report of the Games. 'The Americans were magnificent athletes, but were not aware how to tie an anchor or how to place their men. They were, in fact, not used to the game at all, and were very naturally surprised to find how little their strength availed against skilful combination.'[22]

Manager Halpin called in his Commissioner. James E. Sullivan took one look at the policemen's boots and went off to lodge a vigorous formal protest with the Reverend de Courcy Laffan. Perhaps, he suggested to his press contacts, the 'higher officials would do something to stop the unfairness with which … the officials of the Amateur Athletic Association who are conducting the games are treating their visitors'.

The BOC referred the complaint back to the AAA organisers of the event. 'As these officials had already decided in favour of their own team,' fumed the *Chicago Tribune*, 'the protest of course was not allowed. The members of the American committee, the American athletes, and everybody connected with the team are thoroughly disgusted and almost disheartened, but are going to fight it out to the end.'[23]

'The footwear worn by the United Kingdom team would never have been permitted if there was any desire to have a fair pull,' agreed the *New York Evening Post*.

The contest was supposed to be the best of three pulls but the American Committee declared that their men would not continue unless the rules were adhered to. The Liverpool team offered to take off their boots and pull in their socks. The American managers refused to respond; they marched their men off the field. To their annoyance, as they left, an official with a megaphone announced to the crowd that the Americans were retiring 'because they have had enough of it'.

The size of the policemen's shoes grew in the telling. They were 'immense', according to the *New York Evening Post*. These were shoes which could not 'under any circumstances be used for ordinary purposes'. They had inch-thick soles, and were heavier than those worn in the English navy (though how the reporter knew this is not clear). 'The headman had spikes fastened to his shoes' (there was no evidence of this from non-American sources).[24]

They were 'so heavy … that it was with great effort that they could lift their feet from the ground', added the *San Francisco Chronicle*. They were boots, not shoes, clarified the *Chicago Daily Tribune*, 'enormous calf affairs that could not by any stretch of the imagination be called ordinary'.

Martin Sheridan's version, published in the *New York Evening World*, stirred the pot further. The English team wore 'shoes as big as North River ferryboats', he wrote with comic exaggeration. The offending footwear had 'steel-topped heels and steel cleats in the front of the shoes, while spikes an inch long stuck out of the soles'. The Liverpool policemen, he claimed, 'had to waddle out on the field like a lot of County Mayo ganders going down to the public pond for a swim. The shoes they wore were the biggest things over here and were clearly made for the purpose of getting away with the event by hook as well as crook.'[25]

The poor policemen were much upset by all this impugning of their good faith. Mr J. Park, secretary of the Liverpool Police Athletic Society, was moved eventually to write with painstaking formality to the British Olympic Association to put on record that his team had worn their ordinary duty boots, 'as it is their invariable custom to pull in such boots which have gone too shabby to be worn on street duty. The boots were not prepared or altered in any way.'[26]

The tug-of-war added to the growing catalogue of American mistrust – over the secrecy of the 1,500 metres draw, 'whereby the best American runners were put in the same heats', over the refusal to allow the pole vaulters their hole, over the tone in which their protests were dismissed and now over the 'unfairness' in the tug-of-war. All the Americans wanted was fair play. It seemed that the British officials were determined they were not going to get it.

The US camp was further disappointed when their favourite, J.D. Lightbody, the 1904 Olympic champion, lost the sixth heat of the 3,200 metre steeplechase to the British runner Harry Sewell. But, as his hometown paper, the *Chicago Daily Tribune*, reported, it was not Lightbody's fault. He had slipped on the stairs in his Brighton hotel and put his kneecap out. And 'although he kept up to the Englishman throughout today, his knee bothered him when he attempted to sprint, and he was compelled to fall back, but he ran the pluckiest kind of a race'.[27] In any case the Americans had not expected to win the steeplechase. The event was mostly popular only in Great Britain (although it had been contested at both the 1900 and 1904 Olympics). Still, John Eisele of the New York Athletic Club won his heat and remained a contender for the final the next day.

That evening, at the Holborn Restaurant, Lord Desborough hosted the third dinner for athletes and officials paid for by the *Daily Mail* subscription. All but one of the American Committee were singularly absent as a sign of their disgust. 'None of the American athletes and only one member of the committee attended banquets or receptions,' reported the *New York Herald*, adding to underline the point, 'one-tenth of the outlay for which was subscribed by Americans.'[28]

The BOC dismissed James E. Sullivan's protest over the tug-of-war. They ruled that the police team were wearing standard police boots with metal rims and had not broken the rules. The *New York Sun* was the sole American paper that made light of the matter. The American protest, it wrote, 'must have been due to ignorance of this form of sport, in which it is a great speciality of the British police and army to wear heavy boots. To wear athletic shoes in a tug of war would be regarded as the same error as to wear heavy boots for a sprint.'[29]

The American Committee called in their press contacts to express the fear 'that this unfair treatment of the Americans would dishearten the team'. Sullivan had made a careful examination of the shoes worn by the British team. 'It is absolutely illegal,' he declared in his usual vigorous style, 'and there is no justification to allow the men to anchor themselves' with such shoes.[30]

⊶⊸◯ ◯⊶⊶

'The BOA has concluded not to decide the championship of nations competing in the Olympic Games held in London this year and the same decision applies to the sports now going on in the stadium,' reported the American papers regretfully. 'The difficulty of arriving at an equitable method of allotting the points was so great that the matter has been dropped.'[31]

The truth was that no previous Olympiad had made such an award. The idea itself had probably originated with James E. Sullivan. Captain Wentworth Jones issued a statement on behalf of the BOA. 'The newspapers of the different countries will have to decide the matter to their own satisfaction,' he said. 'America probably more than any other nation would have cause for complaint if we attempted to award a championship', for 'if points were awarded for every event, the United Kingdom would have a walkover'.

The 'Trouble over the Tug-of-War' put the London Games on the front pages. The *Gaelic American* and Irish-American supporters back in New York could hardly contain their glee as the controversy presented the English tyrants as cheats. They worked hard to prolong the story, emphasising the treatment of the heroic American athletes at the hands of the duplicitous British.

Saturday 18 July, despite being cloudy and dull, saw the biggest attendance yet at the stadium. A 45,000-strong crowd, 'similar to that which attends football matches on half-holidays', joined Queen Alexandra, Princess Victoria, the children of the Prince of Wales and the ever faithful Crown Prince of Sweden to watch the competitors in the classical discus event balance on the prescribed board in order to 'throw the discus as at Athens'. The rules were precise:

The discus is thrown from a rectangular pedestal 80 centimetres (31½ inches) long and 70 centimetres (27½ inches) broad, sloping forward from a height of 15 centimetres (6 inches) at the back to a height of 5 centimetres (2 inches) at the front ...

The thrower places himself on the pedestal with the feet apart, and holding the discus in either hand. He then grasps it with both hands and raises them without letting go the discus with either, extending the rest of his body at the same time in the same direction. After that he turns the trunk to the right and bends sharply, so as to bring the left hand, which has now left hold of the discus, to the right knee, and the right hand, still holding the discus, as far back as possible. At this moment the right foot should be drawn forward and both legs bent; the right foot rests full on the sole, and the left on the toes only. Then by a sharp and simultaneous extension of the whole body the thrower throws the discus forward.

(The thrower may leave the pedestal at the moment of throwing.)[32]

Classical scholars have come to the conclusion that these 'Athens rules' were a misinterpretation of archaeological evidence and that the ancient Greeks never actually threw the discus in that fashion. Still, at around a quarter to three, the Athens champion, the Finn Verner Järvinen, stepped into the arena to defend his title. When Martin Sheridan and Bill Horr walked out, the large contingent in the American section of the stands gave them an ovation. All the four top finalists broke Järvinen's standing record (as did Järvinen himself) – although the spectators, including the Americans rooting for their boys from the covered stands, were unaware of the fact as the programme printed an incorrect figure for the record to beat. Martin Sheridan won the gold with a throw of 124 feet 8 inches (37.99 metres), Bill Horr took silver and the displaced champion, Verner Järvinen, collected the bronze for Finland.

Though he had already run three hurdle races that week, the USA's John Eisele came third in the final of the 3,200 metre steeplechase – and this despite tearing a toenail off during training, which made it doubtful he would be able to compete. As Joe Hickey wrote in the *San Francisco Chronicle*:

> He was the only American that compared with the Englishmen in the distance runs, and each race he had to fight against odds, being handicapped on each occasion by having several Englishmen pitted against him ...
>
> With just a little more stamina and a little more luck Eisele would have captured some of the distance events for America. As it was he ran a splendid and plucky race. There were four of the United Kingdom team, Russell, Robertson, Holloway and Sewell in this contest in addition to Eisele and Galbraith, the other representing Canada. The Englishmen took turns in trying to wear down the two others and succeeded in doing so with Galbraith, but Eisele held on despite a nasty fall in the water jump in the first lap and managed to annex third place, well up.[33]

In the semi-finals of the tug-of-war Liverpool Police beat Sweden, while City of London Police beat K Division by two pulls to one. The latter was a 'grand contest', the 'first pull being a very lengthy affair'.[34] The Swedish team declined to turn out again and conceded bronze to K Division. In the final the Liverpool Police team were defeated by their London colleagues. 'The winning team owed much of their victory to the splendid coaching of Inspector Duke,' recorded Theodore Cook. 'He trained the men for five months, and their condition was much admired.'[35]

There followed a ten-minute exhibition of diving by Miss Valborg Florstrom of Finland and Miss Ebba Gisico of Sweden, and a water polo exhibition match between the English Reserves and the British Isles. Emil Voigt of Great Britain won the 5 mile flat race in 'fine style' and the Olympic programme closed for the weekend with gymnastics displays by the Bristol Secondary Schools and the Yorkshire Amateur Gymnastic Association.

At an emergency meeting that morning the BOC had agreed with the Exhibition Company to a reduction in ticket prices. In an interview with the *Daily Mail*, Imre Kiralfy was keen to emphasise that no one was to blame for getting the prices wrong. 'We called in the best expert opinion,' he told the reporter, 'and the prices were fixed on those of the Horse Show and the Military Tournament.'[36] The BOC had also decided that something must be done to placate the American Committee. The Amateur Athletic Association was persuaded to allow American team manager Matt Halpin to witness the draw for the sprints and hurdles to take place the following Monday. As Lord Desborough sat in the nave of St Paul's Cathedral that Sunday he must have hoped that the concession might soothe the suspicions of the American camp and convince them of the good faith of English sportsmen. In a further gesture, an American had been chosen to preach the sermon at the special 'Olympic' service. The Bishop of Central Pennsylvania, who was in town for the Pan-Anglican Congress, did his best to ignore any controversy.

'The Games themselves,' he assured his congregation, 'are better than the race and the prize.'*

A couple of days later, on 21 July, the *Sporting Life* published a challenge from Inspector Duke, captain of the City Police team, inviting the Americans to another match in which both teams would pull in their stockinged feet. The US team managers made no formal response but the next day the *Sporting Life* printed a short paragraph:

> Mr Duke, who captained the winning team in the tug-of-war, has been provoked into issuing a challenge in reply to the complaint about the boots of the men of whom he is so proud. They are sportsmen to the backbone, but the incident must be considered closed by the statement of a member of the USA team that they are satisfied with the result, and they knew that they had met better men at the game than themselves.

'We know really nothing about tug-of-war,' the anonymous source was supposed to have said. 'And before we can hope to hold our own with such a clockwork team as you can put in the field we must have considerable practice. Your men won easily, and they would win easily again, and what more needs be said. I have nothing to say, at any rate, and there will be no more pulling by us.'[37]

---

* Words sometimes erroneously attributed to Baron de Coubertin and which form the basis of the Olympic creed. The service itself was arranged at extremely short notice. The BOC minutes record a discussion of the offer made by the Dean of St Paul's to organise the service at the daily meeting on the previous Thursday.

400 METRES AND FAIR PLAY

A Critical Time

Oh! British Empire, great and free,
Attend! The moment's psychic:
Rome fell, and so it seems shall we,
Unless we win the high kick.

Our fame, once great, will wholly go
To pot – a thought that curdles –
If in the sprints we make no show,
And fail across the hurdles.

Men will forget our Art, our Laws,
Our Trade (secured by dumping),
If for some may be trivial cause
An alien wins the jumping.

'Tis sad, 'tis pity, to achieve
What many would find baffling,
And fail because we cannot heave –
Free style – the blooming javelin.

BYSTANDER, 22 JULY 1908

At the mid-point of the stadium Games Great Britain led the United States by 14 points (according to James E. Sullivan's own accounting). But the American Commissioner was confident his men were about to even the score. In the coming week Sullivan knew he was fielding a clutch of potential gold medallists. He repeated his bullish mantra to the Associated Press: 'We are here to win the championship in field sports and we are going to do it.'[1]

The new week began with a fresh character. The gymnasts gave way to the wrestlers as the Graeco-Roman and catch-as-catch-can competitions were mounted on a pair of stages set up at the north and south ends of the arena. The cyclists no longer circled the cement track. Instead fencers and épéeists were in evidence with their foils and sabres and padded jackets as they moved to and from the fencing grounds. The poles went up for the high jump and sand pits appeared as the hammer and weight men gave way to the jumpers.

The reduction in ticket prices worked. Despite gloomy weather and the threat of rain, 30,000 spectators came to watch the Games that second Monday. At the daily meeting of the BOC, the AAA presented a formal report of its decision over the American Committee's protest against the boots worn by the British competitors in the tug-of-war. The complaint had been ruled invalid, it was explained, on the grounds that 'ordinary ammunition boots' were worn by the English competitors. A French protest lodged by cyclist M. Rousselot, a competitor in the ill-fated 1,000 metre bicycle race (the one where the leaders refused to pick up the pace), was also dismissed. The time limit had been exceeded and the race was therefore void. The British Olympic Council reiterated its firm line that with any complaints 'the final decision must rest with the Association governing each sport'.[2]

Relations with the American Committee had thawed a little since the AAA allowed Matt Halpin to witness the drawing of places in the heats for the races in which his boys were contestants. A potential incident blossomed when the two New York star runners, Mel Sheppard and John Halstead, were drawn together in the first round of the 800 metre race – just as they had been in the 1,500 metres the previous week. The New York newspapers pounced on the story as fresh proof of British foul play and the American Committee lodged its usual protest. For a moment it seemed the dispute might escalate. But the AAA officials had learnt discretion. They agreed to make an adjustment. The original heat was

'Peerless Mel' Sheppard beating the British favourite, Harold Wilson, into second place in the 1,500 metres final on a cold afternoon with a strong wind blowing across the field.

split. That Monday afternoon in the first round of the 800 metres, Mel Sheppard ran in heat two against an Englishman and a Canadian, and John Halstead in heat three against an Englishman, an Irishman and a Hungarian. Both the Americans won. In the covered stands their supporters jumped on their seats and waved the Stars and Stripes, raising raucous college yells combined with choruses of 'A Hot Time in the Old Town Tonight'. The Americans were not the only ones with demonstrative fans. When Emilio Lunghi, a 21-year-old naval student from Genoa, romped home in the fourth heat, 'an ardent little countryman vaulted over the rails, made a high jump to the shoulders of his champion, and kissed him on both cheeks'.[3]

Despite the fact that their two champions made it through to the final of the 800 metres, the American press in the main ignored the new amenability of the British officials to American complaints. Only the *New York Sun* reported the AAA's concession.[4] The readers of other papers were left with the impression of yet another piece of British skulduggery.

On the Monday afternoon the first of that week's American dead certs made his appearance in the standing broad jump. Ray Ewry had had a hard start in life. He suffered from polio as a child. His doctors prescribed an exercise regime to aid his recovery. It included jumping in order to restore his wasted limbs. Young Ray was so assiduous in his exercises that he built up formidable leg muscles and a prowess that, as an adult, earned him the nickname of 'the human frog'. Six foot one inch tall, his speciality was the standing jump.

The standing jump events are no longer contested. They were removed from the Olympic programme after the 1912 Games. As the name indicates, in the standing jump there was

Ray Ewry winning the standing high jump.

no run-up. In the standing broad jump, the contestant stood
at the line and simply jumped. In the standing high jump he
threw one leg over the bar and sprang up, pulling the second
leg up and over as the first came down to earth on the opposite side. The manoeuvre took great speed and control as well
as strength. Ray Ewry made his Olympic debut at Paris in
1900 when he was 27 and world record holder in his sport.
Needless to say he took the gold in all three 'standing jumps':
the high jump, broad jump and hop, step and jump. He came
to the White City stadium the unbeaten champion, having
won all his standing jump contests for the past eight years. It
was pretty certain he would win again. And he did – taking his
fourth gold in the standing broad jump with a distance of

10 feet 11¼ inches (3.33 metres). A 19-year-old from Pylos, the Greek Konstantin Tsiklitiras, came second, leaping 10 feet 7¼ inches,* and that impressive all-rounder, the IAAC's own Martin Sheridan, won the bronze, his mark falling just another quarter of an inch shorter.

'Nothing seemed able to stand against the Stars and Stripes,' wrote the *Daily Mail*:

> Four times the flag of victory was hoisted to the masthead … All the college yells of the States resounded through the White City. The 'Rah, rah, rahs' turned the music of the band into an apologetic murmur … It became almost monotonous to see the shield of the United States blazoned on a white racing shirt, breaking the tape well in advance of the other colours.
>
> 'Will you shout for me? I'm beat!!' exclaimed an enthusiastic American on the grand stand. His voice was a hoarse whisper. But he still had his Stars and Stripes tied to the top of his gold mounted umbrella, and it was waving every few minutes.

James E. Sullivan's boys were proving their worth:

> On Saturday, England won eight finals out of ten. Yesterday, America won three out of four, and made herself reasonably safe for two more. Thus does the tide of victory shift and change.[5]

---

* Tsiklitiras would become Ewry's successor as champion of the standing jump events in 1912 after the latter had retired.

The atmosphere was building and the weather was picking up too. Tuesday dawned warm and sunny. Attendance at the White City stadium swelled to 50,000. There were some disputes. The French were upset about the 100 kilometre cycle race the previous week and the tug-of-war debacle was still reverberating. The *Daily Mail* published a brisk editorial in defence of British fair play, responding to aspersions cast by 'critics in certain of the French sporting papers, and also, we add with regret, in some few American journals, though these are not of the highest class or the most responsible character'. The French sporting papers attacked the time limits put on the cycle races as 'absurd'. 'The fact is that without a time-limit cycle races degenerate into a mere crawl,' responded the *Daily Mail* commentator, demonstrating his recognition that sport was as much about entertainment as sportsmanship.

Tandem cycling is no longer considered an Olympic sport. In 1908 gold went to the French champions, M.Schilles and A.Aufray.

Nothing more depressing can be imagined than a cycle race of 100 kilometres in which the competitors have adopted the waiting tactics, which, when introduced ten years or more ago into England, rapidly killed cycle races as an athletic event. The public stayed away sooner than watch five, ten, or twenty men moving round the course at so slow a pace it was difficult for them to keep their balance.

There was muttering in the French camp about the treatment of their champion, Octave Lapize, in the 100 kilometre cycle race. The race was considered to be the major championship of the 1908 Olympic cycle programme. The accusation was that Lapize, who had come away with the bronze medal, had been boxed in by two other leaders, both Englishmen. The *Daily Mail* writer brushed that criticism aside, for Lapize himself, apparently, was on record saying that he had no complaint. Turning to the American objections the writer spotted a theme: the protests did not appear to be coming from the athletes themselves. The press, it seemed, were largely to blame:

> The most serious complaint of all, perhaps, is that the draws for the heats were unfairly made, so that the British competitors were given a walk-over in their preliminary heats, while the best Americans were drawn together in the same heat. But here, again, there is no ground for insinuations, which do not appear to find any support from the competitors themselves. It will be observed that the swimmers of all nations have agreed at a meeting that never had they met with such fair treatment and such fair judging.

The accusations were 'frivolous or ill-founded', pronounced the *Mail*:

> and, though there will be every wish to make large allowances for foreign journals' ignorance of British rules and conditions, they should never have been entered ... the athletes of the nations themselves acknowledge that they have met with perfect justice and fair play at the hands of the Olympic judges. British fair play stands completely vindicated.[6]

Sullivan's boys kept piling up the wins. On Tuesday morning Harry Porter, another member of the Irish American Athletic Club, cleared 6 feet 3 inches (1.90 metres) in the running high jump, beating the standing Olympic record by a quarter of an inch without ever taking off his sweater. The British favourite, 'Con' Leahy, who jumped a respectable 6 feet 2 inches (1.88 metres), tied for second place with Hungarian István Somodi and Georges Andre of France. (Leahy, holder of the AAA title and the previous Olympic champion, having won gold at Athens, was another Irishman compelled under protest to compete for the British flag.)

The official contest over, Harry Porter took off his sweater and attempted to beat the standing world record of 6 feet 5¾ inches (1.97 metres). He made three attempts but did not quite make it. (For a modern comparison to Porter's 1.90-metre gold medal winning jump in 1908, the current Olympic high jump record is 2.39 metres set by Charles Austin of the USA at Atlanta in 1996.)

At five o'clock it was time for the much-anticipated final of the 800 metre race. Ivo Fairbairn-Crawford of Great Britain set out in front with a storming start, but he made the pace too hot for himself. He was 15 yards ahead in the first 200 metres when his race collapsed, and he was unplaced at the finish. Instead the 'greatest middle distance champion in the world', New Jersey's own Mel Sheppard, beat young Emilio Lunghi of Genoa into second place, winning with a nine-yard lead in 1 minute 52⅘ seconds. According to *The Sportsman*, Lunghi did particularly well to come second, for he was not said to have trained 'with any particular severity for these Games'. It was Sheppard's fastest time to date, cutting over three seconds off the previous Olympic record. (The modern Olympic record, for comparison, is some ten seconds faster. Vebjørn Rodal of Norway ran the same distance in 1 minute 42.58 seconds at Atlanta in 1996.)

This was Mel Sheppard's second gold medal, in addition to the one he secured for the 1,500 metre race the week before. The 26-year-old New Yorker would eventually leave London with three golds (his third was won in the 1,600 metre medley relay race).

The stadium assumed a strangely summery air. The sun shone and the crowds held up. The mood was cheerful. On Wednesday morning the cheerfulness of the British crowd, indeed, caused some offence at the fencing ground where the preliminaries of the sabre team event were taking place. The Hungarians were the reigning champions – two members of their team had just walked off with gold and silver in the individual sabre events. It was the Germans' misfortune to face them in the first round. The German team was so clearly outmatched that the British crowd ended up hooting with laughter at the sight of the portly German team captain 'being whacked all over his body in sabre play'.[7] The Hungarians won by nine points to nil. In his official report Theodore Cook noted blandly that nobody could recall another team fencing match in which one team never scored a single hit. When the incident was relayed back to the Fatherland, Berlin expressed itself offended by the discourtesy. At least the German team was defeated by the ultimate champions. Hungary would dominate sabre events at the Olympics for the next couple of generations, winning all the gold medals in this event from 1908 to 1960 (barring the medal awarded at the 1920 Olympics to which they were not invited, being regarded as one of the aggressors in the First World War).

By Wednesday of the second week – the ninth day of the stadium Games – the Fourth Olympiad seemed at last to be running smoothly. Business was light at the daily meeting of the BOC at the Imperial Sports Club. The Council finalised arrangements for the prize-giving, endorsed a ruling of the Amateur Wrestling Association in respect of a protest against a judgement in the catch-as-catch-can contest, and agreed to award a silver medal to each of the three men who tied for second place in the running high jump.

There was yet more rejoicing in the American stand as Francis Irons of the USA won the long jump, with fellow American Dan Kelly winning the silver. The final of the 100 metre foot race followed half an hour later. One of Imre Kiralfy's sons, Edgar, competed in the 100 metres as a member of the US team. (The Kiralfys had spent twenty years in America and several of their children were born there.) Kiralfy junior was knocked out in heat four of the first round on Monday afternoon. By Wednesday afternoon the last of the British hopes for the race had also been eliminated when the top British sprinter of the day, John Morton, an AAA championship winner for four years between 1904 and 1907, was defeated in the semi-final.

The record to beat in the 100 metre sprint was 10⅘ seconds, set by Frank Jarvis of the USA at the Paris Olympics in 1900. Four men took their marks for the final, two of them Americans. James Rector had equalled the Olympic record in the preliminary round but Nat Cartmell, a 24-year-old from Union Town, Kentucky, was the one tipped by Alonzo Stagg as the winner. The third finalist was the Canadian Robert Kerr – the man who had won the 100 and 200 metre titles at the AAA championship in the week before the Stadium Games. The fourth in the line-up was a 19-year-old born in Natal, South Africa: Reggie Walker.

Walker almost did not make it to the 1908 Olympics. When he was recommended for the South African team in May that year, he did not have the money to make the trip to England. Jim Wallace, a Natal sportswriter, took up the teenager's cause in his column and raised the money to send young Walker to London just in time.

At the starter's pistol James Rector sprang in front. Halfway down the track Reggie Walker put on a magnificent spurt of speed. The pair ran side by side for some six yards and then Walker shot ahead. He won by a clear three feet. Rector, unable to reproduce in the final the same turn of speed he had achieved in the preliminary rounds, came in second; Kerr finished third, just a shade in front of Nat Cartmell. Walker had equalled the standing Olympic record of 10⅘ seconds. (The modern Olympic record, set by Donovan Bailey of Canada at Atlanta in 1996, is 9.84 seconds,[*] but given that he was just 19 years and 128 days old when he ran his race, Reggie Walker still remains the youngest ever winner of the Olympic 100 metres.)

---

[*] The world record is even faster. Asafa Powell of Jamaica ran the 100 metres in 9.74 seconds at Reiti, Italy in September 2007.

*Reggie Walker, winner of the 100 metres, celebrating
on the shoulders of his supporters.*

By Thursday 23 July, day ten of the London Games, the
temperature was climbing. 'Tropical clothes' were spotted out
and about in London. Ladies shopping at the sales, reported
the *Daily Mail*, 'although they wore the lightest cottons for the
most part, felt the heat very much and, as the manager of a
Kensington shop remarked, were too "fidgety" to buy much'.[8]

Attendance at the stadium was the highest yet. Sixty thousand ticket holders filled the stands. In the morning Ray Ewry
added the 1908 standing high jump to his growing collection
of Olympic gold medals. This time he leapt over a bar set at
5 feet 2 inches (1.57 metres). Young Tsiklitiras of Pylos was
again his capable second, jumping 5 feet 1 inch (1.55 metres) in
a dead heat with J.A. Biller of the United States. It was Ewry's

fourth consecutive Olympic double (that is, winning gold for both the standing broad jump and standing high jump), but for him it was not a spectacular success. He failed to beat the Olympic record he had set at Paris in 1900 (5 feet 4¼ inches) and he came nowhere near the world record, which – according to Theodore Cook – was 6 feet, jumped from standing by a professional named J. Darby with his ankles tied together.

The win brought Ray Ewry's Olympic gold medal count up to ten; and that record – for the most Olympic gold medals won by a single athlete – still stands. It was the height of 34-year-old Ewry's career; 1908 was his last Olympic Games.

The British organisers were preparing for the climax of the Fourth Olympiad. At their regular one o'clock meeting in the Imperial Sports Club that Thursday the Council agreed to engage 30 extra policemen for crowd control on the day of the marathon race. Just 24 hours before the contestants were to gather in Windsor for the marathon, the BOC announced that 'the Canadian runner, Longboat, should be allowed to run, but under protest'.

James E. Sullivan's campaign to have Longboat ruled a professional had raised an outcry in Canada, where the native Indian runner was regarded as one of the country's strongest contenders for Olympic glory. It so happened that the dispute fell in the midst of a power struggle between two rival bodies for control of Canadian amateur athletics. The Canadian Amateur Athletic Federation came out in support of the American AAU's bid to disqualify the Iroquois runner. The move would cost the Federation dear. The rival Canadian Athletic Association backed Longboat, vouching for his good standing as an amateur. Their endorsement satisfied the British Olympic Council's printed rule that an athlete's amateur standing rested with the guarantee of his national body, and on that basis they permitted Longboat to run.*

It was four o'clock when the finalists lined up for the 200 metre flat race. A mere 22⅗ seconds later, the race was won by 26-year-old Robert Kerr for Canada, repeating his win over the same distance at the AAA championships two weeks earlier. (Kerr was in fact another Irishman, born in Enniskillen, but he emigrated with his family to Hamilton, Ontario, as a child.) The *Sporting Life* commented that the Canadian sprinter 'seemed slightly overtrained in the Olympic Games'. It was a hard-won race. Kerr flagged visibly towards the end, pressed by two Americans – Robert Cloughen and Nat Cartmell. But he held on, crossing the line nine inches in front of Cloughen. Cartmell took the bronze. G.A. Hawkins of Great Britain came in fourth. The Olympic record established in Paris in 1900 still stood – 22.2 seconds, set by Walter Tewksbury of the USA.†

At ten past four, the Americans proved their supremacy in the 110 metre hurdles, winning every heat in the second round and thus ensuring an all-American final. James E. Sullivan could add another nine points to the rapidly mounting American score.

---

* The specific rule, as printed, was that the national governing association 'will be responsible to the BOC … to guarantee that the competitors entered [by their amateur clubs] are amateurs within the conditions laid down'. The row had significant repercussions in Canada, contributing to the rise of the Canadian Athletic Association and the demise of the Canadian Amateur Athletic Federation.

† Although there was no official body to recognise world records at the time, John Maybury, again of the USA, was said to have clocked 21.4 seconds in a 200 metre sprint at the Western Intercollegiate Athletic Meet in 1897. The modern Olympic record for the 200 metres, at the time of writing, is that set by Michael Johnson (USA) – 19.32 seconds at Atlanta in 1996.

Just over an hour later, while the American stands still reeled with the joy of yet another lifting high of the Stars and Stripes, their throats hoarse with cheering and the rest of the stadium growing a little tired of the constant 'Rah! Rah! Rah!'s from their massed college men, the finalists gathered on the cinder path for the final of the 400 metres. The 400 metre race is the longest sprint distance – precisely one lap of the inside of a track, equivalent to the 440 yard, quarter-mile distance. It was the last major contest of the tenth day of the 1908 Games. The Americans had been amassing medal wins all day; they had the British Empire on the ropes and the 'championship' was within their grasp.

Four finalists lined up, their places drawn by lot. John C. Carpenter was placed in the first position, on the inside track next to the verge. Carpenter, a 23-year-old student from Cornell (a university famous for its track team), was considered the best American intercollegiate 'one-lapper'. Next to him in second position, carrying the honour of the British Empire on his slim shoulders, was 26-year-old Lieutenant Wyndham Halswelle. It is worth mentioning that in the second round of the 400 metre contest, Great Britain suffered precisely what the American Committee had complained of with such vigour. Although there were four separate heats in the round, their three crack runners were drawn against each other in a single heat. Halswelle was the sole survivor. The Americans, however, had three of their best quarter-milers in the final.

Born in London, Halswelle described himself as Scottish. He was a career soldier and he looked the part, the pattern of the upright defender of the Empire, with his even features, slicked-down hair and trim moustache. Having indeed first come to prominence winning the Army 880 yards championship in 1904, by 1908 he was the top British quarter-miler.

He had been AAA champion in 1905 and 1906 and again in 1908. He won silver for the 400 metres and bronze for the 800 metres at the 1906 Athens Olympics. In that same year at the Scottish AAA Championships he won the 100 yards, 200 yards, 440 yards and 880 yards all in the same afternoon. While competing in Glasgow just before coming to the London Games, he had broken by a fraction of a second the world record for 440 yards, set by Edgar Bredin in 1885. (Bredin's time was 48.5 seconds; Halswelle's was 48.4.) Halswelle repeated his time in the second round of the 400 metre contest at the White City stadium, setting a new Olympic record.* He was easily the fastest of the qualifiers that day.

Next to Halswelle in the third lane stood William C. Robbins, a 22-year-old student at Yale who had the reputation of being 'a splendid finisher'. (A few months later, having finished his university course, Robbins would become an active member of the Irish American Athletic Club in New York.) And, then, in fourth position, came 25-year-old John Taylor, one of only two black men competing at the London Games, a veterinary student from the University of Pennsylvania. Having won the Eastern Olympic trials that year, Taylor was considered America's top 400 metre runner. It was an impressive field. In the well-filled stands the rival banks of American and British supporters were keyed up, anticipating a great race.

The men took their marks. According to the *Sporting Life* 'peculiar rumours' had been circulating before the race, though this may be an embellishment woven after the event. The starter, the splendidly named Mr Harry Goble, a member of the Manchester Athletic Club, was instructed by the referee

---

* The current Olympic record for the men's 400 metres is 43.49 seconds, set by Michael Johnson of the USA at Atlanta in 1996.

A picture of the controversial 400 metres final published in the US Spalding's report. It shows the British officials on the track having pulled down the tape. Carpenter looks back over his shoulder, while Halswelle slows down before an official with his raised hand. Note the position of the other two US sprinters at the opposite side of the track, well out of the way of the contested British and US champions.

to caution the competitors that any wilful jostling would result in the race being suspended and the culprit disbarred. There were officials posted every few yards along the track to watch out for just such behaviour. Then Mr Goble fired the starting pistol and they were off.

Carpenter darted to the front with Robbins at his heels. Halswelle, who was known as a slow starter, trailed them for the first 50 metres with John Taylor behind him. Dr Michael J. Bulger of the Irish Amateur Athletic Association, a member of the British Olympic Council and an umpire of the race, was standing by the side of the track some 100 yards from the start. He saw William Robbins shift out of his lane. To Bulger's eyes, Halswelle was forced to drop back in order to move to the outside of Robbins.

As they approached the second bend, 'Robbins and Carpenter were in such a position as to compel Halswelle to run very wide all around the bend,' according to Dr Arthur Roscoe Badger, another umpire and a vice-president of the AAA, who was posted by that section of the track. 'As they swung into the straight Halswelle made a big effort and was gaining hard.'

For a second Halswelle seemed to draw ahead but then John Carpenter ran wide. With growing indignation Dr Badger watched as 'running up the straight the further they went the wider Carpenter went out from the verge, keeping his right shoulder sufficiently in front of Mr. Halswelle to prevent his passing'.[9]

Carpenter's elbow seemed to make sharp contact with the Scotsman's chest as he shouldered him to the outer side of the track. Dr Badger had no doubts. It was a clear case of 'boring'. He ran up the track, waving his hands at the judges.

Another umpire standing nearby, Mr David Basan, an official of the London Athletic Club (the race was remarkably vigilantly policed), joined him. The referee, Mr David Scott Duncan, was standing opposite the winning post behind Mr Pennycock, one of the judges. Mr Duncan saw Halswelle, 'dispossessed' of his position in the second lane by Robbins, struggling to break through the pack and a couple of red-faced umpires lumbering up alongside the track waving their arms. An outraged official (no one was sure who) pulled down the tape* at the finish line before Carpenter could pass

* Contemporary accounts referred to 'the worsted', which suggests that at the time wool was used instead of tape.

the post. Halswelle, Robbins and Taylor slowed down but Carpenter pressed on at full tilt and crossed the line, recording an unofficial time of 48⅖ seconds. Halswelle came next, followed by Robbins and then Taylor.

For a moment the arena was silent and then a furious row broke out. The Americans howled that they had been robbed, that the British officials would do anything to cheat them of victory. The British supporters cried that it was the Americans who were the cheats. As officials with megaphones walked up and down the stands declaring the race null and void, the judges crouched over the footprints left by the runners on the cinder track. They were satisfied that the evidence was

John Carpenter, the crack quarter-miler, who was disqualified during the disputed 400m final.

clear. (The next day the *Daily Mirror* published a photograph showing the footprints of the runners as they entered the home straight. It does seem to show Carpenter's prints running wide and approaching the outside edge of the track off the turn – demonstrating that he had moved from his proper position in the inside lane well towards the outer edge of the track. Another photograph of the finish, according to Mallon and Buchanan, confirms Carpenter forced Halswelle to within 18 inches of the outside of the track.)

The American Committee stormed up with a formal protest. The judges and officials retreated to the Garden Club to hold an inquiry. James E. Sullivan and his managers were furious that they were excluded from the meeting. The AAA stated firmly that it was a private inquiry 'into the allegations of unfair competition by which Mr. W. Halswelle was said to be wilfully obstructed'. The rules, after all, printed and distributed in advance, and agreed by the IOC at the Hague meeting in 1907, were quite clear:

> The competition shall be held under the Laws and Rules of the Amateur Athletic Association of England, who shall appoint all the officials and be responsible for the conduct of each competition ...
>
> The Judges and Referees so appointed shall have sole control over the competitors after the start, with power to disqualify, and their decision shall be final.[10]

The committee took signed statements from all the official witnesses, from the umpires, from the referee, from the judges. The accounts were all British and they all corroborated one another. Halswelle had been fouled. After an hour the officials emerged to issue a statement signed with great solemnity by each of the three judges:

We, the undersigned, being Judges of the Final of the
Four Hundred Metres, declare the race void, and order the
same to be re-run on Saturday next (25th July), without
Carpenter, he being disqualified, and further order that
the race be run in strings.*

The American camp would have none of it. John Carpenter
had crossed the line first and they would regard him as
Olympic champion. The managers ordered John Taylor and
William Robbins to boycott the Saturday re-run; they would
not give legitimacy to a blatant effort to rob America of
victory.

The controversy ignited all the nationalist emotion that
had been accumulating over the past two weeks. The newspapers piled in with glee. American papers declared the death
of British fair play: 'Carpenter of Cornell Easily Beats English
Crack, but is Disqualified', 'Stadium of Strife', 'English
Crowds Boo American Performers for No Reason Whatso-
ever'. The US trainer, the proudly Irish Mike Murphy, stirred
the pot: 'Highway robbery is pretty strong language, but there
are no other words for it,' he confided to the *Daily Tribune*. 'I
have been up against the English officials for years, and it has
always been the same story – they would have robbed us of
everything they could.'[11] He expanded on his theme to the
New York Evening Post:

It shows what the boasted 'fairest sportsmen' in the world
will do to win. I would rather have seen this happen than
win fifty races. It proves what I have always said, that these

---

* That is, that each lane would be marked out with string so that no runner
would leave his lane.

English officials will do anything to prevent an American or anybody besides their own people from winning a race. You bet we won't run it over, and, if I had my way, every American athlete at the Stadium would leave here right away, and never return, either to this arena or to England.[12]

'Trainer Murphy declares that Carpenter had the right of way,' commented the *New York Sun* blandly. 'In his opinion the Englishmen are all things quite unprintable.'[13]

The *Gaelic American* could rejoice that for once the mainstream New York papers were seeing the world their way. (The one difference was that only the Irish weeklies went so far as to demand a formal break in diplomatic relations with Britain over the affair.) Incensed by the hyperbole coming from across the Atlantic, the British newspapers too splashed on the colour. Carpenter had struck Lieutenant Halswelle so hard that he had bruises on his chest, marks he had shown to British team-mates in the dressing room afterwards. The mutual recriminations lasted for weeks and the sour impressions left on both sides lingered for much longer.

The American version was that Carpenter had pulled away from Halswelle before the turn and did not impede him. It was 'because of my long stride', Carpenter told the *Daily Mail*, '[that I] was unable to stick to the inside berth'. He claimed Halswelle was behind him as he entered the final straight:

From this point my path was absolutely straight to the finish line. For about 10 or 15 yards – at eighty yards from the finish – Halswelle was running absolutely abreast of me, with plenty of room on the outside of him, and he could have passed on the inside of me if necessary.

I do not know of any contact between us at any point during the race. I always know exactly what I do during a race, and I am perfectly certain we did not touch.

I do not see how a race could have been more fairly run.[14]

In a moment so filled with testosterone and ego, perceptions differed radically. Halswelle put his version of the affair on record in a letter to the *Sporting Life*. 'Carpenter did not strike me any vigorous blows with his elbow, nor were there any marks on my chest, nor did I say that Carpenter struck me or show the marks to any Press representative,' he clarified, a touch wearily.

I did not attempt to pass the Americans until the last corner, reserving my effort for the finishing straight. Here I attempted to pass Carpenter on the outside, since he was not far enough from the kerb to do so on the inside, and I was too close up to have crossed behind him. Carpenter's elbow undoubtedly touched my chest, for as I moved outwards to pass him he did likewise, keeping his right in front of me.

In this manner he bored me across quite two-thirds of the track, and entirely stopped my running. As I was well up to his shoulder, and endeavouring to pass him, it is absurd to say that I could have come up on the inside. I was too close after half way round the bend to have done this; indeed, to have done so would have necessitated chopping my stride, and thereby losing anything from two to four yards.

When about thirty to forty yards from the tape I saw the officials holding up their hands, so slowed up, not attempting to finish all out.[15]

Within the overheated crucible of the stadium, the image of the English gentleman pressed and harried by boisterous Americans was vividly evocative of British feelings about the pushy, aspiring, ascendant new nation that had sprung from its erstwhile colonies. They just did not know how to play the game.

Alonzo Stagg suggested that although Carpenter 'certainly took the route complained of', he had not committed a deliberate foul. 'Technically America was within its rights to force Halswelle to run wide at the turn,' he wrote in the *Chicago Tribune*. Although, he admitted, 'it would have been more creditable not to have done it',[16] Stagg nonetheless maintained that Carpenter's behaviour 'would have been considered an acceptable tactic at a track meet in America'.[17] The referee at the controversial race, David Scott Duncan, was moved to publish a response to this argument pointing out that the American AAU rules were even more explicit than the British on the subject. In particular:

> **Rule III**. – The Referee – When in a final heat a claim of foul or interference is made, he [the referee] shall have power to disqualify the competitor who was at fault if he considers the foul intentional or due to culpable carelessness, and he shall also have the power to order a new race between such competitors as he thinks entitled to such a privilege.

> **Rule XVIII**. – The Course – Each competitor shall keep in his respective position from start to finish in all races on straightaway tracks, and in all races on track with one or more turns he shall not cross the inner edge of the track except when he is at least six feet in advance of his nearest

competitor. After turning the last corner into the straight in any race each competitor must keep a straight course to the finish line, and not cross, either to the outside or the inside, in front of any of his opponents.

'In the face of the above rules of the Union of which Mr. Sullivan is president,' Scott Duncan ended bitingly, 'he is surely left without a leg to stand upon.'[18]

Alonzo Stagg's argument highlighted the division between American and English concepts of sportsmanship. According to the code of the Edwardian sporting gentleman, a true amateur should never seek to gain any advantage over an opponent that he would not expect his opponent to take over him. If a penalty was awarded against them, those symbols of Edwardian amateurism, the Corinthian Casuals (founded in 1882 to bring England's best public school footballers together for international matches) would withdraw their goalkeeper and give the opposition an open goal on the principle that it would be wrong not to accept the consequences of a foul, even if it had been accidental. This attitude, of course, was exceptional; but it represented the ideal the English sportsman liked to believe he believed in.

Michael Oriard, in his study of the development of American football in the 1880s and 1890s, traces the evolution of an American sporting culture that assumed that while it was the referee's duty to enforce the rules, it was the business of the athlete to press those rules as hard as he could, for to do so was a measure of his winning determination.[19] As one contemporary American sports commentator, Robert Edgren, put it, writing in *Outing* in 1903: 'In America everything is given up to sharp competition. In England a man is supposed to remain always in the same class ... It is a well-known axiom that nothing stands still. Where there is no advancement there must be some retrogression.'[20]

From the perspective of James Sullivan and his AAU such behaviour as that of the Corinthian Casuals was a sign of lack of seriousness rather than nobility. The American sportsman would never have so little respect for his sport as not to do his very best to win. In that light, John Carpenter's single-minded focus on the winning post was admirable – evidence of his youthful athletic vigour. From the perspective of the Edwardian gentleman amateur, this was looking down the binoculars from the wrong end. Sportsmanship was dead as soon as one assumed that players were naturally inclined to 'trip, hack and push their opponents and behave like cads of the most unscrupulous kidney'[21] in the blind fury of winning.

The tenth day of the London Games ended at the Holborn Restaurant, where the BOC hosted its fourth and final dinner for competitors and officials. According to the *Daily Mail*, the various national anthems played during the dinner 'evoked scenes of enthusiasm'. Lord Desborough, presiding, attempted to end a trying day on a positive note. He told his assembled guests that the Games of London would stand out as the most memorable gathering of athletes ever seen in the world.

'There must be,' he said, 'owing to the variations in the manner of conducting sports in various countries, differences of opinion, but when those differences did arise the BOC endeavoured to settle them according to a policy of a "fair field and no favour".'[22] His remarks, however, were not heard by those they were perhaps aimed at; the American managers had boycotted the affair.

If Mike Murphy had had his way the American team would have packed up and left that night. That they did not, James

E. Sullivan later assigned to the courtesy and diplomacy of Lord Desborough. However, the American Commissioner had another reason to stay. Since becoming president of the AAU he had been determined to develop a new breed of American long-distance champion to challenge the British in the last athletic discipline they called their own. He was eager to see whether his efforts would be vindicated, for the next day would bring the ultimate championship of athletic endurance, the marathon.

CHAPTER

8

THE MARATHON

It was a spectacle the like of which none living had ever
seen, and none who saw it expect ever to see it repeated.

NEW YORK TIMES, 25 JULY 1908

I N THE FLAT LIGHT before dawn relays of horse-drawn
watering carts trundled out of Shepherd's Bush. Dragging
heavy roller brushes, they dampened the dusty road past the
deserted platforms of Wembley and Sudbury stations and on
by Harrow on the Hill. Full-blown poppies stirred in fields of
ripening corn on either side of Eastcote Road as the carts rat-
tled by: on through the idyllic villages of Ruislip and Ickenham, past woods and pasture land, into the silent streets of
Uxbridge and through Slough – tracing 26 miles of road up
to the gatehouse of Windsor Castle.

As residents of Windsor unfurled their newspapers over
their breakfast tables they were promised a fair to very fine day:

With the barometer inclined to rise, a rather high temperature may be expected between Windsor and London.
If the warmth proves somewhat oppressive it should suit

the competitors from southern climes. The roads are dry and in fine order after the recent rains. Everything points to exceptionally fast times.[1]

It was Friday, 24 July 1908. The day of the marathon: 'the greatest long-distance event in the history of the world'.[2]

As Joe Hickey of the *San Francisco Chronicle* assured his readers back home, the marathon contest was to be 'the crowning feature of the track and field events at the Olympic Games'.[3] The closing ceremonies of the main Games were to take place the next day. The US team would scatter and this round of the Anglo-American grudge match would be over. The marathon was not only the supreme test of athletic endurance – the emblem on the winner's jersey would demonstrate to the international community which nationality really had what it took.

Spectators began to assemble along the route. Householders with homes fronting the course hung out flags and bunting and shops informed their customers that they would be closing early. Two thousand policemen were on duty to marshal the anticipated crowds – although in those golden days of Empire the good behaviour of the British public was assumed:

It is not expected that it will be necessary to divert the traffic at any point within the metropolitan area, and the authorities are confident that the crowds who will view the race will do all they can to keep the course free from obstruction … the various omnibus and tramway companies plying along the line of the route have instructed their drivers to do all they can to assist the police.[4]

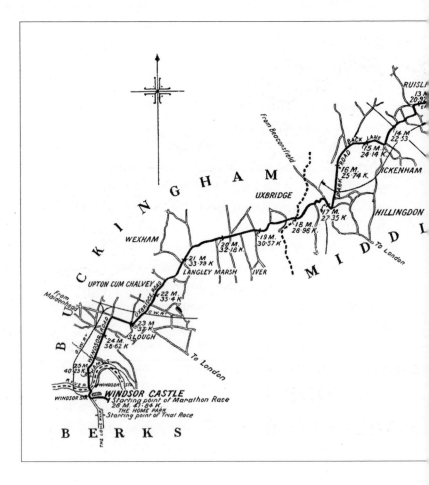

The competitors began to arrive at Windsor railway station soon after 9 am. The first stop was the station master's room where a dozen doctors stood by. To qualify for entry each contestant had been required to supply a current certificate of medical fitness and the examinations were cursory. 'All in good fettle,' a jovial doctor informed the waiting reporters. From the station the racers went to a mid-morning meal under the watchful eye of their trainers – steak, toast, a cup of

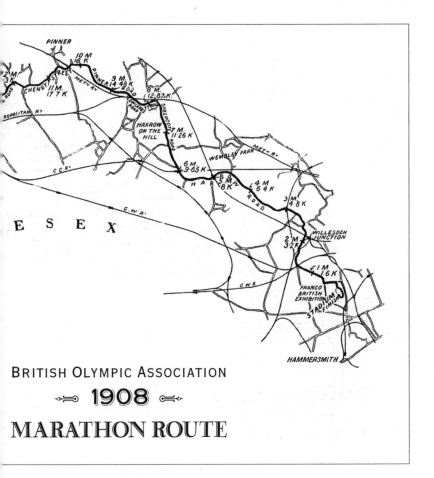

BRITISH OLYMPIC ASSOCIATION
⊷⊷ **1908** ⊷⊷
MARATHON ROUTE

tea and the occasional raw egg. At exactly 1.27 pm a special train arrived from Paddington carrying more contestants. The station's waiting rooms and cloakrooms served as dressing rooms. Under AAA rules each competitor dressed in 'complete Clothing from the shoulder to the knees (i.e. jersey sleeved to the elbows and loose drawers with slips)'[5] and donned, back and front, the number supplied to him – 'a distinctive number corresponding to his number in the programme'.

As the time of the start approached they made their preparations. Each national team had its own preferences. The Americans put on socks soaked in tallow and high-sided shoes with a strip of rubber between sock and leather sole. The Canadians ran in boots. Their trainer, Bill Sherring, the 28-year-old winner of the 1906 Olympic marathon, had his charges bathe their feet in whisky and alum and sprinkle the inside of their socks with talcum powder.

The original plan had been to start the race in the town of Windsor. J.N. Andrews, secretary of the Polytechnic Harriers, set a course of 26 miles. The story is told that a few days before the race was to take place, the formidable 40-year-old Princess Mary, Princess of Wales, mentioned to Lord Desborough that it would be nice if the young princes could have a proper view of the historic occasion. So the starting line was moved into the private grounds of Windsor Castle, in sight of the windows of the royal nursery. The course – which was to finish in the stadium in front of the royal box – was thereby stretched to 26 miles 385 yards, a distance that eventually became the standard for the Olympic marathon. If the tale is true, the extra yards added at royal whim were to prove crucial to the dramatic outcome of the race.*

The Oxo Company provided booths along the course offering sustaining refreshments: an 'Oxo Athletes' Flask containing Oxo for immediate use; Oxo, hot and cold; Oxo Soda' (although – should an athlete lack the taste for Oxo – rice

---

* The distance for the Olympic marathon of 26 miles 385 yards (42.195 kilometres) was finally adopted by the IAAF in 1921. Sadly, recent research by Hugh Farey has been unable to find any evidence to support the widely told tale of the Princess of Wales's involvement in the addition of the extra 385 yards. According to his research, the Harriers made a request to Windsor Castle to be allowed to start the race there.

*Mary, Princess of Wales, waiting for the start of the marathon race
while the runners assemble at Windsor; thirteen-year-old Prince Albert,
the future George VI, stands in front of the table with his eight-
year-old brother Henry.*

pudding, raisins, bananas, soda and milk were on offer too).
There were stimulants 'in case of collapse', and on request
eau de cologne and sponges could be obtained from one of
the Oxo representatives stationed along the course. The Oxo
Company sponsored the marathon programme, in which its
advertisement was prominently displayed: '68 of the Competitors chosen to represent Great Britain in the Olympic
Games have given written testimony to the sustaining value
of OXO. Let the Experience of Britain's healthiest sons teach
you the value of OXO as a strengthener.' (The other sponsor
was WAWKPHAR Antiseptic Military Foot Powder, as recommended by the War Office: 'Strengthen the Feet! Free samples
available to competitors in the dressing room.')

It was a hot day. The thermometer had risen to 78 degrees when, soon after two o'clock, the contestants filed up through Sovereign's Gate to the East Terrace of the castle.

Princess Mary and her children were gathered under the shade of a hawthorn tree on the manicured lawn. Twelve-year-old Prince Albert, the future King George VI, had his camera and autograph album at the ready. Five-year-old Prince George sat with three-year-old John in an elaborate baby carriage. Their elder sister Mary and brother Henry stood nearby. The American reporter for the *New York Evening Post* was much struck by this tableau of royalty. The Crown Prince of Sweden was also present and the two courtly entourages provided an aristocratic supporting cast, the scarlet coats of the Coldstream Guards a foil to the pastel summer gowns of the ladies, and here and there the short, top-hatted figure of an Eton boy. Standing respectfully apart, members of the castle staff and their families, dressed in their Sunday best, lined the gravel drive.

Seven hundred yards from the imposing statue of Queen Victoria, 55 runners lined up in four rows, their places drawn by lot: 'The world's best runners are competing; they are in splendid condition; international rivalry is acute.'[6]

'The world' in this case was represented by 16 nations. The United Kingdom and Canada had the largest national contingents, each fielding the maximum of 12 runners; next came the Americans with seven contestants. There were runners from Australia, Bohemia, Belgium, Finland, Germany, Holland and Italy. George Lind, an Estonian residing in London, was running for Russia; there were a couple of Greeks – Anastasios Koutoulakis was a veteran of the Athens Olympics. In the back row stood Charles Hefferon, a 35-year-old South African – reputedly 'an excellent stayer' – alongside

Johan Svanberg of Sweden who had come second to Bill Sherring in the 1906 Athens marathon. There were no ethnic Africans, Orientals, Asians or Arabs. All the competitors were white save three 'redskins', two Canadian Indians – Tom Longboat and Fred Simpson – and one American, Lewis Tewanina. Nonetheless it was then the most cosmopolitan entry ever gathered for a sporting event.

The *Daily Mail* published a handy guide listing each man with his nation and number. (The contestants bore national emblems on their jerseys – the maple leaf for Canada, the Stars and Stripes for the USA and so on.) The predominant colour was white although the two South Africans were dressed in gold and green, the Swedes sported blue running trunks and Italian Dorando Pietri red ones. With the complacent assurance of representatives of the Empire, the UK runners simply wore their numbers on a plain white ground.

Princess Mary was escorted to a gilt chair by a round oak table on which was placed an electric button and a floral arrangement. Lord Desborough, who was serving as referee, got into his official car. Prince George was lifted out of his perambulator to get a better view. At 2.33 pm precisely Princess Mary pushed the button. Responding to the signal, Lord Desborough fired a starting pistol out of his car window at the same time as Mr Andrews, the chief clerk of the course, fired his, and the runners were off.

The *New York Evening Post* reporter was a little disappointed: 'It was a decorous gathering of spectators, for when the group of athletes sprang forward only a faint clapping of hands applauded the beginning of the event.'[7]

As the contestants passed the gauntlet of spectators waiting by Queen Victoria's statue, Tom Longboat led the pack with two other Canadians, the seven Americans close at their heels. The runners swept through the castle gates and there was a rush to the station to catch the special train laid on to take spectators to Old Oak Lane Halt, just over a mile from the finish of the course.

In a gradually loosening phalanx the contestants thundered down the hill over the rough paving stones of Windsor High Street towards the Thames. The river was dotted with skiffs and punts, their occupants straining to get the best view of the runners as they passed over the bridge.

The American managers, with their scientific approach to sporting excellence, ran their men as a team. They had their chief opposition identified. Only a couple of their contestants were picked out as potential winners of the race. The business of the rest was to get close to the rival favourites in the race and periodically, over the long miles that followed, to try to tire them out by driving up the pace.

The US management had highest hopes for T.P. Morrissey, a young runner for the Yonkers club Mercury AC who had shot to prominence a few months earlier as the unforeseen winner of the 1908 Boston marathon. The 19-year-old stormed home in 2 hours 25 minutes 43 seconds and some officials thought that if he had not been obstructed by the crowd of cars following the course he would have lowered Longboat's figures. After that, they thought Joseph Forshaw a contender. The veteran of the US team, 28-year-old Forshaw had completed the 1906 Olympic marathon in Athens and was said to be much improved since then. Other commentators – including Bill Sherring – were keeping an eye on 20-year-old Lewis Tewanina, from the Carlisle Indian School, although it was said that Tewanina was feeling the effects of the British climate and complaining that his knees were giving him trouble.

In contrast, in the UK the press discussed British prospects with quiet assurance. Even James E. Sullivan, interviewed by the *New York Sun* in the first week of the stadium Games, accepted that 'England should win the Olympic Marathon, and if [it] does not finish one, two, three [it] should be well up'.[8] Great Britain, after all, was the land of Alf Shrubb, the man regarded as the leading long-distance runner in the world at the time. Although Shrubb could not compete in the Games, having turned professional, the British Empire was thought to be fielding a clutch of home-grown champions.

The general favourite was Fred Appleby of the Herne Hill Harriers, a wiry little man who beat Shrubb over a 15 mile course at Stamford Bridge in the record time of 1 hour 20 minutes 4¾ seconds. Another fancied entry was Alexander Duncan from Kendal in Cumberland – the 'flying market gardener of the North' – holder of the British record over 10 miles and the winner of that marathon qualifier race held by the Polytechnic Harriers the previous April. Then there was the Scottish 10 mile champion, Thomas Jack, who was, the journalists faithfully reported, 'a great believer in fruit, especially apples and bananas'.

The heart of British long-distance running came from the industrial working class – embodied in men such as Tom Lord, winner of the Northern trials, a 'wiry coal-miner, tough, tenacious, half-greyhound, half-bulldog';[9] and J. Price of the Small Heath Harriers, winner of the Midland marathon trial. These were tough men, the sportswriters assured their readers, men who would stay the course. It was said that 'the Spartan' Jack Beale, who came second in that muddy trial in the April sleet, did so with 'four loose toenails in his stocking'.

It was Thomas Jack, runner number 61, who took the lead

as the pack loped through narrow Eton High Street and down past the ancient gateway and red walls of Eton College. To the left of the road the very playing fields where the gentleman amateur's code of sport was forged were lined with cheering boys. At the fifth mile, just before the Crooked Billet inn, a sea of cyclists waited, one foot to the pedal.

At 3.02 pm, Jack passed the five-mile post, closely followed by Price and Lord. One hundred yards behind them, the slight, boyish figure of the 22-year-old Italian, Dorando Pietri, ran in a strange, pattering gait. He was followed by Alexander Duncan, Britain's champion, matching stride for stride with Charles Hefferon of South Africa.

Two by two the cyclists fell in behind their man.* Alexander Duncan's escort carried 'muscatels and distilled water'. Pietri was showered from a wet sponge. Baker, a South African runner, had a special bottle of calves' foot jelly and lemon, while George Lind's attendant carried new-laid eggs in tea and grapes. There was none of the modern focus on rehydration. The contemporary language was rather of 'stimulants'. (The use of drugs was prohibited by the rules of the race, although there was no such thing as drug testing at the time.) North American trainers disdained the idea of liquid refreshment; for their men, a 'wet Turkish towel passed over the head and face' and the occasional orange segment to suck, was officially considered all the sustenance needed for a gruelling 26 miles in the heat.

Many of the riders were competitors in the Olympics themselves. Lou Marsh, who pulled out alongside Longboat, was a sports journalist. A stocky, bull-headed, aggressive man, Marsh was a pal of Tom Flanagan's from the Toronto Irish

---

* Each runner was allowed two cyclist attendants.

Canadian Athletic Club. He was in London to report on the Games for the *Toronto Daily Star*. Flanagan had enlisted his help in preparing Tom Longboat for the marathon. Marsh enjoyed his influence, although he continued to report to *Star* readers without mentioning his dual role. His cycling companion was a Toronto man named Doc Morton, a bicycle racer in his own right. Morton's job was to speed ahead and report back about the state of the opposition in front.

It was at this five-mile point that the Shepherd's Bush stadium, crammed and expectant, began to receive news of the race. As the *Daily Mail* reporter explained:

> The name of the leader will be telephoned direct to the Stadium … These messages will be received as each successive mile is covered by the runners, or, roughly speaking, about every five minutes, so that visitors to the Stadium will know more about the race than the spectators along the course or even the privileged people in the motor cars following the competitors.[10]

A capacity crowd was engrossed in the ebb and flow of the cross-Atlantic contest. The morning saw the finals of the pole vault – that rubbing point between US managers and British Olympic officials. Sir Arthur Conan Doyle, the creator of Sherlock Holmes, sat in the stands, a celebrity reporter for the *Daily Mail*, having been tempted, as he recorded in his memoirs, 'chiefly by the offer of an excellent seat'[11] from Lord Northcliffe. Jolly and enthusiastic, Doyle was resolutely oblivious to the controversy:

> It is incredible that a human being with the aid of a small pole could clear such a height. Eleven feet, eleven and a

half, twelve feet go up. The Americans are closely pressed
by the Swedes. There is a Canadian, too, as active and
strong as a deer. But there seems a clean finish and a
mastery of the game in the American style, which I see
nowhere else. The great bank of people in front of them
roar with applause at every leap. It is a great audience to
play to, impartial, enthusiastic, whole-hearted ...

After all the dark mutterings about handicaps and alien
practices from the American managers, their college athletes
won with ease. A.C. Gilbert of Yale University and E. Cooke
of Cornell tied for first and second place, while a colleague
from the University of Chicago shared third with a Swede and
a Brit.

Great Britain redeemed her honour in the swimming
relay race.

In the centre is a great relay race of swimmers. It sways and
vacillates. Red cap wins all the way then blue cap closes on
him. Within a few yards of the mark they are neck and
neck. Blue cap has the staying power. He wins by a length
and shouting comrades drag him from the water. He roars,
also, like a joyous boy. Only when the British flag is run up
on the staff does the crowd gather what it has all been
about. Another point for the old country and Taylor, dripping but exultant, is carried with shouts to his quarters.[12]

Whole stands of massed spectators stood to acclaim the
victory, a shimmering sea of fluttering Union Jacks. The
Americans still made it to the final.

That day the Olympic Games of London were a success. The sun shone, the seats were filled; the Crown Prince of Sweden saw his countrymen dominate the high diving; Great Britain won the catch-as-catch-can wrestling and the American team beat the British and Canadian teams in the third heat of the 1,600 metre medley relay race. And from time to time, the progress of the marathon race was shouted through the stadium by officials with megaphones, the leader and mile post displayed on large boards paraded around the stands in the arms of sturdy attendants. The home crowd was buoyant. Early forecasts were of a British victory.

In a series of articles in the *Daily Mail* before the race, Bill Sherring, that diplomatic international sportsman, had been enthusiastic about the 1908 course. 'Never have I seen a better track than the one between Windsor and the Stadium,' he wrote. 'In no other country in the world could you find 26 miles of road with a better surface or a fairer course for all runners.'

Other commentators pointed out that the newly laid macadam surface that covered much of the marathon route was 'hard as flint'. 'It is much better for a man running in a race of this description over a long distance that the road should be winding and that the scenery should be as varied as possible,' Sherring pronounced with sunny optimism, 'for a long, straight, stretch with nothing to relieve its monotony breaks a man's heart.'[13]

Sherring was not running that day. The men who were discovered that the route was a twisting one, featuring several sharp turns and narrow stretches where two could not run side by side. In addition, the heavy rain earlier in the week contributed high humidity to the enervating glare of the sun.

In the first five miles, Englishman Albert Wyatt, Dutch

runner Wilhelmus Braams and two Australians, including George Blake, who finished sixth in the Athens marathon, all abandoned the race. After seven miles, Thomas Jack, the Scottish runner who had begun so strongly, stopped too.

At the nine-mile mark, the Georgian market town of Uxbridge, the English runner Lord was in the lead. The marathoners filtered through the Old High Street where the crowd was 'wedged in long, cheering lines beneath the flaunting flags of all the nations'. On the chalk-white road between Uxbridge and the Common, Price wrested the lead from Lord. A few seconds before half past three he passed the ten-mile post a few strides ahead of his countryman. Behind them Hefferon strode on, strong and steady, and in his wake

Runner no.8, Charles Hefferon (South Africa), at 35 the oldest of the marathon runners that day, the man whom Dorando Pietri considered his main opposition.

Dorando Pietri, whose odd pattering steps sent up little puffs of dust.

Pietri, a 22-year-old confectioner baker from Carpi, had not registered previously in the British or American press. A slight young man with round, soulful dark eyes, a shock of curly black hair and a dapper moustache, he was said to be self-trained (although his father was known as a runner back in his home village). In 1906 he won the Rome marathon but his failure to finish the Athens Olympic marathon the same year meant that the cross-Atlantic sports commentators knew little of him. One journalist watching him could not believe the diminutive Italian could last long, 'his breath coming in great heaves and his mouth all awry'.

Although the Anglo-Saxon press regarded him as unknown,
22-year-old Pietri held all the Italian long-distance records and had won
the Paris marathon in 1904 at the age of 18 by a clear six minutes.

Alexander Duncan, too, was giving his supporters concern. The British champion was white to the lips and beginning to roll in his gait. The American Indian, Lewis Tewanina, moved up alongside him, quickening the pace. Duncan tried to respond to the challenge, but he could not. He collapsed. His race was over before the eleventh mile.

Back at Shepherd's Bush notices were being posted on the gates. The stadium was full. All tickets were sold out. There was not even standing room left. The police called in reinforcements to cope with the tide of humanity, swelling as each 'special' train disgorged its load of spectators from further down the course. Around the royal box the cream of fashionable society from across Europe was taking its place under lace parasols and straw boaters. Thousands of Americans clustered in flag-waving bands, cheering their boys to the echo. Up on the boards, Runner 55: Great Britain was leading the marathon.

The race had left Uxbridge Common, following a switchback road through plantations of dark pine to Ickenham, a Miss Marple village of red-roofed houses grouped around its village pond. Beyond the landscape opened out again for another mile or so to Ruislip. This was the heart of golden England; the England of nostalgia and storybooks. Vistas of parkland, grand houses glimpsed down avenues of elm. Ancient oak trees and fields of new-mown hay. A landscape of 'snug farmhouses, pretty cottages in gay gardens and quiet manor houses, dreaming away the golden afternoon'.[14]

By the 14-mile post, passing Eastcote Post Office, Price was flagging. The green-and-gold-clad figure of Charles Hefferon was closing the gap. Seven seconds behind him; then five. Price faltered and Hefferon passed at an easy stride.

Some way behind the leaders, Joseph Forshaw and his running mate, Lewis Tewanina, began to move up through the pack. 'We passed men time after time.'[15] The Italians lost one of their two entrants, Umberto Blasi, the English team lost another two runners (Henry Barrett and Frederick Thompson) and, in a great blow to the Americans, Thomas Patrick Morrissey, the 19-year-old of whom the managers had had such hopes, too abandoned the race.

Dorando Pietri was plodding along steadily at his uniform pace in fourth place. Tom Longboat was also up near the front. But the Indian Wonder was behaving oddly, interspersing 'brilliant spurts' with walking.

There is a mystery attached to Longboat's race that day. Flanagan, his manager, had not allowed him to train for the race with the rest of the Canadian team. He had taken him off to Ireland to prepare in seclusion. The week before the marathon reports of an accident appeared in the press. While out for a '15 mile spin', it was said, the young Indian had collided with a wagon at a sharp turn in muddy conditions, slipped and hurt his shoulder, knee and arm. Flanagan was quick to telephone journalists with reassurance that Longboat was not seriously hurt and would be in form for the race. But it was noticeable that Bill Sherring, who had previously tipped Longboat as Canada's strongest contender in his articles in the press, suddenly ceased mentioning him, transferring attention to Fred Simpson.

British newspapers reported that the bookmakers were doing brisk business in the run-up to the marathon. Rumour had it that there was a lot of money riding on the Indian. Now, just over halfway through the race, Longboat, who had never before been seen to falter in any of his major long-distance races, was behaving as if in distress.

By Pinner gas works, at three minutes past four, on a rough piece of road littered with stones for remetalling, Charles Hefferon made the 15-mile post. Ten minutes later Pietri and Longboat ran past together, then the Englishmen Lord and Appleby three minutes behind them.

Suddenly Tom Lord collapsed in the arms of his trainer. The crowd roared for Fred Appleby who ran on, apparently still in good heart. The trainer poured stimulants down Lord. He got up and 'pluckily resumed'. There were 40 runners left, the last of them – Lister of Canada – running three-quarters of an hour behind the first.

News filtered back to the stadium, under siege from the massing crowds. By four o'clock it was estimated that 20,000 people had been turned away and 100,000 were watching inside. 'Disquieting reports' began to eddy around the stands. It was said that Alexander Duncan, the much-fancied Cumbrian market gardener, had collapsed at 15 miles, and Lord and Price had stopped. The boards gave runner number 8 the lead. Consulting their programmes the spectators translated this information into Charles Hefferon, South Africa.

The British press had always had a fall-back position. Should the 'cream of English running' prove outmatched in the marathon there was the comforting thought that – as Conan Doyle put it – 'if England fails, the oak leaves of victory may perhaps still remain in the family'. Charles Hefferon, after all, was born in Newbury in England. (As it happened, he could be claimed by the Canadians too, since he had emigrated to Canada as a child.) He had only moved to South Africa in his early twenties, at the time of the Boer War. UK athletic fans could console themselves that under the green and gold beat a British heart.

Along the course, countryside gave way to pavements and

street lamps. Houses drew nearer to the street and joined up in brick rows. The route avoided Harrow Hill and the famous school, taking the lower road to Sudbury. At the foot of the hill Harrow boys in their long tailcoats and low-crowned straw hats gave Hefferon a noisy reception as he strode past, half a mile in the lead. They cheered still louder as the boyish figure of Dorando Pietri came by contesting second place with Longboat, his short, clockwork steps a contrast to the Indian's alternation of fitful sprints and periods of walking.

The Indian Wonder won the struggle for second place. He was 300 yards behind Hefferon in the twentieth mile. It was an open stretch of road without shade and the sun was still strong. All at once, Longboat threw up his arms and staggered. Apparently convulsing, he tumbled, collided with Lou Marsh's bicycle, fell in the road and passed out. Marsh ran to his side, taking out a flask he carried. He poured champagne into Longboat's slack mouth. An Olympic medic arrived to find the Canadian athlete just coming round. He pronounced the young man 'dead beat' and ordered he be withdrawn from the race. Longboat, weak and shaky, was bundled into the contestants' omnibus and driven off towards the stadium.

There has never been a satisfactory explanation of what happened that afternoon. In the post-mortem press coverage Lou Marsh argued that Longboat was exhausted by the twisting nature of the course. 'If the race had been over a road with a straight stretch where Longboat could have seen the leader,' he told reporters, 'he would have won handily.'[16] Tom Longboat himself cited the heat and humidity and said that 'the pounding on the hard pavement knocked me out'.

J. Howard Crocker, manager of the Canadian Olympic team, however, had a different story. He examined Longboat soon after he arrived at the Shepherd's Bush stadium. He described the Indian runner as having a weak pulse and pinpoint pupils. After the Olympics, Crocker wrote in the official *Report of the First Canadian Olympic Athletic Team*: 'I think that any medical man knowing the facts of the case will assure you that the presence of a drug in an overdose was the cause of [Longboat's] failure.'

His assumption was that Longboat had ingested strychnine, which was known to be in regular use among runners at the time as a performance enhancer. Taken in tiny doses strychnine acts as a stimulant. Get the dose slightly wrong and it causes painful convulsions. A little more results in paralysis of the respiratory system and death. Strychnine is odourless and colourless – although it has a bitter taste which would be apparent in water. It might be administered without a runner's knowledge. After Crocker's damning report, Flanagan admitted that 'stimulants were resorted to', but claimed that he was referring to the champagne administered by Marsh after Longboat collapsed. Some years later Flanagan told an interviewer that 'if Longboat had not failed us in the English marathon and had won, I would have toured the world with him and he would have retired worth a quarter of a million. I had the financial backing and I had the tour all arranged.'[17]

Tom Longboat came from poverty. He was said to have learnt to run chasing his mother's cows across scrubland on the reservation. When he lined up for his first public race at the age of 19, the 'Around the Bay' marathon in Hamilton, Ontario, in 1906, the other competitors sniggered at the young Iroquois's droopy cotton bathing suit and cheap sneakers. He won that race with a full three-minute lead, but the racism that surrounded him would always blur perceptions of his ability as an athlete. In his people's tradition Tom

Longboat was a Runner of Messages in the Iroquois Confederacy, a member of the Wolf Clan. In the Six Nations tradition runners were key members of their community. As one historian put it, they were 'communicators of culture' and 'safe-keepers of accurate information'. In the days when the Iroquois Confederacy dominated Upper New York State, the runners carried messages from one end of the Confederacy to the other, along the 240-mile Iroquois Trail from the eastern Atlantic seaboard to the Niagara frontier, spreading word of new chiefs and treaties and keeping the Six Nations united. This was not running for mere sport; it was an activity connected to the very soul of a people. But 'redskin' athletes were outsiders in an all-white athletic establishment which regarded their stamina as legendary. 'In their case,' wrote Sir Arthur Conan Doyle with a flourish, 'it is nature and instinct against the art of the trained white.'[18] Others were less elegant. In the opinion of Lou Marsh, the *Toronto Daily Star*'s number one sportswriter, redskins were stubborn, dumb half-savages too foolish to see the superiority of the 'scientific' white civilisation. Neither Marsh nor Longboat's manager Flanagan had any understanding or sympathy for the distinctive native running traditions.

Tom Longboat, although he was a modest and good-tempered youth, was stubborn enough to keep to his own way of doing things. And his white handlers resented it. While the young white athletes listened to their trainers, meekly rehearsing their speed and building their stamina in regimented degrees, Longboat hiked and played handball and drank beer with his friends. To his handlers, his 'stubbornness' was another instance of his underlying stupidity. He just 'did not have a white man's business brain', said Lou Marsh.[19] Perhaps the simplest explanation for Longboat's collapse that day was that while Flanagan had the young athlete secluded in Ireland away from his friends, he forced him to over-train. Then, seeing him flagging, resorted to strychnine.

⇢⇒ ⇐⇠

The omnibus labelled 'competitors' was nearly full. There were just 29 men left in the race. With the Indian Wonder gone, runner number 26 – Johnny Hayes, a diminutive 22-year-old from the Irish American Athletic Club – moved up into third place.

Hayes was another runner largely overlooked in the pre-race coverage. Born in New York, the son of Irish immigrants from County Tipperary, Hayes had run the 1907 Boston marathon – the race where Tom Longboat broke all the

*Born in New York, the son of Irish immigrants from County Tipperary,
Johnny Hayes worked as a backroom boy in New York's famous
Bloomingdale's department store.*

records. The 21-year-old Hayes had come 'a plucky third' in that race. He finished second to T.P. Morrissey in the 1908 Boston race. Johnny Hayes was probably the smallest runner in the London marathon that day. At just under 5ft 4in he was, as the *New York Sun* described him, a 'slim, little nickeled steel athlete from his toes to the crown of his head … as Irish as you find them, with black hair, blue eyes, a good humored and freckled face and a ton of confidence in himself'.[20]

At half past four, the crowd waiting at the 20-mile post by Sudbury station saw Charles Hefferon pass, having extended his lead to almost a mile. Three and a half minutes later Pietri followed looking exhausted. Fred Appleby, England's last best hope, arrived fourth, only to stop running at the mile post. A coaxing voice cried out 'Keep on!' Appleby did his best. He started off again but he had barely run out of sight of his encouragers when he gave up for good.

It was coming up to five o'clock. The sun's glare had mellowed. Harrow had been left behind for open country and the grateful shade of a tree-lined stretch of straight road.[21]

> … a capital place for a semi-final sprint for good position. It is about the last chance before the Stadium is reached, for at Stonebridge Park the tramway lines begin. Laid on stones, these will trouble the runners not a little, and from here to Wormwood Scrubs the course is all through streets, where great speed is not possible.
>
> *Daily Mail*

Hefferon was beginning to tire. Dorando Pietri, running in his odd, 'low, stealing action', was gaining on him. Back down the road, Joseph Forshaw and Lewis Tewanina began to move up the line of runners. They passed Fred Simpson, the third

Native Indian runner, picking up the pace 'with a view to taking the heart out of the Canadian'.

Simpson saw off the challenge and Forshaw got a severe stitch for his pains. His accompanying cyclists produced some brandy which he sipped, hoping to ease the cramp, as he ran on clutching his side.

Just before five o'clock, as Hefferon approached the 23-mile post at the Midland Railway's Stonebridge Park goods office, the royal party arrived in the stadium. The 63-year-old Queen, resplendent in a large hat, her features softened by a veil and carrying a fashionably tall parasol, settled herself in the royal box. The applause went up a notch. The Union Jack, run up the flag pole in response to another swimming victory, was greeted with a roar of enthusiasm.

An official appeared on the track, shouting through a megaphone, 'Clear the course for the marathon race!'

> With these words the people braced themselves for the culmination of the most exciting event of the Olympiad. Outside the crowds were pressing around the gates, while the police pushed them back, shouting time and time again that there were no more tickets to be had.
>
> *New York Evening Post*

At six minutes (and 28 seconds) past five, Hefferon ran past the 24-mile post at no. 28 Railway Cottages, Willesden Junction. An admirer ran alongside and offered him champagne. The South African took a gulp, much to the crowd's delight. A rocket went up – a signal to the stadium that the race was nearing its end. From Willesden Junction the course left the main road, taking a sharp turn towards Old Oak Common

The packed north end of the stadium as the crowd waits for the first marathon runner to arrive.

and Wormwood Scrubs. The runners were within a mile of home.

Just as Hefferon's number was being displayed on the stadium boards, spectators along Old Oak Lane watched his race fall apart. The champagne he had drunk had given him a cramp. The South African's stride grew shorter and shorter until he was barely able to stagger along. Dorando Pietri was gasping, his eyes glazed, and yet his pace never seemed to vary. Miraculously, he was closing the gap. Out of sight, back in third place came Johnny Hayes, running with mechanical rhythm, regularly wiping his face with a towel dipped in Florida water handed to him by his cyclists and occasionally gargling with brandy.

The route followed narrow cow paths across the grassland of Wormwood Scrubs, between the prison and the Hammersmith Infirmary and then on to the hard surface of Ducane Road. Both South African and Italian were limping badly. In sight of the domes and turrets of the Exhibition, Charles Hefferon dropped into a walk. For the first time, the Italian changed pace. Galvanised, Pietri spurted past the South African.

It was estimated that nearly a million people were crammed along the road leading to the stadium. The reporters had their notebooks out:

> A motorcar brought the news to the huge throng through which the police kept the track that Hefferon was leading but Dorando staggered past first, livid and dazed, oblivious to cheers.
>
> There seemed a long interval. At last Hefferon came only slightly fresher than Dorando. Two minutes elapsed and Hayes, moving with remarkable vigour and freshness, passed. 'He will catch Hefferon', was the comment. Then came Forshaw and another cheer went up for the Stars and Stripes.
>
> *Daily Mail*

Through the lines of boisterous, flag-waving humanity the North Gate appeared. Beyond that there was two-thirds of the cinder track to cross to reach the finishing tape in front of the royal box.

The vast arena of the stadium had stilled. The swimmers left the pool. Pole vaulters, wrestlers, sprinters – coats over their costumes – gathered near the stands. In the distance gun shots were heard. Then a rocket burst. The megaphone man, coat flapping, raced across the grass to announce before the royal box that the first runner was in sight.

The board no longer carried the identity of the leader. No one knew who he was.

> The crisis in a battle on which the life of a nation hung could hardly have been more impressive … An intense silence overhung the Stadium, while the thousands waited breathlessly the approach of the first man.
>
> *New York Times*

There was a commotion. Figures appeared through the North Gate. A false alarm. It was Tom Longboat, supported by two friends, who had arrived by motor car. He flopped full length on the grass.

> We are waiting, eighty thousand of us, for the man to appear; waiting anxiously, eagerly with long turbulent swayings and heavings, which mark the impatience of the multitude. Through yonder door he must come.
>
> Every eye in the great curved bank of humanity is fixed upon the gap. What blazoning will show upon that dust-stained jersey – the red maple leaf, the blue and yellow, the Stars and Stripes, or the simple numbers of the Britons? Those figures on the board tell us nothing. It is the man who has a dash in him at the end who may head the field. He must be very near now, speeding down the streets between the lines of shouting people. We can hear the growing murmur. Every eye is on the gap …
>
> *Sir Arthur Conan Doyle*

The suspense seemed intolerable. The band struck up 'See, the Conquering Hero Comes'. Then out of the shadow of the gate a figure in red running drawers and white top staggered down the incline. A tiny, boy-like man, Chaplinesque with his little black moustache. He paused, stunned by the force of the roar that met him. The journalists were scribbling furiously.

> He stood for a moment, as though dazed, and then turned to the left, although a red cord had been drawn about the track in the opposite direction for the runners to follow. It was evident at once to everyone that the man was practically delirious. A squad of officials ran out and expostulated with him, but apparently he was afraid that they were trying to deceive him, and fought to go on to the left. At length he turned about and started on the right path along the track.
>
> *New York Times*

At first no one recognised him. They consulted their programmes. In the vast, sky-open space, 100,000 pairs of eyes were fixed on the little man wearily trotting round the track.

> The colours and the number told the spectators that it was Dorando and his name was on every lip. He staggered along the cinder path like a man in a dream, his gait being neither a walk nor a run, but simply a flounder with arms shaking and legs tottering. By devious ways he went on. People had lost thought of his nationality and partisanship was forgotten. They rose in their seats and saw only this small man clad in red knickers tottering onward with his head so bent forward that the chin rested on his chest.
>
> *New York Times*

Francis Peabody, a Boston lawyer, was sitting in a front row seat. To his eyes Pietri was near death. 'If he could have been told to simply walk for the one-third of a mile on the track to the finish he could have done so. But some excited individuals rushed up to him and shouted to him to run, which he attempted to do.'[22]

A large group of track officials and policemen – some said 30 or 40 – drew into a fascinated half-circle around the man, who hardly seemed aware that they were there. His pace diminished to a crawl, so slow his escort almost stopped. Then he fell. A shiver of disappointment circled the stadium.

'There were wild gesticulations,' Sir Arthur Conan Doyle recorded. 'Men stooped and rose again. Good heavens! He has fainted! Is it possible that even at this last moment the prize may slip through his fingers?'

Pathé still from footage of Pietri's entrance into the stadium showing track officials – the clerk of the course, J. Andrews with megaphone in hand and the race's doctor, Michael Bulger, in the tweed cap behind him – urging the confused Italian to turn the right way around the track.

Everyone looked to the North Gate. No sign of a rival yet. Pietri was getting up. A communal sigh rose from the stands.

> The band ... could scarcely be heard amid the tumult of excited talk – admiration for the man's splendid courage and sympathy for his pitiful condition ...
>
> *New York Evening Post*

Photograph showing Pietri apparently in a faint and the track officials quite clearly giving him assistance.

He was on his feet again – the little red legs 'going incoherently but drumming hard driven by a supreme will within'.[23] It was a 'pitiable and pathetic exhibition', wrote the correspondent for the *New York Evening Post*. Amid the cheers of encouragement, there were shouts of 'Let him alone!' 'Don't kill him! That's not sport!'

'It is horrible and yet fascinating, the struggle between a set purpose and an utterly exhausted frame,' wrote Conan Doyle.

> A vast groan filled the air. The little figure had fallen again. According to the rules of the race, physicians should have taken him away, but the track officials, lost in their sympathy for such a man and such an effort, lifted him to his feet and with their hands at his back gave him support.
>
> *New York Times*

Dorando Pietri got up. He was weaving towards the part of the stand where Conan Doyle was on his feet. 'Again, for a hundred yards,' recorded Conan Doyle breathlessly, 'he ran in the same furious and yet uncertain gait, then again he collapsed, kind hands saving him from a heavy fall.'

> He was within a few yards of my seat amid stooping figures and grasping hands. I caught a glimpse of the haggard, yellow face; the glazed, expressionless eyes, the lank black hair streaked across the brow. Surely he is done now, he cannot rise again …

Pietri had fallen on the bend entering the last straight. Dr Michael Bulger of the Irish Amateur Athletic Association, who was serving as track doctor, was holding him up. Another medical man appeared to be massaging his chest.

A volley of shouts drew everyone's attention back across the stadium. Another runner had emerged from the mouth of the North Gate. Jimmy Hayes, the Stars and Stripes blazoned on his chest, came on, covering the ground in a steady rhythm.

The fallen Italian was only yards from the tape. If he could crawl, he could win.

An artist's impression of Pietri's fall at the final bend from the Illustrated London News.

The next incident happened in the full view of thousands of people near the Royal Box. Carried away by the excitement of the moment, two officials raised Dorando to his feet and supported him while he covered the ten feeble yards.

Daily Mail

The knot of police and track officials fractured and Pietri was up, his face frozen and blank. 'Again the red legs broke into their strange automatic amble.'[24] The whole stadium held its breath. Across the vast expanse of grass Hayes was gaining, yard by yard of cinder track.

The tape was before him. His face waxy, the skin pulled over the bones of his skull, the diminutive Italian swayed within a half-moon of policemen and track officials. J.N.

Andrews, secretary of the Polytechnic Harriers and clerk of the course, gripped one elbow, Dr Bulger shepherded him in an air embrace at the other, willing him on.

Pietri caught his balance and staggered forward. He broke the tape and fell to the ground. The stadium erupted.

Thirty-two seconds later Jimmy Hayes crossed the line, almost tripping over the doctors and officials crowding round Pietri. The Italian's inert body was lifted on to a stretcher and hurried away. Hayes was left to walk off unaided as the Italian flag was run up the winner's pole, the Stars and Stripes beneath it.

> In the excitement of the moment [Hayes] failed to get even from his own countrymen the reception he deserved.
>
> *New York Times*

To the American managers the raising of the Italian flag was a deliberate insult. Everyone had seen Pietri receive assistance in direct contravention of the rules – and from J.N. Andrews, the clerk of the course, no less. What more blatant example of the bias of the British judges? While team-mates congratulated Hayes, the American Committee rushed to lodge their protest. Why, they demanded, did the course doctor in attendance not order Pietri to withdraw from the race when he was so evidently risking his health? James E. Sullivan and his colleagues were certain it was a conspiracy. They had heard that Pietri had fallen even before he entered the stadium. He should have been ordered to withdraw from the race on medical grounds. The fact that he was not could only suggest that the British would do anything to deny the Americans victory. It was all photographed in black and white. The evidence was incontrovertible.

Pietri being hurried off on a stretcher. Various ladies watching were reported to be in tears thinking he had imitated the mythical herald Pheidippides and died.

They had difficulty finding a BOC official free to attend to them. They were told they would have to submit their protest in writing.

Forty-eight seconds after Hayes, Charles Hefferon crossed the line. Around the stadium the American fans were cheering themselves hoarse as Joseph Forshaw came in fourth, hardly a minute behind the South African. The 28-year-old was 'so fresh that he walked off shaking hands and laughing'.

Great Britain's reputation for long-distance running was in tatters. Another American – Alton Roy Welton – came in next. The American swimmers tore off their cloaks and waved them over their heads, hooting in celebration. Still no Brits in sight. Instead three Canadians – including Fred Simpson – arrived in the next five minutes. In the royal box the Queen rose to her feet, beating a tattoo on the floor of the stand with her parasol. At least these champions were 'of the family'.

Despite the climate and his troublesome knees, Lewis Tewanina came in tenth, soon after the Swedish champion, Johan Svanberg. The first Briton to make it home was 35-year-old William Thomas Clarke, another runner who was scarcely mentioned in the pre-race coverage. He came twelfth. Of the dozen home-grown champions who began the race, only four survived to finish it. It was North America's day.

As the stadium crowds began to disperse, the Olympic officials were in parlay with the American Management Committee. The American managers grew strident.

'Why, my dear sir, Dorando was not assisted,' replied one British official, looking down his nose. Gustavus Kirby, shaking with raging emotion, pointed to Mr Andrews: 'There is the man who picked up Dorando and carried him across the finish.' Andrews – like St Peter – denied it.

The kindest interpretation that can be put on the affair is that the moment epitomised the clash between two different interpretations of the marathon movement. When his managers asked Charles Hefferon, the South African, to endorse a similar complaint to the American objections, he refused. 'I will not seek to gain second place on a protest,' he declared nobly.

'In such a race as this,' he said, 'I will either win by being first past the post, or I will not win at all. Dorando has won; he deserves the great victory, and I will not do anything to rob him of it. Dorando was the best man. Let the best man have the honour. No protest for me.'[25]

The American management committee were invited to a meeting at which evidence would be taken in relation to the marathon race. The American managers absolutely refused to be part of such a conference and heated language was exchanged among minor members of the drama. The British Olympic officials withdrew to the Imperial Sports Club and after a couple of hours issued their statement. Dorando Pietri had been disqualified. Johnny Hayes was the official winner of the 1908 Olympic marathon.

At half past nine that evening the news was delivered to Pietri, lying exhausted in his lodgings in Church Street, by Count Brunetta d'Usseaux, a prominent Italian member of the International Olympic Committee. Pietri protested that he had never asked for help. He insisted on lodging a formal protest of his own. He had suffered 'official interference' from the committeemen and members of the Olympic Council who had clustered around him at the finish. 'I never lost consciousness of what was going on, and if the doctor had not ordered the attendants to pick me up I believe I could have finished unaided.'[26]

His protest was rejected by the Olympic judges. 'Certainly you are the moral victor,' Count d'Usseaux consoled him, 'and you will be regarded as such throughout the world.'

CHAPTER
9

THE QUEEN AND THE
SUGAR BAKER

This should prove a restful month after July. There will
be one or two regattas for sportsmen to turn to, but
nothing feverish like the Stadium events. And, by the
sea one will be able to forget and forgive the White
Elephant City.
Of course, it has taught us things. Our athletes realise
now that a hot sun doesn't suit them best, and that the
Czechs and the Merovingians and the Sioux can give
them points at hopping, and that England should wake
up to combined fancy diving. But altogether the Stadium
was, so to speak, Rah-rah-rahther too much with us.

BYSTANDER, 5 AUGUST 1908

LORD DESBOROUGH found the time to send flowers to
Dorando Pietri's lodgings, wishing the exhausted Italian
a speedy recovery. As the young runner lay disconsolate, with
his faithful brother, Ulpiano, by his side, he had no inkling
of the impact his heroic effort had made. The evening of
the marathon race, at yet another Olympic banquet at the

This photograph of Queen Alexandra presenting her cup to Dorando Pietri became a best-selling postcard in Italy.

Holborn Restaurant (this time hosted by His Majesty's government), Lord Desborough made a surprise announcement. Her Majesty Queen Alexandra had been so moved by the scenes she had witnessed that afternoon that she had decided to add a gift of her own to the prize-giving ceremony the next day.

'Her Majesty,' Lord Desborough explained, 'felt so keenly that the Italians should have some honour for the success of their champion' that she had decided to present Dorando Pietri with a special cup at her own expense. 'The Italian champion was beaten on technical grounds and quite rightly but after all they must feel great sympathy with the Italians in the closeness of their defeat.'[1]

Count de Bosdari rose to respond on behalf of the Italian ambassador. In an unsteady voice, a tear gleaming in his eye, he expressed his profound emotion at this 'notification of the Queen's intention'. The Queen, it was felt, had intervened with grace in a sticky diplomatic moment.

The American managers – who were not present at the banquet – meanwhile were revelling in their success. 'Wasn't it great?' crowed manager Matt Halpin to the *New York Times* reporter. 'We not only won the big race of the Olympic Games, but also got third, fourth, and ninth places, and, what is more, our Indian beat the much lauded Canadian Indian Longboat. Well, we can forget what has gone before, although we will always feel that we have been unfairly treated.'[2]

'America has been hysterical with joy,' reported the *Daily Mail*'s correspondent from New York.[3] When news of the marathon reached Johnny Hayes's home town, the winner's employer, Samuel Bloomingdale, ordered his famous store to be decorated in young Hayes's honour. His club president, Pat Conway, shouted: 'That squares us for yesterday!', and threw his hat in the air for the benefit of the press corps.

The marathon was not quite the end of the stadium games. On Saturday, before a crowd of 60,000, Irishman Timothy Ahearne won the hop, step and jump for Great Britain and in his final jump set a new Olympic record. (By the time the next Olympic Games came around Ahearne would have emigrated to the United States.) In late morning the all-American final of the 110 metre hurdles was run on the grass track. Forrest Smithson, a 23-year-old six-footer from Portland, Oregon, won with a five-yard lead, setting a new world record of 15 seconds. He was later photographed mid-jump with a Bible in his left hand, prompting a story that he ran the same way.

At noon the final of the disputed 400 metre race was rerun. The Americans refusing to turn out, poor Lieutenant Wyndham Halswelle was forced to the weird indignity of running solo around the track. He won gold in 50 seconds – nearly 1³/₅ seconds slower than his time in the second heat – and made Olympic history as the only finalist ever to run against himself. The moment was soon over. The final of the 1,600 metre medley relay race, the first Olympic relay race ever introduced, took centre stage. Teams from Hungary, Germany and the USA competed with four runners per team. The first two ran 200 metres each, the third 400 metres and the last man 800

Forrest Smithson (USA) winner of the 110 metre hurdles on the closing day of the Games jumping a hurdle with a Bible in his hand in a posed photograph to publicise his objection to Sunday meets. (Within a year he would abandon sport to become a protestant minister.)

metres. (The runners did not carry a baton; transfer was by touch alone.) The Italians had originally been tipped as favourites in the first round but the second-round contest was scheduled at noon the day before, just when the marathon runners were getting ready at Windsor. The Italian team decided to abandon their race at the last minute in order to provide support for their team-mate, Dorando Pietri. In the final the US team extended its lead at every leg and won easily. John Taylor, who had finished fourth in the controversial 400 metre final,* ran the 400 metre leg of the relay, thereby making history by becoming the first black man to win an Olympic gold medal.

---

* In which he behaved impeccably. There was never any suggestion that Taylor participated in the disputed behaviour of Robbins and Carpenter.

Wyndham Halswelle breaking the tape in the rerun the final of the 400 metres. Although he ran alone, Alonzo Stagg, a member of the American Committee, noted with some admiration that the Scotsman insisted on running all out.

The contests of the London stadium Games closed with the 1,500 metre freestyle swimming final. Great Britain won.

It was time for the prize-giving. In 1906 the Greek king presented the winning athletes with olive branches from the groves of Elis. In 1908 the English king substituted oak branches from Windsor Forest tied with red, blue and white ribbons. Edward VII himself was absent. A couple of days previously Buckingham Palace had issued a terse statement that 'the King would not give the prizes, as had been planned, nor participate in the finish of the Games'.[4] *Vanity Fair* announced that he had left London for Sandringham that morning to inspect trees damaged in a gale the previous spring.[5] There was a suspicion that His Majesty had been annoyed by the press coverage. Instead his popular wife, Queen Alexandra, presided with her customary grace. Even with the rowing and

Great Britain's Henry Taylor winning the 1,500 metre freestyle race and being urged on by his trainer to keep going to try to break the standing mile record. Taylor stopped but silver medallist and fellow Brit Sydney Battersby kept swimming to set a new world record for one mile of 24 minutes and 33 seconds.

yachting races and the winter Games to come, there were plenty of prizes to give out; no less than 1,320. The Queen distributed the gold medals in their red Moroccan leather cases and the trophies and the cups.* Each gold medallist also received two copies, rolled up in tubes, of the diploma designed by Bernard Partridge (an illustrator well known for his cartoons in *Punch*) – the winner's personal copy in a deep crimson tube, and a smaller version in a blue tube for 'presentation to his Club or Association as a memorial of his success'. Tables were set up at the foot of the royal stand to cope with the rest: the silver prize medals in their dark blue leather boxes were distributed by the Duchess of Rutland; the bronze medals (yellow leather box) by the Duchess of Westminster. Lady Desborough handed out the diplomas of merit and gave each competitor his commemorative medal with its 'winged figure of Fame' representing the London Games.

The Queen arrived to begin the ceremonies at four o'clock. The athletes were drawn up in phalanx on the green turf. To an endless accompaniment of 'See, the Conquering Hero Comes' from the band of the Grenadier Guards, the Olympic gold medal champions filed up the stairs of the royal box to receive their prizes one by one. The sun shone on a cheerful, good-humoured scene. The small daughter of Clarence Kingsbury, winner of the 20 kilometre cycle race, was made a fuss of when she was brought up to collect her father's medal

---

* Twelve new Challenge Cups and trophies were donated for four-yearly contests at the London Olympic Games, including the Marathon Trophy with a figure of the dying herald, donated by the Greeks. Apart from two – the Prince of Wales Cup, presented for the 100 kilometre cycling event, and the Hurlingham Trophy, awarded to the winners of the polo tournament, neither of which event was contested at the next Olympics – these trophies were also presented at the 1912 Games in Stockholm.

Lt Halswelle returning from the podium holding his diploma in its tube in one hand, while balancing his boxed medal, sheaf of oak leaves and straw boater in the other.

from the Queen (he having left for another competition in Leipzig).* There was much laughter when Lord Desborough was presented with a medal by his wife. Then, just before the distribution of the trophies and cups, the Queen turned to her equerry and asked: 'Where is Dorando Pietri?' A summons was passed down the line and Pietri, looking remarkably recovered from his pitiable state the previous afternoon, dressed in a neat suit with a grey tweed cap confining his curly black hair, emerged from the mass of waiting athletes.

---

* As not every competitor could stay for the prize-giving, the British Olympic Council announced that they would accept postal claims for the uncollected prizes.

After a moment's silence the air was rent by shouts, shrieking, whistles, screeching horns, and the rattling of clappers. Flags were vigorously waved, hats were thrown in the air, sticks and parasols were held aloft, while tears rose to the eyes of many ladies, who had memories of the preceding day's scene. Count Brunetta d'Usseaux, the Italian Secretary General of the International Olympic Council, walked across the grass and shook hands with the hero.

An Italian with a blue-embroidered banner of the arms of Italy rushed to his compatriot. This was borne in front of Dorando until, on nearing the royal box, he crossed on to the cycle track, his face ablaze with pleasure, and beneath the dais awaited his summons.[6]

True to her word, the Queen had produced a silver gilt cup overnight. There had been no time to engrave it, so Alexandra had written out a card in her own hand: 'For P. Dorando, In Remembrance of the Marathon Race from Windsor to the Stadium, From Queen Alexandra'. The presentation over, Pietri made a lap of the stadium holding up his cup and oak leaves. According to the Italian papers, the applause was 'unstoppable'. 'Long live Dorando!' they cheered, waving hats and handkerchiefs, and 'Long Live Italy!'

The American team, unsurprisingly, were a little miffed at the attention lavished on the disqualified marathon winner. Johnny Hayes had to mount the podium in the wake of all this acclamation. When he returned to the turf, his teammates lifted him on to a kitchen table and carried him around the stadium in his turn, clutching the marathon trophy of the dying herald donated by the Greek Olympic Committee. 'The public applauded courteously,' recorded the Italian reporter for *L'Illustrazione Italiana*, 'but the applause lacked the warmth and spontaneity of that which an instant earlier had acclaimed the Italian champion. Here and there in the crowd there were boos.'[7] After the ceremony was over Pietri was driven back to his rooms where he handed his cup to Mr Cremonia of Romano's Restaurant for safekeeping.

The British crowd were clear in their preferences. They put on a special show of applause for young Reggie Walker, the 100 metre sprint winner, for British champion swimmer Henry Taylor and for George Larner, the star English pedestrian; and they cheered long and loud when Lieutenant Halswelle, smart and correct in his suit, marched up for his gold medal for the 400 metres.

Johnny Hayes may have been the official winner of the Olympic marathon, but by apparently nearly killing himself, the small-town confectioner's assistant from Carpi had provided a moment of public drama perfectly expressing the emotion encapsulated in the story of the mythical ancient herald. Hayes's success established the winning superiority of the Americans' strategies and scientific training methods, but it was Pietri who won the public heart. The black and white photographs of his final struggles – images of the pitiable little figure of the shattered Everyman – seemed to carry a universal meaning. The Italian marathon runner became a symbol of the resilience of the human spirit, which despite the odds, despite statistics, despite scientific predictions and past evidence, fought on in hope.

The Queen's cup caught the public mood. Dorando Pietri became the public darling of the moment. 'As the English say,' he commented, 'I am the one who won and lost victory.'

Pietri made an attractively grateful interviewee. 'When I was called to Her Majesty,' he told the British reporters through a translator, 'I was trembling all over. I felt as if I

A postcard of Johnny Hayes being carried by his team-mates on a victory lap around the stadium, displaying the marathon trophy of the dying herald donated by the Greeks.

should fall just as I did the day before. Then she spoke to me very kindly. "Bravo!" was the only word I could understand, but I knew what she meant by her smile. I tried to thank her in Italian, but I could not. I wept. This cup is balm to my soul. I shall treasure it to the end of my life.'[8]

The young Italian provided the newspapers with copy for weeks. There were stories of mysterious ladies unclasping their precious jewellery to thrust into his hands; Italian waiters from the West End took up a collection for him. He was given dinners and the offer of a music hall engagement (although he 'signed the agreement in a moment of excitement', the *Daily Mail* assured its readers, 'and has no intention of becoming an artiste'). Sir Arthur Conan Doyle sponsored another *Daily Mail* appeal to raise a subscription for the young Italian as a token of British respect for his achievement. On

*Pietri's epic run was celebrated on the covers of popular
weekly papers across Italy.*

31 July Conan Doyle and his wife, Jean, met the runner at
the *Daily Mail* offices. Mrs Doyle presented Pietri with a gold
cigarette case and a cheque for £308 10s. In a few well-chosen
words (which Pietri, who spoke only Italian, did not understand) the writer praised the athlete's sportsmanship on
behalf of 'all the English nation'.

◄══ ══►

A DAY AFTER THE FAIR.

Mr. Punch (to Peace). "GLAD TO SEE YOU, MADAM; BUT I WISH YOU COULD HAVE COME A LITTLE EARLIER—WHILE THE OLYMPIC GAMES WERE ON."

'Mr Punch (to Peace). "Glad to see you, madam; but I wish you could have come a little earlier — while the Olympic Games were on." *Punch's comment in the aftermath of the games of 1908. (Published August 5, 1908.)*'

As the *Daily Mail* put it on Monday, 27 July: 'Although the regatta races and winter sports have yet to be decided, most people will regard Saturday's closing scenes at the Stadium as the practical ending of the Olympic Games.'

Britain had come an 'easy first' with 38 points, the Americans following in second place with 22 points. 'Britain on the aggregate, comes out best, and America takes second place,' summarised the *Mail*:

Sweden third, thanks to its superiority in gymnastics, to Johannson's high diving and to Lemming's ability with the javelin; France comes fourth, but except tandem-cycling without a single win in track events. Hungary, thanks to superior skill with the sabre, secures fifth place in the list. Norway, Germany, Canada and Italy come next, though had Dorando been officially declared the winner of the Marathon Race Italy would have tied with Hungary for fifth position. Belgium, South Africa and Finland bring up the rear.

Lord Desborough, reviewing the games in response to the *Daily Mail* reporter, spoke of the 'numerous records' that demonstrated, he felt, 'the quality of the competitors':

> I think, from the expressions of thanks we have received from the managers of the various teams, that the efforts of the Rev. R.S. de Courcy Laffan, the honourable Secretary of the British Olympic Council and others who have worked so hard and for so long to make the games a success, have been appreciated and that allowances have been made where allowances were required.
>
> 'It is to be hoped,' he ended a little wistfully, 'that for those who took part in them the abiding memory of the games will be the feeling of international good fellowship arising from friendly athletic rivalry.'[9]

At first glance, an overview of the assessments of the London Games in the foreign press suggests this hope was in vain.

'The British are incomparable athletes,' conceded the voice of Paris, *Le Figaro*:

> but they are not imbued with the breadth of view, independence, and impartiality of the chivalrous Latins.

The English jury disqualified Dorando and gave the victory to the Americans as compensation for the previous misunderstanding. Thus the Anglo-Saxon race is made to triumph over the Latins. The famous sporting spirit of the English is more legend than reality.[10]

'Although individual events were highly interesting,' considered Vienna's *Zeit* newspaper, 'the games as a whole did not fulfil expectations, owing to defective management and a badly arranged programme.'

The Swedes were annoyed that their champion wrestler Andersson had been declared defeated in spite of their representatives' protest. In the main their journals felt that the bad weather, high ticket prices and the British public's general indifference meant the Games had been overshadowed by the White City, which they rather liked.

As for the Norwegians, 'The Press is unanimous that the games, apart from the weather, were a complete success,' declared the royalist newspaper *Christiania*, 'and that the Norwegians learned much from the gathering.' (Although they felt that their champion, Kam, should have won the gymnastic competition.)

The Danes were less diplomatic. 'The games, which began as a disappointment, finished as a scandal,' announced a leading newspaper. The civilised Danes were repelled by 'the desperate hunt for records', and their commentators did not like the marathon race, considering it neither healthy nor beautiful as a sport. 'Our London experiences show,' declared one of their experts, 'how necessary it is to maintain health and beauty in sport.'

The Italians, at least, were much touched by Queen Alexandra's gesture and the British response to Dorando Pietri. It was

Dorando with the Queen's Cup.

A Souvenir of
The Marathon Race 1908.

Davidson Brothers'
Copyright.

Souvenir postcards of Pietri sold by the thousands – the one of him holding the Queen's cup was one of the most popular.

reported in Britain that Italians had gone mad for the British Queen, buying up postcards of her image, with Italian retailers placing large orders for a particular card showing her in the act of bestowing her cup on Pietri. But Italian journalists also made acid references to the Anglo-Saxon media's general disregard for any non-Anglo-Saxon sportsman. The British press might regard Pietri as an unknown, but as they pointed out, he was in fact the Italian long-distance champion who had won the prestigious Paris marathon in 1904 aged 18.

> The idea that international assemblies of any kind do the State good in promoting peace is one which is rapidly being blown into splinters. More bad blood was caused between otherwise friendly nations by the late Olympic Games than by all the diplomatic incidents in the last ten years together ... The only consolation is that, for some reason or other, we do not seem to have fallen foul of Germany.
>
> *Bystander*[11]

The American newspapers carried reports of the Shepherd's Bush disputes for months. The tone of the returning athletes' remarks was, in general, less vitriolic than that of their managers, but there was a general opinion that the British officials had been officious and arrogant.

'In nearly every event the boys had to compete not only against their competitors but against prejudiced judges,' Harry Porter, winner of the running high jump, told the *New York Times*:

> The judges may not have been intentionally unfair, but they could not control their feelings, which were antagonistic to the Americans. This was especially true in the

field events where the boys came in closer contact with the judges. The Americans were constantly nagged and made uncomfortable. The officials were discourteous to our men, and, further, by their encouragement of the other men, tried to beat us.[12]

Some British commentators did admit, grudgingly, that too much impartiality had been expected of ordinary men. Though barely giving ground, the *Tatler* conceded:

We do think that the patriotic enthusiasm of the officials overcame their sense of official responsibility in one small point, and that is that when an English competitor was winning they not only cheered him up the straight but showed the most unbounded enthusiasm after he had succeeded. We think it would have been more judicious to have left the cheering to the crowd and as officials to have preserved an attitude as unbiased as their treatment of the competitors.[13]

The first member of the American management committee to arrive home in New York, one Captain Charles J. Dieges, made an illuminating comment. He was clear that the AAA officials had been out to get the American athletes, although he had nothing but praise for Lord Desborough: 'The Chairman is the type of sportsman every country loves,' he told the *New York Times* with warmth. 'Nothing was too much trouble for Lord Desborough ... and he showed in many ways how he appreciated the efforts of the American athletes in making the games a success.' The problem lay with the British club officials given charge of the games – or to be specific, the British AAA officials: 'They were ignorant of the rules of

Souvenir postcard of Canada's Olympic heroes at a Toronto parade including Tom Longboat, despite the fact he was unable to finish the marathon race.

athletics and too wrapped up in their own importance to consult with those who knew what to do. It was to this fact largely that the meeting was so badly mismanaged.[14]

And that was, perhaps, the crux of the matter. James E. Sullivan made his position clear:

> It is a pity that the Amateur Athletic Association had control of the games. It should not have been necessary for America to have to be protesting and protesting, and put in a position where letters were necessary every day. It looked as though the officials of the Amateur Athletic Association wanted to control everything themselves, and would not take other countries into their confidence. They were working under the old customs, and thought those the best.[15]

'As a matter of fact,' he concluded, the Games were 'entirely too big a proposition for the men handling it, and they would not look anywhere for help'.

'So far as I personally am concerned,' declared the president of the AAU, 'this is the last international meeting I shall recommend the Americans to take part in until assured that every country competing shall have some say in the management, so that we shall not hereafter be placed in the false position that we have here.'[16]

The Americans had once again proven themselves sporting champions of the world. James E. Sullivan and Mike Murphy returned to New York with a PR triumph. In place of the old Happy Hooligan stereotype they brought Irish-American champions. The American team had won 13 out of a possible 23 firsts in track and field events, 'scoring more firsts than the athletes of the entire world'.[17] And of those 13 victories, members of the Irish American Athletic Club accounted for eight.[18]

The highly coloured stories of the gallant Irish-American heroes and their triumph over the cheating Brits, propagated in particular by the *Gaelic American*, Sullivan and Murphy, with the able assistance of Martin Sheridan, became engrained in the American record. By 1946, when London was announced as the site of the 1948 Olympics, *New York Times* commentator Arthur Daley related most of them as fact. The 400 metre final was established as a story about British tyranny and class war: Halswelle, 'the little tin god of the toffs', was pictured looking down his nose at the wholesome American college boys, 'J.C. Carpenter of Cornell, W.C. Robbins of Harvard and J.B. Taylor of the Irish American

A.C.'* Halswelle was the cheat helped by British officials as dastardly as the standard moustache-twirling villain.

> The British officials suspected that there would be plenty of sharp practice and that the United States operatives would gang up on their hero. But the shrewd James E. Sullivan, the father of the AAU, Mike Murphy, the United States coach, and the other Americans took no chances. They warned our boys to give the leftenant [sic] all the running room he needed. They did … [Halswelle] was given so much running room that a couple of tanks always could have been driven between him and the nearest American. But an official rushed out on the track screaming 'Foul'.

Daley also introduced a new story explaining Ralph Rose's refusal to dip the Stars and Stripes (he did not name his sources). In his version, Rose was taken out for a drink the night before the opening ceremonies by his fellow weight men of Irish descent, including John Jesus Flanagan, Martin Sheridan and Matt McGrath.

> The more ale they consumed the more vehement they got. The glorious Stars and Stripes, they informed him, never should be bowed to anyone, particularly a British King … If Mr. Rose dared lower that magnificent banner even a fraction of an inch he would be torn limb from limb and his bones cast into the Irish Sea … Needless to say, the American flag was not dipped the next day. Nor has it ever bowed to a foreign ruler in the Olympics since.[19]

It was a good story, but not necessarily true.

---

* Robbins was actually a Yale man who later ran for the IAAC. John Taylor ran for the University of Pennsylvania.

Pat Conway, president of the Irish American Athletic Club, orchestrated lavish preparations to welcome the returning heroes. 'It's all for the good of the Stars and Stripes,' he said. On 29 August 1908 a quarter of a million people took part in 'the greatest ovation in the history of athletics', celebrating those 'brawny representatives of young America [who] faced the multitudes in the London Stadium perfectly unconcerned and won the most glorious victory in the annals of athletics'.[20]

At ten o'clock in the morning a parade set off from 46th Street and Broadway. The Grand Marshal, General George Wingate, escorted by 16 high-ranking officers, led groups representing the US Army, the National Guard, the Marines and the Navy – some 15,000 troops in all. Behind the militia came 95 athletes from the US team on floats, followed by representatives of the city's athletic clubs and schoolchildren drawn from James E. Sullivan's Public School Athletic League.[21] The float carrying John J. Hayes, P.J. Conway and James E. Sullivan was decorated with American and Irish flags.[22] Accompanying bands played 'The Star Spangled Banner' and 'Hail, Columbia', along with the 'The Wearing of the Green'. It was a proud day for the Irish Americans of New York. The *Gaelic American* published a poem, 'How the Yankees Beat the World', to celebrate. It began:

They stood within the Stadium so proud, so tall, and straight,
From New York town, from Maine they came and from the Golden
    Gate,
To do honor to their country, and the land that sent them o'er,
And show the world that athletic crowns belong on Columba's shore.
The Gods on High Olympus smiled, as they saw them take their place

At banner, shot and discus, and in long heart-breaking race,
We'll bate these pigmy furriners, be the powers or we'll croak,
And we'll set the pace for the British race, they swore in their Kerry
  brogue.

And five verses later ended with:

At jumping too, and running they showed the English tricks,
Although they knew John Bull could sprint since back in '76.
They chewed them up, and spat them out, and trounced them good
  and sound,
That's how the Yankee beat the world in good old London town.
So let the Eagle scream, me boys, from 'Frisco to New York.
From Dublin town to Galway Bay, from Derry down to Cork.
Hang out the starry banner and never take a dare,
For they still raise brawny Yankees in Donegal and Clare.[23]

The parade arrived in front of City Hall where a stage, decorated in the colours of the clubs to which the victorious athletes belonged and displaying in prominent position the flag Ralph Rose refused to dip to the British king, was erected for 500 athletes, officials and guests. Acting Mayor McGowan delivered a rousing speech on behalf of 'the people of the United States', congratulating 'those of our countrymen who have won victories in athletic sports against the world' and extolling the 'uplifting role of amateur athletics' in producing a 'strong and manly race' of courageous and patriotic men. He proceeded to present each athlete with a gold medal and the freedom of the city. For John J. Hayes, J.C. Carpenter ('who was unjustly disqualified in the 400 metre run after defeating the champion English quarter-miler') and W.C. Robbins of Yale ('who finished second in that event, but declined to compete in a run-off'), there were in addition silver cups, presented 'as special marks of distinction'.

The parade organisers had hoped that President Roosevelt would endorse the affair with his presence. He declined their invitation but sent his congratulations, expressing his 'desire to shake every man by the hand and tell them personally what he thought of their wonderful work at the Olympic games if they would arrange to visit him at Oyster Bay'.[24] President P.J. Conway, as 'Chairman of the Executive Committee of the athletes' parade', and James E. Sullivan swiftly arranged just such a visit.

At eight o'clock in the morning on Monday, 31 August, 95 members of the US Olympic team boarded the Long Island

The New York welcome-home parade for the Olympic victors on 29 August 1908 taken by a businessman watching from his office overlooking City Hall.

steamer from the dock at the foot of East 31st Street accompanied by their trainer, Mike Murphy, their manager 'Matty' Halpin and 'several members of the athletes' parade Committee' (the Irish-American lobby were eager to make the most of this extraordinary presidential access). There seem to have been journalists in the party too, because the day trip was closely documented.

They landed at Sagamore Hill. Sullivan marshalled the men into double file and marched them up to the President's summer home whistling their favourite anthem, 'There'll Be a Hot Time in the Old Town Tonight'. President Roosevelt, in his white duck suit, waited for them on his porch accompanied by members of his family (the athletes were nearly an hour late). Sullivan stepped forward to be 'warmly greeted by the President as an old friend'.

The first athlete to be introduced was Johnny Hayes. 'Here is the top notcher,' declared the President, wringing his hand. 'This is fine! Fine! And I am so glad that a New York boy won it. By George!'[25]

Some years later, Gustavus T. Kirby, a member of the expedition that day, reminisced in a letter to Roosevelt's sister, Corinne:

> I shall never forget the enthusiasm of the gathering, nor how, no sooner had either Sullivan or I presented a member of the team to the President, than he would, by use of his wonderful memory and his most inspiring manner, tell the special athlete all about his own performance, how far he had put the shot to win his event, or how gamely he had run; by how much he had beaten his competitor; his new world record time, and the like.[26]

'America is proud of you,' the President told the athletes standing in his library under his own trophies – the mounted deer antlers and bear heads. 'I think it is the literal truth, Mr Sullivan, to say that the feat that this team has performed has never been duplicated in the history of athletics. I think it is the biggest feat that has ever been performed by any team of any nation, and I congratulate all of you.'

It was a great day for James E. Sullivan. The President publicly thanked him for his work – 'Without you we could never have got together and sent over such a team.' He sat in a window seat beside his President, who listened carefully to his account of the Games. When Sullivan turned to his catalogue of British injustices, Roosevelt offered some avuncular advice:

> Well, we won and the less talking we do the better. We don't need to talk, we've won. There never has been a team like this one. You fellows have won a place for all time. I feel like giving you the advice I gave my regiment when it disbanded.
>
> Remember … that you're heroes for ten days, but when that time is up drop the hero business and go to work.[27]

Sullivan was not quite able to take his President's advice. On 21 September, 500 men prominent in the New York Irish-American sporting community gathered for the Irish American Athletic Club dinner to celebrate their own Olympic victors at the Waldorf Astoria. Over a feast of clams and celery soup, crab meat in the shell, Irish bacon with cabbage, squab guinea hen roasted in a casserole, fillet of beef Longchamps and string beans sautéed in cream, washed down with Moet et Chandon and Olympic sherbet (and not forgetting the obligatory Waldorf salad), they heard a brief address by the

The US team and managers posing outside Theodore Roosevelt's summer home at Oyster Bay on August 31 1908 with James E. Sullivan in prime position next to his President.

Democratic candidate for Governor, Lieutenant Governor L.S. Chanler. (He did not stay long; it was the first stop on his campaign tour.) The principal speaker was James E. Sullivan. 'The American people think we raised too many objections, but my opinion is that we did not object enough,' he declared.

'The American Committee protested only when it was necessary to protect American interests, and even then we had good reason to protest. I am glad a few members of the team have had the courage to declare that they were treated well, but my experience at the games is at variance with their views.

'Athletically speaking it was the most remarkable event in the world's history ... the American athletes just swept England off the athletic map.'[28]

⊶ ⊷

Johnny Hayes, like Dorando Pietri, became an overnight celebrity. The pair of them, along with Tom Longboat, made a good deal of money for a while from the London Olympics. All three turned professional and contributed to a marathon craze in New York and across various American cities for the next couple of years. They were much in demand from promoters eager to match them against one another in various combinations. Hayes and Pietri first met to compete over another marathon distance under the electric lights of Madison Square Garden in November 1908. Pietri won. When he met Longboat, a few weeks later, Longboat won. All three earned substantial sums through purses and endorsements – Longboat endorsing Indian tonic, Hayes promoting O'Sullivan's Live Rubber Heels (for a 'graceful, easy stride').

Hayes, young as he was, grew a little arrogant, sacked his manager, neglected his training and stopped winning. On being offered $1,500 and expenses to run in a marathon in Berlin, Hayes went to Europe and, as he later reminisced, 'mooned around' Italy, 'looking at Roman ruins and picture galleries'. He tried to look Pietri up but failed. At the time Pietri 'lived in a little town way off in the hills. It would have taken me three days to get there over narrow roads.'[29]

Hayes returned to New York to settle down to marriage. He served as a trainer to the American Olympic team in 1912 and eventually made a prosperous career as a food broker in New Jersey. Johnny Hayes was the last American to win the Olympic marathon until Frank Shorter in 1972. He lived until 1965, sprightly to the end, and regularly attended athletic reunions.

Dorando Pietri married his childhood sweetheart in 1909. He continued to compete professionally for a few years in the capitals of Europe and up and down the United States. He

The business of sport: a solemn Johnny Hayes shakes hands with Dorando Pietri in a publicity pose to advertise an agreement that was to bring the Italian to New York to run against Hayes at Madison Square Garden.

retired in 1911 and moved to San Remo, a fashionable holiday resort on the coast, where he invested his prize money in a car hire business. In 1932 a reporter spotted him, now a stout, middle-aged man, waving the starter's flag at a marathon in San Remo. Pietri died ten years later. He is buried in San Remo. The silver gilt cup Queen Alexandra presented to him is still kept in a security box in the UniCredit bank in Carpi, the treasured possession of his athletic club, Carpi's branch of Gymnastica La Patri.

Tom Longboat's professional athletic career was blighted by racism. 'In my time, I've interviewed everything from a circus lion to an Eskimo chief,' Lou Marsh reminisced late in life, 'but when it comes to being the original dummy, Tom Longboat is it. Interviewing a Chinese Joss or a mooley cow is pie compared to the task of digging anything out of Heap Big Chief T. Longboat.'[30] It was his manager Tom Flanagan who turned Longboat professional, but within a year he had sold his contract for $2,000 to a New York entrepreneur. Tom Longboat was as surprised as anybody. Two weeks previously Flanagan had been best man at his athlete's wedding. (Longboat later told his son that Flanagan had sold him just as if he was a racehorse.) Longboat raised the money to buy out his contract. Having served as a despatch runner during the First World War, he returned to Canada to find his wife, thinking him declared dead, had married again. By the 1920s he was living in poverty. He ended up following a Toronto garbage truck picking up bins. In the last years of his life, sports fans belatedly raised a subscription on his behalf and he ended his days back on the reservation where he was born, cared for by his daughter. He died there in 1949. He is now recognised as one of Canada's greatest long-distance runners.

A faded photograph that according to the handwritten notation on the back shows Tom Longboat and his wife living in rural poverty in Canada in the 1920s. His wife sold the baskets she made to the local farmers.

Wyndham Halswelle's experience in the 1908 Olympics so soured him that he ran only one more race, later that year, before quitting competitive sport entirely. A career army officer, he was killed by a sniper's bullet in France on the last day of March 1915. He was 33. John Carpenter's racing career also seems to have finished with the London Games. He too served in the First World War. He was decorated for bravery, receiving the Croix de Guerre at Mons. He survived the war but died in 1933 at the age of only 49.

Ralph Rose, the famous flag bearer and shot putter, continued to set records until he was felled by typhoid in October 1913 and died within days. John Taylor, the first black athlete to win an Olympic gold medal, died of the same disease, just months after his return from London, in December 1908.

⊷☞ ☜⊶

'The fact that England is twenty-five years behind America was proven in the Marathon Race,' said Gustavus Kirby, the college administrator from Columbia and member of the American Committee. 'They simply relied on traditions and expected to win the race, when their records show they have not had a Marathon Race in dozens of years up to 1908.'[31]

The British were forced to accept that the American methods showcased in the London Games produced better athletes. *Vanity Fair*, at least, was prepared to face the truth:

> Giving ourselves the greatest credit for showing the best all-round performance, there can be no doubt at all that in the feats upon which we have specially prided ourselves hitherto, the Americans have beaten us decisively. Ask any boy at Eton or Harrow what events he would like to win

in the sports and he will tell you he would like to win one of the races, or one of the jumps. To the English boy, and indeed, the English man, these tests are the true tests, and measured in this way one can only confess that the American team have done extraordinary things.

Up Against It

A San Francisco Chronicle cartoonist's impression of what the London Olympics had done to Great Britain's reputation for fair play.

If Britain wished to continue to compete in the Olympics it was clear that British athletes would have to adapt to American methods and American-style trainers:

> Of course there is a great deal to be said for the British way of taking the matter comfortably, and yet doing pretty well thank you. It speaks volumes for the sense of rivalry in us and the love of hard exercise that we have done as well as we have with half-trained men … The root fact of the whole business is that a first-rate trainer improves his whole team. The individual does not see his little fault; perhaps indeed he cherishes it; but the trainer won't have it; gets it corrected, and the man's time improves. Our teams must put themselves under trainers if they would win the next Olympic Games.[32]

International sport, it seemed, required the abandonment of some piece of the British character. 'You now pass a policeman,' complained *Bailey's Magazine* a few years later, 'and show a season-ticket or pay for entrance into a ground furnished with a path of cinders, or fenced with grim barriers in order to look at athletes who have been training systematically, instead of runners who take off their coats and go in with glorious uncertainty as to who's going to win what.'[33]

'No friends are closer, no friendships last longer,' wrote Theodore Cook, 'than those made in the honest struggle for victory in manly sports.' His vision of the Olympic idea – that international festival of sport played out on a green sward under a blue sky, like some vast summer sports day carried on under the approving eye of a firm but benevolent headmaster in the guise of a king, was not an idea that could survive in an age that rendered monarchs redundant. It was the embodiment of a nostalgic dream about an ordered, balanced society, unthreatened and secure in itself; the dream of an aristocratic society that sensed its end.

The Franco-British Exhibition was seen by 8.4 million people before it closed on 31 October 1908. Contemporary opinion was that the event was an outstanding success. Although the original lease ran for just one year, the White City continued by popular demand, more or less intact. Kiralfy produced seven further exhibitions on the site between 1908 and 1914. After that the exhibition buildings surrounding the stadium were gradually demolished. Imre Kiralfy himself died in April 1919, aged 74, having amassed a considerable fortune earned through his production of imperial exhibitions and spectacular displays.

Detail from cartoon published in the Bystander, *August 12 1908.*

The White City stadium never again saw the overflowing crowds of the final of the 1908 marathon but it long outlived the white palaces and the exhibition that gave it its name. Kiralfy's grand, all-encompassing sporting venue never quite found its market. Bookings dried up. Its seating capacity was reduced. Over the years its gently rotting stands witnessed greyhound racing, cheetah racing, speedway racing, boxing, soccer, rugby, American football and show jumping. In 1927 it was taken over by the Greyhound Racing Association, which in a nod to the glorious past held an annual 'Dorando Marathon' for dogs. In 1932 the stadium returned to its roots. Mr Fisher's ⅓ mile track was refurbished and White City became the centre of British athletics, until in 1971 the Amateur Athletic Association moved their championships to Crystal Palace. The last event to take place at the Shepherd's Bush stadium was a greyhound race, held at 10.15 pm on 22 September 1984. The race was won by the blue brindle bitch, Hastings Girl. A few days later, demolition began. The site became the White City headquarters of BBC Television.

Theo Cook was knighted for his services during the First World War and went on to become an affectionately remembered editor of the *Field*. He lost his enthusiasm for the Olympics in the war. He felt that politics had intervened and proved the ideal impossible.

William Henry Grenfell, Baron Desborough of Taplow, KCVO, served as a member of the International Olympic Committee from 1906 to 1913. He too, like Cook, grew disillusioned by what the Olympics became. The world he knew died in the First World War. He lost his two eldest sons within a month of each other in the trenches in France. His surviving son was killed by modernity in a car crash in 1926. When Desborough died in January 1945 at the age of 89, his name would die with him.

James E. Sullivan never quite fulfilled his ambition to impose his rules on international sport. The cross-Atlantic tension over the standardisation of rules would not be resolved until the International Amateur Athletics Federation was established years after his death. Sullivan did, however, help make track and field the centrepiece of the Olympic Games and he initiated the modern Olympic organisation in America. He served as American Commissioner to the 1912 Games but died suddenly of complications following an operation for appendicitis in September 1914. In 1930 the AAU established the James E. Sullivan Award, presented annually to the best amateur athlete in the US. Known as the Oscar of sports, the Sullivan Award still honours America's top amateur athlete each year, selected on the basis of athletic accomplishments and strong moral character.

Despite all the arguments, disputes and complaints the Olympics of 1908 were the best run so far. The enthusiastic amateur efforts of Desborough, Cook and their colleagues brought into relief the areas requiring reform and James E. Sullivan and the Americans pressed for that reform, initiating changes that helped preserve the movement through the impact of the First World War. Indeed the revived Olympic Games might not have survived until today without the London Games of 1908.

Notes

PREFACE

1 Estimates of contemporary values
are calculated using the Retail Price
Index formula from Lawrence H.
Officer, 'Five Ways to Compute the
Relative Value of a UK Pound
Amount, 1830–2006',
MeasuringWorth.Com, 2007.

CHAPTER 1

1 Unless otherwise identified, all
quotes in this chapter come from
Theodore Cook, *International Sport*
(Constable & Co., 1910).
2 *Vanity Fair*, 15 July 1908.
3 *The Times*, 16 May 1906.

CHAPTER 2

1 Baron Pierre de Coubertin: *Mémoires
Olympiques*, Lausanne (1932), p. 46.
2 Quoted in Steve Bailey, 'A Noble
Ally and Olympic Disciple: The
Reverend Robert S. de Courcy
Laffan', *OLYMPIKA: The
International Journal of Olympic
Studies*, Vol. VI (1997), 51–64.
3 Revd Robert Laffan, handwritten
speech delivered at the banquet for
Olympic competitors and officials,
31 October 1908. Archives of the
British Olympic Association.
4 Imre Kiralfy, 'My Reminiscences',
Strand Magazine, June 1909.
5 Unless otherwise identified, quotes
in this chapter are from London
and the Franco-British Exhibition
1908 (Ward, Lock & Co., 1908).
6 'Musings without Method',
Blackwood's Magazine, August 1908,
p. 277.
7 Kiralfy, 'My Reminiscences'.

CHAPTER 3

1 'City of Splendid Palaces', *Daily
Mail*, 11 May 1908, p.102.

2 Cook, *International Sport.*
3 *Country Gentleman*, 27 June 1908.
4 *Sporting Life*, 5 February 1908.
5 *Evening Standard*, 24 November 1906.
6 'Athletic Alliance with Great
Britain', *New York Times*, 25
December 1905.
7 Cook, *Sunlit Hours*, p. 244.
8 *Country Gentleman*, 27 June 1908.
9 *Daily Telegraph*, 27 April 1908.
10 *Vanity Fair*, 20 May 1908.
11 *Bystander*, 20 May 1908.
12 *Bystander*, 15 July 1908.
13 *Tatler*, 17 June 1908.
14 *Daily Mail*, 22 June 1908.
15 *Bystander*, 20 May 1908.
16 *Tatler*, 8 July 1908.
17 *World*, 8 July 1908.
18 *Daily Mail*, 9 July 1908.
19 *Daily Mirror*, 9 July 1908.
20 Appendix to Minutes of the
meeting of the BOC, Wednesday 2
September 1908. Archives of the
British Olympic Foundation.
21 *Tatler*, 8 July 1908.
22 *Daily News*, 11 May 1908.

CHAPTER 4

1 This and other quotes about the
AAU dinner from 'Sullivan
Testimonial', *New York Times*, 10
January 1907.
2 Figures from David Nasaw, *The
Chief: The Life of William Randolph
Hearst* (Houghton Mifflin, 2000),
p. 135.
3 Quoted in Bill Mallon and Ian
Buchanan, *The 1908 Olympic Games:
Results for All Competitors in All
Events*, with Commentary
(McFarland & Co., 2000), p. 10.
4 *New York Times*, 14 April 1907.
5 *Theodore Roosevelt, The Wilderness
Hunter* (G.P. Putnam's Sons, 1893),
quoted in Dr John Lucas, 'Caspar
Whitney: The Imperial Advocate of

Athletic Amateurism', *Journal of Olympic History*, May 2000.

6 *Collier's Weekly*, 13 March 1909.
7 Zona Gale, 'Editors of the Younger Generation', *Critic*, 44 (April 1904), 318.
8 S.W. Pope, *Patriotic Games: Sporting Traditions in the American Imagination, 1876–1926* (New York: Oxford University Press, 1997), p. 34.
9 'First Revival of the Olympic Games: How Americans Got into the Athletic Contest', *Warren Evening Mirror* (Pennsylvania), 24 July 1908.
10 Quoted in Robert K. Barney, 'Coubertin and Americans: Wary Relationships, 1889–1925'. LA Foundation website.
11 *Outing*, March 1907.
12 Caspar Whitney, 'The View-Point', *Outing*, September 1905.
13 *New York Times*, 3 and 26 May 1906, quoted in William Johnson, *All That Glitters Is Not Gold: An Irreverent Look at the Olympic Games* (G.P. Putnam, 1972).
14 G. S. Robertson, 'The Olympic Games By a Competitor and Prize Winner', *Fortnightly Review*, June 1896.
15 Cook, *International Sport*, p. 89.
16 *New York Times*, 7 June 1908.
17 Corinne Roosevelt Robinson, *My Brother Theodore Roosevelt* (New York: Charles Scribner & Sons, 1921), p. 245.
18 'Conway of the IAAC', *Gaelic American*, 25 July 1908.
19 'Irishmen at the Olympic Games', *Irish-American Advocate*, 18 July 1908.
20 *New York Times*, 30 June 1908.
21 Baron Pierre de Coubertin speaking at the meeting of the Union des Sports Athlétiques at the Sorbonne on 25 November 1892, reported by Theodore Cook in the official report of the 1908 Games, p. 16.
22 *World*, 28 June 1908.
23 'America Against the World at London', *San Francisco Chronicle*, 12 July 1908.

CHAPTER 5

1 Cook, *International Sport*, p. 94.
2 Cook, *International Sport*, p. 17.
3 'Arrangements at London Not Satisfactory – Men to be Lavishly Entertained', *World*, 8 July 1908.
4 *New York Evening Post*, 7 July 1908.
5 'The Olympian Games', *Chicago Daily Tribune*, 13 July 1908.
6 *Bystander*, 15 July 1908.
7 *Irish News*, 8 July 1908.
8 *World*, 12 July 1908.
9 'America's Turn Next', *New York Daily Tribune*, 20 July 1908.
10 *The Fourth Olympiad, London 1908: Official Report* (British Olympic Association, 1909), p. 49.
11 'Rain Mars the Opening', *Chicago Daily Tribune*, 14 July 1908.
12 Official Report, p. 47.
13 *Sporting Life*, 3 July 1908.
14 'Rain Mars the Opening', *Chicago Daily Tribune*, 14 July 1908.
15 Minutes of BOC meeting, 8 July 1908. Archives of the British Olympic Foundation.
16 'Yankees Win First Blood in Olympic Games', *World*, 14 July 1908.
17 Quoted in Jack Batten, *The Man Who Ran Faster Than Everyone* (Tundra Books, 2002).
18 'AAU is Menaced … the Irish-Americans May Secede', *New York Times*, 13 September 1905.
19 'For Long-Distance Running', *New York Times*, 20 January 1907.
20 *Vanity Fair*, 15 July 1908.

CHAPTER 6

1 'The Olympian Games', *Chicago Daily Tribune*, 13 July 1908.
2 Quoted in Mallon and Buchanan, *The 1908 Olympic Games*, p. 96.
3 Official Report, p. 49.
4 *Bystander*, 15 July 1908.
5 *Daily Mail*, 13 July 1908.
6 Various, including *Chicago Daily Tribune*, *New York Times* and *World*, 14 July 1908.
7 *San Francisco Chronicle*, 17 July 1908.
8 *Daily Mail*, 17 July 1908.

9 *Daily Mail*, 18 July 1908.
10 *Chicago Daily Tribune*, 13 July 1908.
11 *Tatler*, 29 July 1908.
12 *Daily Mail*, 17 July 1908.
13 'The Men Who Set the Marks', *Outing*, July 1908.
14 *Daily Mail*, 17 July 1908.
15 *San Francisco Chronicle*, 17 July 1908.
16 Various papers carry the same AP report; this quote from *San Francisco Chronicle*, 17 July 1908.
17 Official Report, p. 100.
18 Official Report, p. 408.
19 *Daily Graphic*, 18 July 1908.
20 *San Francisco Chronicle*, 18 July 1908.
21 *New York Evening Post*, 17 July 1908.
22 Official Report, p. 92.
23 *Chicago Daily Tribune*, 18 July 1908.
24 *New York Evening Post*, 17 July 1908.
25 *New York Evening World*, 18 July 1908, quoted in Mallon and Buchanan, *The 1908 Olympic Games*, p. 269.
26 Letter dated 26 October 1908, quoted in Mallon and Buchanan, *The 1908 Olympic Games*, p. 269.
27 *Chicago Daily Tribune*, 18 July 1908.
28 'America's Best are Again Drawn for the Same Heat', *New York Herald*, 20 July 1908.
29 'Off Day for Our Athletes', *New York Sun*, 18 July 1908.
30 *New York Evening Post*, 17 July 1908.
31 *San Francisco Chronicle*, 18 July 1908.
32 Official Report.
33 *San Francisco Chronicle*, 19 July 1908.
34 Official Report, p. 408.
35 Official Report, p. 92.
36 *Daily Mail*, 18 July 1908.
37 *Sporting Life*, 22 July 1908.

CHAPTER 7

1 *San Francisco Chronicle*, 20 July 1908.
2 Minutes of BOC meeting dated Monday 20 July 1908. Archives of the British Olympic Association.
3 *Daily Mail*, 21 July 1908.
4 'America's Day in Stadium', *New York Sun*, 21 July 1908.
5 *Daily Mail*, 21 July 1908.
6 'The Outlook', *Daily Mail*, 21 July 1908.

7 E.E.P. Tisdall, *Unpredictable Queen* (Stanley Paul & Co., 1953).
8 *Daily Mail*, 23 July 1908.
9 Official Report, p. 56.
10 Official Report, p. 403.
11 'New Olympic Disputes', *New York Daily Tribune*, 24 July 1908.
12 '400-Meter Race Controversy', *New York Evening Post*, 23 July 1908.
13 'Yankee Runner Disqualified', *New York Sun*, 24 July 1908.
14 *Daily Mail*, 24 July 1908.
15 Quoted in Mallon and Buchanan, *The 1908 Olympic Games*, p. 54.
16 *Chicago Daily Tribune*, 24 July 1908.
17 Quoted in Mallon and Buchanan, *The 1908 Olympic Games*, p. 53.
18 *Field*, 29 August 1908.
19 Michael Oriard, *Reading Football: How the Popular Press Created an American Spectacle* (University of North Carolina Press, 1993).
20 Robert Edgren, 'The Modern Gladiator: Why the American Succeeds – Brute Strength Superseded by Scientific Cleverness', *Outing*, March 1903.
21 In the words of C.B. Fry, a famous sportsman in the *Boy's Own* hero mould playing in the 1890s, quoted in Richard Holt, *Sport and the British: A Modern History* (Clarendon Press, 1989), p. 99.
22 *Daily Mail*, 24 July 1908.

CHAPTER 8

1 *Daily Mail*, 24 July 1908.
2 *Daily Mail*, 20 July 1908.
3 *San Francisco Chronicle*, 19 July 1908.
4 *Daily Mail*, 24 July 1908.
5 From official instructions to competitors, marathon programme. Archives of the British Olympic Association.
6 *Daily Mail*, 24 July 1908.
7 *New York Evening Post*, 24 July 1908.
8 'Sullivan's Olympic Views', *New York Sun*, 13 July 1908.
9 Sir Arthur Conan Doyle, *Daily Mail*, 25 July 1908.
10 *Daily Mail*, 21 July 1908.

11 Sir Arthur Conan Doyle, *Memories & Adventures* (Greenhill Books, 1988), p. 229.

12 Sir Arthur Conan Doyle, *Daily Mail*, 25 July 1908.

13 *Daily Mail*, 21 July 1908.

14 'Scenes from the Course', *Daily Mail*, 24 July 1908.

15 Tewanina speaking to Associated Press, reported in *New York Times*, 25 July 1908.

16 Quoted in Batten, *The Man Who Ran Faster Than Everyone*, and in Bruce Kidd, *Tom Longboat* (Fitzhenry & Whiteside, 2002).

17 Quoted in Batten, *The Man Who Ran Faster Than Everyone*, and in Kidd, *Tom Longboat*.

18 *Daily Mail*, 25 July 1908.

19 Quoted in Batten, *The Man Who Ran Faster Than Everyone*.

20 *New York Sun*, 25 July 1908.

21 Quotes in the following account are from the *Daily Mail* of 24 and 25 July 1908, and the *New York Times* and *New York Evening Post* of 25 July 1908.

22 Letter in *Boston Daily Globe*, 24 September 1908.

23 Sir Arthur Conan Doyle, *Daily Mail*, 25 July 1908.

24 Sir Arthur Conan Doyle, *Daily Mail*, 25 July 1908.

25 Various, but in particular *Daily Express*, *Sporting Life*, 25 July 1908.

26 'Signor Dorando: I Believe I Could Have Won', *Daily Mail*, 25 July 1908.

CHAPTER 9

1 *Daily Mail*, 25 July 1908.

2 *New York Times*, 25 July 1908.

3 *Daily Mail*, 27 July 1908.

4 Quoted in Mallon and Buchanan, *The 1908 Olympic Games*, p. 13.

5 *Vanity Fair*, 29 July 1908.

6 *Daily Mail*, 27 July 1908.

7 *L'Illustrazione Italiana*, 2 August 1908.

8 *Daily Mail*, 27 July 1908.

9 *Daily Mail*, 27 July 1908.

10 Translations supplied by *Daily Mail* correspondents, 27 July 1908.

11 *Bystander*, 5 August 1908.

12 *New York Times*, 26 July 1908.

13 *Tatler*, 29 July 1908.

14 'First of Olympic Party to Arrive', *New York Times*, 31 July 1908.

15 'Sullivan Scores Britons', *New York Times*, 26 July 1908.

16 'Cable Is Sent to Roosevelt', *Chicago Daily Tribune*, 26 July 1908.

17 'Sullivan Scores Britons', *New York Times*, 26 July 1908.

18 'Fine Example of Self-Development', *New York Herald*, 25 July 1908.

19 'The Battle of Shepherds Bush', *New York Times*, 24 February 1946.

20 'Thousands Cheer Victors of the Olympic Games', *New York Times*, 30 August 1908.

21 'New York Welcome to Olympic Victors', *Gaelic American*, 5 September 1908.

22 'Thousands Cheer Victors of the Olympic Games', *New York Times*, 30 August 1908.

23 E.P. McKenna, 'How the Yankees Beat the World', *Gaelic American*, 25 July 1908.

24 'To Meet the President', *New York Times*, 31 August 1908.

25 *New York Times*, 1 September 1908.

26 Quoted in Corinne Roosevelt Robinson, *My Brother Theodore Roosevelt* (Charles Scribner, 1921), p. 245.

27 *New York Times*, 1 September 1908.

28 *New York Times*, 22 September 1908.

29 John Kieran, 'Sports of the Times', *New York Times*, 2 April 1930.

30 Lou Marsh quoted in Batten, *The Man Who Ran Faster Than Everyone*, p. 36.

31 Caspar Whitney, 'Viewpoint: The American Committee Report', *Outing*, November 1908.

32 'The Olympic Games at the Franco-British Exhibition', *Vanity Fair*, 29 July 1908.

33 Quoted in Holt, *Sport and the British*, p. 100.

Index

Note: page numbers in **bold** refer to illustrations/photographs.

aboriginal games 90
Acropolis 11, 12
Adlerz, Erik 121
Ahearne, Timothy 228
Albani, Mme 63
Albert, Prince VI
Albert, Prince *see* George
Alekna, Virgilijus 144
Alexandra, Queen 7, 10, 16–17, **16**, 19, 116,
    117, 120, 155, 212, 224, 227–8, **227**, 231–4,
    235–6, 240–2, 254
Alington, Lord 52
Allen, Maud 110
Amateur Athletic Association (AAA) 32,
    54, 112, 114–15, 129, 134, 145–6, 151, 158,
    161–3, 170, 178, 180, 191, 243–4, 260
    Championships 58, 105–8, 134–5, 145,
    170, 174, 176
Amateur Athletic Union (AAU) 53–4, 76–8,
    82, 84, 88–90, 92, 112, 114, 127, 129–30,
    145, 173, 184–7, 245–6, 261
American Olympic Committee 92, 96–7,
    112, 114, 115, 118, 140–1, 151, 154, 158, 161–2,
    175, 180, 222, 252, 256
Andersson (wrestler) 240
Andre, George 168
Andrews, J.N. **xii**, 62, 192, 195, **217**, 219–20,
    222, 224
Appleby, Fred 197, 206, 211
archery 59, 147, 148
Argyll, Duke of 29, 117, **117**
Argyll, Louise, Duchess of 117
Arnold, Thomas 12, 22
Ascot 66, 67
Associated Press 146, 161
Athens Olympics 1906 1–19, **11**, **14**, **16**,
    92–4, 108, 110, 119, 123, 124, 126, 139, 146,
    176, 192, 194–5, 202, 203, 231

Atlanta Olympics 1996 168, 169, 171
Aufray, A. **166**
Austin, Charles 168
Australian team 122, 123, 143, 194, 202
Austrian team 120, 123
Avéroff, Mr 10

Babcock, John 81
Badger, Arthur Roscoe 178
Bailey, Donovan 171
Bailey's Magazine 258
Baker (runner) 198
Barnum, Phineas 26
Basan, David 178
baseball 80, 83
basketball 83
Beale, Jack 'the Spartan' 62, 197
Beaupaire, Henry 143
Belgian team 123, 194, 239
Bennett, James Gordon 80
bicycle polo 58, 131, **131**
Bieberstein, Arno 148
Biller, J.A. 172
Blackwood's Magazine 45
Blasi, Umberto 205
Bloomingdale, Samuel 228
Bohemia 119–20, 123, 194
Bonhag, George V. 129
Bosanquet, Mr 7
Bosanquet, Mrs 15
boxing 59, 80, 83
Braams, Wilhelmus 202
Branwen (yacht) 6, **7**, 8, 9, 15
Bredin, Edgar 176
British Empire Exhibition 27
British Empire League 27–8
British Olympic Association (BOA) 4,
    18–19, 23–4, 32, 53, 59, 145, 153, 155
British Olympic Council (BOC) 24, 31–2,
    48, 54–5, 58, 60–1, 67, 71, 93, 101, 108–12,
    118–19, 121–2, 130, 140, 143, 146, 151, 154,
    158, 161, 170, 173–4, 177, 186, 223, 239

British team 122-4, **123**, 132-4, 138, 141, 143, 145-54, 157, 159, 161, 168-70, 174-5, 177-86, 194, 197, 200-2, 204-6, 223-4, 231, 238, 256-8
broad jump, standing 132, 163-5
Brock, Sir Thomas 55
Buchanan, Ian xv, 180
Buermeyer, Henry 81
Bulger, Michael J. **xii**, 177-8, **217**, 219, 220
Butterfield 126
Bystander (magazine) 66, 110, 136, 160, 226, **259**

Canadian Amateur Athletic Federation 173
Canadian team 122-4, 133, 135, 140-1, 157, 173-4, 192, 194-6, 200-1, 206-12, 224, 228, 239, 254-5
Carpenter, John C. 175, 177-81, **177**, **179**, 182-4, 186, 245, 248, 256
Cartmell, Nat 171, 174
Casey, Captain Kellogg 111
Cassel, Sir Ernest 29
Chanler, Lieutenant Governor L.S. 252
Chicago Daily Tribune (newspaper) 105, 109, 134, 142, 151, 152, 153, 184
Christiania (newspaper) 240
cigarette cards **99-100**
Clarke, William Thomas 224
Cloughen, Robert 174
Cockburn, Sir John **117**
Coe, Harry 103-4
Coldstream Guards 47, 194
Committee of Honour 97
Conan Doyle, Sir Arthur 95, 199-200, 206, 209, 215, 217, 218-19, 236-7, 238
Conan Doyle, Jean 237, 238
Connaught, Duke and Duchess of 117
Conway, P.J. 79, 97, 98, 228, 247, 249
Cooch Behar, Maharajah of 70
Cook, Theodore Andrea 1-3, **2**, 5, **6**, 7-10, 12-15, 17-19, 48, 54-5, 58-9, 69, 75, 93-4, 108, 114-15, 119, 126-7, 136, 150-1, 157, 169-70, 173, 258-61
Cooke, E. 200
Cooper, Charlotte 64
Cope, Sir Arthur 55
Country Gentleman (magazine) 58
Cowes 66, 67
Cremonia, Mr 235

cricket 71-2
Crocker, J. Howard 207-8
Crown Prince of Greece 15, 16, 20, 117
Crown Prince of Sweden 117, 118, 141-2, 155, 194, 201
Curtis, 'Father Bill' 81
cycling 48, 49-50, 59, 93, 135, 141, 143, **144**, 161, 166-7
tandem **166**

Daily Graphic (newspaper) 150, 165
Daily Mail (newspaper) 42, 68, 69, 70, 71, 73-4, 110, 112, 132, 136-7, 142, 145, 154, 158, 166-8, 172, 182-3, 186, 195, 199, 201, 211, 214, 219, 228, 236-9
Daily Mirror (newspaper) 179-80
Daily News (newspaper) 74-5
Daily Tribune (newspaper) 181
Daley, Arthur 245-6
Dana, Charles 80
Daniels, Charles **100**
Danish team 120, 123, 137-8, **138**, 240
Darby, J. 173
de Bosdari, Count 228
de Coubertin, Baron Pierre 3-4, **3**, 8, 12, 20, 21, 22, 23, 31, 54, 59-60, 64, 74, 75, 81, 87, 88-93, 102, 118, 120, 124
de Fleurac 124
de Manneville, Count H. 29
de Walden, Lord Howard 6, 6, 8, 9-10
Deakin, Joe 135-6, 140
Derby, Earl of 29
Desborough, Lady Ettie Grenfell 6, 26, 48, 232, 233
Desborough, Lord Willie Grenfell, 1st Baron of Taplow xiii, 4-10, 15-21, 23-4, 26, 29-32, 45, 47-8, 52, 62, 66-72, **73**, 74-5, 81, 86, 101-2, 104-5, 109, 115, 117-18, **117**, 123, 126-7, 130, 140-2, 146, 154, 158, 186-7, 192, 195, 226, 233, 239, 243, 260-1
Dieges, Captain Charles 243
discus 13-14, **14**, 18, 88, 89, 98, 132, 143-4, 155-6
diving 59, 63, 157-8
Dod, Lottie 147-8
Dod, William 147
Drain, General J.A. 97, 111-12
Duff Gordon, Sir Cosmo 5, **6**, 8, 9-10, 17
Duggan, Mickey 98
Duke, Inspector 159

Dull, G.A. 103
Duncan, Alan 62
Duncan, Alexander 197, 198, 204, 206
d'Usseaux, Count Brunetta 225, 234
Dutch team 123, 194, 201-2

Eastlake Smith, Miss 65, **65**
Edgren, Robert 185-6
Edward VII, King of England xv, 6-7, 10,
    15-17, **16**, 19, 28, 29, 36, 45, 67, 95, 105, 116,
    123-4, 126, 231, 248
Eisele, John 153-4, 157
Elliot, H. 116
Emil, Dr xi, xiii
Evening Call (newspaper) 142
Evening News (newspaper) 42, 69
Evening Standard (newspaper) 46, 53
Ewry, Ray 163, 164-5, **164**, 172-3

Fairbairn-Crawford, Ivo 168-9
fencing 1-2, 5-6, **6**, 15, 17-18, 58, 59, 93, 161,
    169-70
figure skating 59, 83
Finnish team 120, 121, 123, 138, 139, 156, 157,
    194, 239
Fisher, Mr 32, 48, 115, 260
Flanagan, John Jesus **91**, 98-9, 103, 110,
    127-8, 130, 134-5, 148-9, 152, 198-9, 205,
    208, 209-10, 246, 255
Flip-Flap 38-9, **39**, 46, 63, 68, 142
Florstrom, Valborg 157-8
Foden, C. 149
football 59, 80, 83
Forshaw, Joseph 196, 205, 211-12, 214, 223
Franco-British Exhibition xiii, xv, 20,
    28-31, **30**, 32-45, **34**, **35**, **39**, **41**, **43**, 46-7,
    47, 53, 63, 63, 68, 69, 71, 72, 109, 118, 259
Franco-British Exhibition Company 31,
    32, 48, 52, 67, 158
French team 120, 123, 124, **125**, 147, 161,
    166-7, 168, 239

Gaelic American (journal) 98, 102, 124, 155,
    182, 245
Garrells, John 145
Garrett (shot putter) 88
George I, King of Greece 3, 7, 10, **16**, 17, 18,
    93, 123, 231
George V (Prince of Wales) 63, 70, **117**
George VI (Prince Albert) 117, **193**, 194

George, Prince 194, 195
German team 120, 123, 131, **131**, 137-8, 148,
    169-70, 194, 229, 239
Gilbert, A.C. 200
Gisico, Ebba 157-8
Goble, Harry 176-7
golf 59, 83, 148
Gould, Jay 64, **65**
Greece, Crown Prince of 15, 16, 20, 117
Greek Olympic Committee 2, 234
Greek team 123, 148, 165, 194
Grenadier Guards 117-18, 124, 232
Grenfell, Gerald 71
Greyhound Racing Association 260
Griffin, Merritt 144
Gustavus, Prince 118
Gymnastica La Patri 254
gymnastics 59, 93, 120, **125**, 135, 137-8, **138**,
    143, 158, 240

Hallows, N.F. 126, 135
Halpin, M.C. (Matt) 93, 97, 103, 108, 123,
    149-50, 151, 158, 162, 228, 250
Halstead, J.P. 113-14, 125, 126, 162-3
Halswelle, Lieutenant Wyndham 108, 175,
    177-80, **177**, 182-4, 229, **230**, **233**, 235,
    245-6, 256
hammer throwing 98-9, 132, 134-5
Harper's Weekly (magazine) 86
Hawkins, G.A. 174
Hawtrey, Lieutenant 18
Hayes, Johnny 99, **100**, 210-11, **210**, 213,
    214, 219, 220-2, 223, 225, 228, 234-5, 236,
    247, 248, 250, 253, **254**
Hearst, Randolph xv, 80, 94, 98
Hearth and Home (magazine) 23
Hefferon, Charles 194-5, 202-3, **202**, 204,
    206-7, 211, 212-14, 223, 224
Henley Regatta 58, 66
Henry, Prince 117, **193**, 194
Herald (newspaper) 80
Hesse, Princess of 117
Hickey, Joe 104, 150, 157, 189
high jump 161
    running 132, 168, 170
    standing 132, **164**, 164, 172-3
hockey 59, 148
Hohn, Uwe 140
Homer 9
hop, step and jump 164, 228

Horgan, Denis 145
Horr, Marquis F. 'Bil' 144, 149, 156
Hungarian team 120, 123, 168, 169–70,
   229, 239
hurdles 132, 144, 174, 228–9, **229**

Illustrated London News, The 26, 66
Imperial Sports Club 37, 50–2, 118, 140,
   143, 170, 173, 225
International Amateur Athletics
   Federation 260–1
International Exhibition 1862 29
International Olympic Committee (IOC)
   4, 16, 21–3, 54–5, 58–60, 64, 81, 87, 89,
   91–2, 101, 118–20, 124, 188, 225, 260
Irish News (newspaper) 110
Irish-American Athletic Club 79, 97–102,
   113, 122, 129–30, 135, 149, 165, 168, 176, 177,
   210, 219, 245–6, 247, 251
Irons, Francis 170
Italian team 120, 123, 137–8, 169, 194, 198,
   203, 205–7, 213–14, 216–22, 224–8, 230,
   234–6, 239–42

Jack, Thomas 62, 197–8, 202
Järvinen, Verner 156
Jarvis, Frank 171
javelin 13, 133, 139–40, **139**
jeu de paume 58, 64
John, Prince 194
Jones, B. **144**
Jones, Captain F. Wentworth 61, 67,
   110, 155

Kam (gymnast) 240
Kelly, Dan 108, 170
Kerr, Robert 105–6, 133, 171, 174
Kingsbury, Clarence **144**, 232–3
Kipling, Rudyard 86
Kiralfy, Bolossy 25–6
Kiralfy, Charles 27
Kiralfy, Edgar 170
Kiralfy, Imre 24–9, **25**, 31, 33, 37, 40–1, 45,
   47–8, 53, 68, 74, 109, 115, **117**, 118–19, 134,
   158, 170, 259
Kiralfy, Marie **25**
Kirby, Gustavus Town 79, 88, 97, 224, 250,
   256
Knott, F.A. 124
Koutoulakis, Anastasios 194

lacrosse 59
Laffan, Robert de Courcy 21–4, **21**, 54, 55,
   58, 61, 109, 112, 151, 239
Lamplough, Wharram 65
Lapize, Octave 167
Larner, George 136, 148, 235
Le Figaro (newspaper) 239–40
Leahy, 'Con' 168
Lemming, Eric 139–40, **139**, 238–9
Life Guards 123
Lightbody, J.D. 64, 113, 124, 126, 153
L'Illustrazione Italiana 234, **237**
Lind, George 194, 198
Lister (marathon runner) 206
Litvinov, Sergey 135
Liverpool Courier (newspaper) 67
London, Jack 86
London Olympics 1908 45
   aftermath 239–61, **249**
   American lead up to 94–104
   attendance 141–3, 147, 161, 166, 172
   and the British sense of 'fair play' xv,
      55, 62, 166–8, 181, 240, **257**
   bronze medals 56, 144, 145, 156, 165, 167,
      232
   climax 173
      see also marathon
   closure 231–8
   contestant numbers and selection 54–5
   costs of xv, 32–3, 50, 96–7
   diplomas of merit **57**, 232
   drug use at 208, 210
   female contestants 64–6, 138
   filming ix–xi, xiv–xv
   fundraising for 69–71, **73**, 110
   gold medals 56, 111, 134–5, 143–4, 148,
      156, 161, 164–5, 169–70, 172–3, 229, 230,
      232, 235, 256
   grounds 46–50, **47**, **49**
      see also White City Stadium
   hospitality crisis 108–10, 111–12
   inspiration for 18–19, 93
   judges 242–6
   medal design 55–6, **56–7**
   mid-point 161
   opening day **106–7**, 115–27, **123**, 131, 132
   organisation 59–60
   points system 145–6, 154–5, 161, 238
   prize giving **227**, 231–8, **233**, **236**, 238
   programme 58–9

publicity **51**, 66-70
raising support for 20-4, 31
silver medals 56, 144, 145, 156, 165, 168, 170, 232
ticket prices 142, 143, 161
unifying purpose 75
weather 136, **137**, 141, 143, 147, 172, 188-9, 194
win predictions 132-4
see also specific teams
London Olympics 2012 xv
Longboat, Tom 127-8, **128**, 129, 130, 133, 140-1, 173-4, 195-6, 198, 205, 207-11, 215, 228, **244**, 253, 254-5, **255**
Lord, F. 62
Lord, Tom 197, 198, 202, 206
Lords 71-2
Louis XV Pavilion 36-7
Louise, Princess 29
Lunghi, Emilio 163, 169
Lyon, George 59

Mackennal, Bertram 55, 56
Mallon, Bill xv, 180
marathon **xii**, 59, 61-2, 99, 127, 129, 140, 173, 187, 188-98, **190-1**, **193**, 201-25, **202-3**, **210**, **213**, **217-18**, **220**, **222-8**, 226-8, 234-7, **236-7**, 239-40, 253-6, 259
Marinaky, Mr 1-3
Marsh, Lou 198-9, 207, 209
Mary, Princess of Wales 192, **193**, 194, 195
McClinton's soap 42, **43**
McGowan, Mayor 248
McGrath, Matt 99, **100**, 103, 134-5, 149, 246
McKinley, William 42, 89, 91
Meadows, F. 124
Mercadier, Monsieur 28-9
Meredith, Leon 141, **144**
Millner, Joshua 111
Mitchell, Robert 116
Morning Journal (newspaper) 80-1
Morning Post (newspaper) 67
Morrissey, T.P. 196, 205, 211
Morton, Doc 199
Morton, John 108, 170
motor-boat racing 59
Murphy, Mike 97, 108-9, 115, 121, 181-2, 186-7, 245, 246, 250
Murray, Henry St Aubyn 122

Naples 8-9, 17
New York Athletic Club 76, 79, 81, 93, 97, 98, 125, 129, 149, 154
New York Evening Post (newspaper) 151, 181-2, 194, 195, 212, 218
New York Evening World (newspaper) 152
New York Herald (newspaper) 154
New York Sporting Times (newspaper) 81
New York Sun (newspaper) 154, 163, 182, 197, 211
New York Times (newspaper) 76, 78, 81, 101-2, 130, 188, 215, 216, 221, 228, 242-3, 245
New Zealand team 122
Newall, Sybil Fenton 'Queenie' **148**
Nightingale, Florence 36
Northcliffe, Lord 69, 199
Norwegian team 120, 123, 133, 138, 139, 146, 239, 240

Olga, Grand Duchess 10, **16**, 17
Olympic records 56, 126, 134-5, 144, 168-9, 171, 173-4, 176, 228
Oriard, Michael 185
Outing magazine 86, 89, 92, 94, 144, 185-6
Oxo Company 192-3

Pain, James 115
Paris Olympics 1900 3, 31-2, 89-90, 146, 147, 164, 171, 173, 174, 242
Park, J. 153
Parthenon 12, **13**
Partridge, Bernard 232
Pathé brothers x, **x**, 44
Payne, E. **144**
Peabody, Francis 217
Pennycock, Mr 178
Perry, Charles 48-9
Pheidippides 61
Pietri, Dorando xii-xiii, **xii**, 195, 198, 203, 203, 205-7, 211, 213-14, 216-22, **217**, **220**, **222-3**, 224-8, **227**, 230, 233-7, **237**, 238, 239-42, **241**, 253-4, **254**
Pietri, Ulpiano 226, 238
Pilgrims 68-9
Pindar xi, 12, 15, 19
pole vault 132, 144, 199-200
polo 58
bicycle polo 58, 131, **131**
water polo 59, 158
Polytechnic Harriers 62

Pope, Steven 87
Porter, Harry 99–101, 168, 242–3
Price, J. 197, 198, 202, 204, 206
Public Schools Athletic League 82
Pulitzer, Joseph 69, 80, 94, 98, 108
Pulitzer, William xv

racquets 58, 62–3, 66
Rector, James 171
Reed, R.C. 132–3
Reid, Ambassador 117
Robbins, William C. 176, 177–9, **177**, 181,
    245, 248–9
Robertson, Archie 140
Robertson, George Stuart 11, 55, 93
Robinson, Charles Newton 5, **6**, 8, 10,
    18–19
Rodal, Vebjørn 169
Roosevelt, Corinne 250
Roosevelt, Theodore 76, 79, 85, **85**, 86–7,
    89, 95, 249, 250–1, **252**
Rose, Ralph Waldo 122, 123, 124, 145, 149,
    152, 246, 248, 256
Rothschild, Lord 29
Rousselot, M. 161
rowing 4–5, 59, 231–2
rugby 59
Ruhl, Arthur 144
running 48, 49, 89–90, 124–6
    3 mile 140
    5 mile 132
    100 yards 105–8
    100m 133, 170–1, 235
    200m 133, 174
    400m 132, 175–87, **177**, 229, **230**, 235,
        245–6
    800m 114, 132, 162–3, 168–9
    1,500m 64, 89–90, 99, 113–14, 132, 135–6,
        153, 162, **162**
    1,600m medley relay 169, 201, 229–30
    3,200m steeplechase 153, 157
    4,000m steeplechase 90
    quarter-mile 108
    see also hurdles; marathon
Rutland, Duchess of 232

St James' Gazette (newspaper) 1
St Louis Exposition 90
St Louis Olympics 1904 3, 31–2, 90–2, 114,
    145, 147

San Francisco Chronicle (newspaper) 104,
    113, 145, 146, 150, 152, 157, 189, **257**
Sandow, Eugen 70, 110
Schilles, M. **166**
Scott Duncan, David 178, 184–5
Seligman, Edgar 5, **6**, 8, 10, 17
Seoul Olympics 1988 135
Sewell, Harry 153, 157
Sheppard, Mel 99, **99**, 113–14, 125–6, 135,
    162–3, **162**, 169
Sheridan, Martin 18, 79, 88, 98–9, **99**, 102,
    103, 129, 143–4, 149, 152, 156, 165, 245, 246
Sherring, Bill 18, 192, 195, 196, 201, 205
shooting 5, 58, 111
Shorter, Frank 253
shot put 145
Shrubb, Alf 130, 197
Simpson, Fred 195, 205, 211–12, 224
Sloane, William Milligan 87, 88, 89
Smith, J.M. 124
Smithson, Forrest 228–9, **229**
Somodi, István 168
Sorbonne conference 1894 87
'Souls' 23
South African team 122, 171, 194–5, 198,
    202–3, 204, 206–7, 212–14, 223, 224, 239
Spalding, A.G. xii, 79, 82–4, 97
Sparta, Duke and Duchess of 116–17
Sporting Life 24, 52, 159, 174, 176, 183
Sportsman, The ix, 169
Stagg, Amos Alonzo 109, 171, 184, 185
Strathcona, Lord 29
strychnine 208, 210
Stud, John Edward Kynaston 122
Sullivan Award 261
Sullivan, James E. 53–4, 76–82, **77**, 84,
    86–7, 88–92, 94, 96–7, 99, 101–3, 109,
    112–15, 124, 127, 129–30, 140–1, 146, 151,
    154–5, 161, 165, 168, 173–4, 180, 185–7,
    197, 222, 244–7, 249–52, **252**, 260–1
Sun (newspaper) 80
Svanberg, Johan 195, 224
Sweden, Crown Prince of 117, 118, 141–2,
    155, 194, 201
Swedish team 120–1, 123, 138–9, **139**, 146,
    148, 157–8, 195, 200, 224, 238–40
swimming 48, 50, 59, 83, 143, 148, 200,
    231, **231**

Talbot, Lee J. 122, 149

Tatler (magazine) 23, 66, 67, 69–70, 71–2, 142, 243
Taylor, Henry 143, **231**, 235
Taylor, John 176, 177, **177**, 179, 181, 230, 245–6, 256
tennis 58, 64, 65–6, 65, 83, 147–8
Tewanina, Lewis 195, 196, 204, 205, 211, 224
Tewksbury, Walter 174
Times, The (newspaper) 12, 17
Toronto Daily Star (newspaper) 199, 209
track and field 59, 64, 88–9, 88–91, 189, 243, 261
see also specific events
Tracy, Louis 141
Tsiklitiras, Konstantin 165, 172
tug-of-war 58, 59, 148–54, **149**, 152, 155, 157, 159, 161, 166

US team 96–104, 108–115, 121–6, 129, 131–5, **131**, 143–4, 146, 148–51, **152**, 153–4, 156–7, 159, 161–5, 168–87, 192, 194–6, 200–1, 204–5, 219–25, 228–30, 234–5, 238, 240, 242–3, 245–53, **252**, 256–8

Vanderbilt 110
Vanity Fair (magazine) 4, 23, 65, 66, 69, 131, 231, 256–7
Vesuvius 8–9, 15
Victoria, Queen 28
Victoria, Princess 116, 155
Voigt, Emil 158

Wales, Prince of see George V
Walker, Reggie 108, 171, **172**, 235

walking races 132, 135, 136, 148
Wallace, Jim 171
Walsh, Cornelius 'Con' 135
water polo 59, 158
Webb, Eric 148
Weeks, Barlow S. 76–7, 79, 97
weights 132, 144
Welton, Alton Roy 223
Westminster, Duchess of 232
Westminster, Duke of 52
White City 28, 32, 40–1, 45, 46–7, 74, 240, 259
White City Stadium 46–50, **47**, **49**, 63, 66, 75, 119, 121, 134, 164–6, 204, 259–60
Imperial Sports Club 37, 50–2, 118, 140, 143, 170, 173, 225
Whitney, Caspar 85–6, 87, 89, 92
Wilhelm II, Kaiser 28, 73, 74
Wilson, H.A. 64, 126, 135, **162**
Wimbledon 147–8
Wingate, General George 247
winter Games 59, 232
World 70, 80, 103, 108, 111, 112, 125–6, 131, 133
world records 18, 134–5, 139–40, 141, 143, 144, 145, 164, 168, 173, 176, 228
wrestling 59, 161, 170, 240
Wyatt, Albert 201–2

yacht racing 59, 231–2

Zeit (newspaper) 240
Zelezny, Jan 140
Zeppelin, Count 73–4
Zilliacus, Bruno 121